A HOUSE WITH FOUR ROOMS

By the same author

FICTION

Chinese Puzzle
The Lady and the Unicorn
Black Narcissus
Gypsy, Gypsy
Breakfast with the Nikolides
Rungli-Rungliot
(Thus Far and No Further)
Take Three Tenses:
A Fugue in Time
The River
A Candle for St Jude
A Breath of Air
Kingfishers Catch Fire
An Episode of Sparrows
Mooltiki: Stories and Poems
from India
The Greengage Summer
China Court
The Battle of Villa Fiorita
Swans and Turtles
(short stories)
In This House of Brede
The Peacock Spring
Five for Sorrow, Ten for Joy
The Dark Horse
Thursday's Children

NON-FICTION

Hans Christian Andersen:
A Great Life in Brief
Two Under the Indian Sun
(*with Jon Godden*)
The Raphael Bible
The Tale of the Tales:
The Beatrix Potter Ballet
Shiva's Pigeons: An Experience
of India (*with Jon Godden*)
The Butterfly Lions

NON-FICTION CONTINUED

Gulbadan: Portrait of a
Princess of the Moghul Court
A Time to Dance, No Time
to Weep: A Memoir

POETRY

In Noah's Ark
Prayers from the Ark
The Creatures' Choir
The Beasts' Choir
A Letter to the World:
Poems for Young People

FOR CHILDREN

The Doll's House
The Mousewife
Impunity Jane
The Fairy Doll
Mouse House
The Story of Holly and Ivy
Candy Floss
St Jerome and the Lion
Miss Happiness and Miss
Flower
Little Plum
Home Is the Sailor
The Kitchen Madonna
Operation Sippacik
The Diddakoi
The Old Woman Who Lived
in a Vinegar Bottle
Mr McFadden's Hallowe'en
The Rocking Horse Secret
A Kindle of Kittens
The Dragon of Og
The Valiant Chatti-Maker
Fu-Dog

Rumer Godden

A HOUSE WITH FOUR ROOMS

William Morrow and Company, Inc.

New York

Grateful acknowledgment is made for permission to reprint the following:

"Cleaning the Candelabrum" by Siegfried Sassoon from *Collected Poems, 1908–1956* (Faber & Faber). Copyright © 1961 by Siegfried Sassoon. Reprinted by permission of George Sassoon.

Siegfried Sassoon's letter to Rumer Godden reprinted by permission of George Sassoon.

"Come Death" by Stevie Smith from *The Collected Poems of Stevie Smith* (Penguin Modern Classics). Copyright © 1975 by Stevie Smith. Reprinted by permission of James McGibbon.

"Ballad of Lost Objects" in *Times Three* by Phyllis McGinley. Copyright © 1953 by Phyllis McGinley, renewed 1981 by Julie Elizabeth Hayden and Phyllis Hayden Blake. Originally published in *The New Yorker*. Reprinted by permission of Viking Penguin, a division of Penguin Books USA, Inc., and by permission of Martin Secker & Warburg Limited.

To the Stanbrook Abbey Press for extracts from "The Path to Peace."

Library of Congress Cataloging-in-Publication Data

Godden, Rumer, 1907–
   A house with four rooms / Rumer Godden.
     p.   cm.
   ISBN 0-688-08629-2
   I. Title.
  PR6013.O2H68   1989
  823'.912—dc20   89-12147
                                CIP

Printed in the United States of America

First Edition

1 2 3 4 5 6 7 8 9 10

BOOK DESIGN BY CLAUDIA CARLSON

For Alan Maclean

My thanks are due to Dido Renoir and Eleanor Wolquitt for their valuable help in checking my remembrances of the filming of *The River*; to Shahrukh Husain who corrected Hindi and Bengali phrases and words that I could not attempt to spell and to Miss Gosling, of the Highgate Literary and Scientific Society, who gave me particulars of The Old Hall's history and identified writers buried in the Old Highgate Cemetery. Thanks to Orville Prescott for allowing me to quote from his book, *In My Opinion,* and to James Kirkup for permission to use his letters and poems from our shared experience of Emily Dickinson and Amherst; also to my editors, Jane Meara in New York and Susanna Wadeson in London, for their skill and patience with my vagaries; and to Sheila Anderson and Ena Logan Brown who never flagged, typing, retyping, managing to decipher my impossible fly-mark handwriting.

Most particularly of all, I thank Alan Maclean who was the first person to read the book and showed me how to put it into perspective.

To me and my kind life itself is a story and we have to tell it in stories—that is the way it falls. I have told the truth and nothing but the truth, yet not the whole truth, because that would be impossible.

R.G.

Contents

There is an Indian proverb or axiom that says that everyone is a house with four rooms, a physical, a mental, an emotional and a spiritual. Most of us tend to live in one room most of the time but, unless we go into every room every day, even if only to keep it aired, we are not a complete person.

R.G.

PART ONE

To Darrynane

We landed at Liverpool in August of nineteen forty-five. I, now thirty-eight, and my small daughters, Jane, who was nine, and Paula, almost six.

Every book I write, a novel, a memoir, that is even remotely connected with our family begins the same way with a landfall, an alighting in a stranger place to start a new life, probably in a new way.

Long, long before—it had been in nineteen twenty, again in the aftermath of another war, the First World War—I and my family, my father, Fa, Mam, my mother and we four sisters had, after a halcyon childhood in India,* come back to England, which they called home. I still remember the feeling of cold and utter desolation Jon, my elder sister, and I had felt as we stood together on the quay at Plymouth watching our luggage being unloaded from the liner that had brought us from Calcutta. I did not want that desolation to fall on Jane and Paula, especially as, for the last few months, they had been tossed about, two helpless jots of flotsam and jetsam; besides we were not going, as Jon and I had then been going, to our grandmother's strict and gloomy house in London; we were going to Darrynane in Cornwall, where Fa and Mam had, at last, retired from India.

"You remember Darrynane," I said to Jane. Jane wrinkled her

*Jon and I have told about that time in the book we wrote together, *Two Under the Indian Sun*.

forehead—too often, for a child, creased with a worry frown. "You remember it?"

"Just. There was a cock called Harlequin."

Jane had left Darrynane—that unique small house in Cornwall —when she was five. Paula, at two years old, had been too young to remember it though Jane had told her over and over again about Mam and her chickens. "Paula, you used to help collect the eggs in a tiny basket."

Darrynane was built into the side of a steep hill so that one side was a storey higher than the other. Fa said the house was ramshackle, which it was, but Mam loved it because it reminded her of a house in an Indian hill station. It looked far down the valley and the river and had at its gate, a small lodge, "Where we used to live when you were babies," I told Paula. "I expect it's ready for us now." The drive that separated the lodge from the house was bordered by hydrangeas, grown higher than Fa's head.

"What are hydrangeas?" asked Paula.

"Big blue flowers, blue as your eyes."

I told her, too, of the rhododendrons, pink, red and white, that grew everywhere and of the garden Mam had made—"The house sits in its flowers"; of how the azaleas in their flame, apricot, and yellow, were so vivid their reflections coloured the walls of the rooms.

Azaleas! Paula must have built a vision on that word. "Where are the azaleas?" she said looking round the Liverpool docks.

We had left Kashmir the October before. As an abandoned family we had lived there for most of the war years, abandoned meaning that the husband or father of the family, enlisted for the army, was serving overseas; though Laurence Foster, my husband, had not left India we were perhaps more abandoned than most; I had not seen him, and barely heard from him, for two years.

The Provost Marshall in Kashmir's capital, Srinagar, had recommended us for immediate repatriation, but the papers had not come until June. Jon and her husband, Roland, in Calcutta had nobly taken us in. By June the war in Europe was over, the Japanese war waning, so that thousands of women and children were trying to get back to England. I suppose the army could not cope with the numbers but nothing could excuse the filth and squalor of the transit camp in Deolali just outside Bombay where we had to wait.

We were given a one-roomed hut in a row of huts, hastily built, bamboo-walled, earth-floored, without water or electricity, which meant no fans in the torrid heat of June and July. There was no sanitation; twice a day women sweepers—ironically called mataranis, rani being a queen—came round and emptied the pots of cess from the bathrooms into the open gully that ran in front of the huts.

In the common dining-room, among the flies and spillages, as the sittings changed, crockery and cutlery were washed up on the floor behind us, the washers having one basin of water and filthy drying-up cloths. I dared not let Jane and Paula, especially Paula who was delicate, eat much of the food and spent my dwindling money at the canteen buying what I could—because of the war, tinned food was in short supply. Everything had to be ready to eat as there was nowhere to cook. I seemed to buy mostly biscuits, dried milk and fruit.

It was a test of survival; each one of us had to fight for ourselves and our children—there were few husbands.

It was harder, cruelly hard, on the families of the B.O.R.s— British Other Ranks—as the non-commissioned officers and men were called. They were herded into dormitories, had separate playgrounds, a separation that made the mothers belligerent.

One evening at children's tea, one of the mothers with four small children came and sat at our table. That day I had bought a jar of Horlicks, dried malted milk, wickedly expensive as were all imported things, but it was nutritious and could not harm Paula.

"What's that?" the mother asked.

"Horlicks," and, looking at the children's pallid little faces, "Would they like some?" I asked and passed the jar over. When she got up to go she took the jar with her and, as I jumped up to protest, "Ours," she said. "Complain if you like. It's my word against yours." She was a corporal's wife and, I was sure, had more money than I, but I knew as a B.O.R. she would have all the sympathy. "Why did you let her?" Jane asked in indignation.

"I couldn't do anything else." An officer's wife could not tussle in the Mess with a lower rank over a jar of Horlicks.

"You could and you should," said doughty Jane.

Jane always made the best of everything. I found her making paper boats and sailing them down the unspeakable gully to amuse the little ones, but soon Paula was ill as I had known she would be with an intestinal infection, perhaps sprue which is worse than dysentery. I, too, was ill.

I think she would have died if a woman army doctor had not come to the camp; so outraged was she by the conditions that she defiantly put down her flashes. She insisted that I, Jane and particularly Paula, be moved out at once and taken onto the ship that was waiting in Bombay harbour.

July 23rd 1945

I shall never forget, I wrote in my diary, coming down the companion way, a sailor carrying Paula, and being met by an English stewardess, clean, wholesome, capable, in a dark blue uniform and starched white apron. I wanted to kneel and kiss her feet.

Four years before, our voyage out from England to India had been an ordeal, five weeks of it going round the Cape, but life on that ship had been luxurious; now this one, another of the Peninsular and Oriental great 'Strath' liners, had been converted to a troopship, capable of carrying four thousand men.

We, in the officers' quarters which were the best, were still six in what had been a two-berth cabin, not counting two babies whose cot cradles were slung on the rail of their mothers' bunks. It was impossible to sleep and a guard had to be kept on tongues and tempers, but our crampedness was nothing to what the men had to endure; they were below decks, and could only be allowed up for a short while every other day; most of them slept in hammocks over the mess tables.

That nineteen forty-one voyage had been one of continual fear, endless boat drills even at night because of enemy submarines— owing to the speed of the ship, we had not been in convoy. Now I had another ache of fear; "You're not going to get that child home," kind fellow wives told me. I had endless offers from them to look after Jane, none to help with Paula; she seemed to them too frail and soon she was put in the ship's hospital, I with her because we had both developed deep abscesses.

In those long nights of pain and sleeplessness in the hospital Paula beside me restless too, now and again giving a little moan, a patient sigh, too patient for a five-year-old, everything seemed to come back; Laurence; money; our time in Kashmir that had ended in catastrophe.

I did not have to shut my eyes to see Dove House where we had lived, out in the countryside, high above the Mogul garden of Nishat and the Dāl lake.

I have had several cherished houses and always, by circumstance not by desire, have had to leave them but never have I loved a house as I loved Dove House.

I had found it in nineteen forty-two when we were desperate, ill and so poor that Srinagar's Mission Hospital had taken us in. For Dove House I paid five rupees, the equivalent then of seven shillings and sixpence, or a dollar and a half, for the house and nine acres of land 'under the trees'—the landlord kept the fruit.

It was a rarely beautiful little house. In spring, all round it, were flowering trees, peach, apricot, cherry, almond, acacia; in summer it was hung with vines and honeysuckle and scented white roses, while along its terraced orchards white iris grew wild. In the court-yard the stream splashed to a small waterfall and, high above, the mountain cut off the sky; the lake below was divided in two by a built-up road and a bridge, like a brooch, pinning the lakes to-gether; the far horizon was broken by the range of the Pir Panjal snows.

We had lived there for nearly three years in almost peasant simplicity and content. If we had kept to that simplicity there would not have been any trouble; as it was, I was persuaded to share it with a friend, Olwen, who was also lonely. Olwen though, brought her British Raj customs with her; it was a different, far more elaborate way of life with different servants and one of them, the cook, proved to be a homicidal maniac. It had ended in a court case and our precipitate flight from Kashmir.

"Are you the family they tried to poison?" the ship's Doctor asked me.

"It wasn't poison, only drugs," which was not quite true—Ol-wen had been given belladonna but I was trying not to make it too sensational—I still could not believe it myself but, "It was only marijuana and ground glass," I said.

"It's a wonder you're alive."

When Paula was well enough to come up on deck, a little skeleton, "All eyes and bones," as Jock the hospital orderly said, I was allotted a sergeant to carry her on a pillow. Light as she was I could not carry her—I only weighed six stone, or eighty-four pounds. 'Allotted' sounds objectionable but the whole ship was regimented and I knew he was glad to get out of the heat below.

Always when I had been on board ship I had done what I most love to do, go forward to stand in the bows, leaning over to watch the prow cleave through the water, sending a high wave each side; feeling the power of a great ship behind us, the clear salt wind in my face, sometimes even at that height, spray. To watch, all round me, the sea meeting the horizon, like a great bowl turned upside down, gives a feeling of loneliness, of such space that worry and concern dwindle to infinitesimalness. This ship though was proportioned into strict areas, most of them forbidden, and certainly the foredeck was out of bounds. There was nowhere to be alone, to get away.

August 1945

There was a time before the war—it seems in another world. Where has it gone? Am I the writer who wrote *Black Narcissus*? Has she gone, just as the money is gone? Is it possible I shall write again?: first I must cope with England. . . . which had never seemed as alien.

We had, too, the lesser sadness of loss. The few possessions I had managed to salvage from those years, things we had all loved—they spelled home—had been put in a warehouse in Bombay while we waited for our passages. The warehouse had been sabotaged so that we did not have as much as a saucer with which to start a new home, with two exceptions; some handmade Kashmiri silver cutlery I had taken with me in my suitcase to Calcutta and an Agra rug I had carried all the way with me. A worse sadness was that we had to leave our two pekingese; even if I had had the money to bring them, they would not have been allowed on a troopship. Moon Daisy, the white bitch, went on for some years giving Jon, who had taken them in, a litter of puppies to her delight, but Candytuft—they were all named for white flowers—the miniature dog I had bred myself, though he had every care, only lived for eighteen months. 'He never settled,' wrote Jon, 'just grieved.'

To despair is traitorous to your gift. "How could you forget?" I say to myself now. Not take into account that you had that silver and the Agra rug, rare as all true Agra rugs are rare, "an invest-

ment against some rainy day," the Kashmiri merchant, my friend
Ghulam Rasool had said when he sold it to me. More importantly
I had in my suitcase a manuscript no-one had seen, a novel called
The River.

I ought too, to have had faith in my children. Jane, at nine years
old, had grown from a solid child to a slim little girl, with the same
red hair, serious aquamarine eyes, the freckles that were such a
grief to her; she had an uncommon mixture of bonté—an untrans-
latable word, the nearest perhaps is good will—bonté and sense.

After our years in remote Kashmir I had expected her to be shy,
perhaps resistant to this new world as was Paula but no, the ship
held no out of bounds for Jane. She came constantly to see us
while we were in the ship's hospital, which for Jane naturally
meant going to see the men in the troops' hospital, the orderlies,
the crowded lower decks. Soon everyone knew her, from the Captain to the cleaners in the engine room.

I had no idea of this until the ship stopped at Port Said. No one
was allowed ashore but the merchants came alongside in their
boats, or even on board, especially what we used to call the 'gulli
gulli' men or conjurers who would turn our handkerchiefs or
watches into day-old chicks.

Most young men and women coming out to India for the first
time used to buy their topees* at Port Said, in its most famous
shop Simon Artz, later taken over by Selfridges. There was another
speciality that used to fascinate me as a child—'Moses in a
basket'—a tiny figure of baby Moses in a miniature gilt or enamel
basket made to look as if it were woven like the one in which his
mother and sister, Miriam, floated him in the bulrushes for Pha-
raoh's daughter to find.

There were no Moseses now, no topees, only cheap Persian
carpets and rugs, probably made in Kidderminster; they and Turkish Delight.

Jane came staggering into our cabin with at least a dozen of the
light wooden boxes oozing stickiness and sugar. "Jane! Who gave
you those?"

"The soldiers," said Jane.

The trouble was, none of us liked it. Having had few bought
sweets—there were none in our village in Kashmir—to us the

---

*Sun hats made of pith which is light and cool.

glutinous pink or green squares were sickeningly over-sweet, especially when they were topped with honey and nuts. Thinking of sugar rationing in England, sweets were rationed too, "We must try and take them with us," I said but they were dusted with such fine sugar that it went everywhere and, in the end, we gave most of them to the little Goanese men who looked after the bathrooms and lavatories.

I had though, to be careful with Jane. She was the family worrier. "When is Daddy coming to England?" she asked me, fixing me with those percipient eyes. For the moment I could answer, "Not yet. He hasn't been demobilised," but I knew the time would come when she would have to know.

As for Paula, "That's the bravest wee bairn I've ever seen," Scots Jock said of her. She had developed another deep abscess on her buttock and was ordered hot kaolin poultices, almost unbearably hot. He would stand her up on the surgery table. "Ready?" and, "Slap it on, Jock," she would say, setting her teeth not to cry.

"Never get that child home." Even the Doctor was discouraging. "She's going to have trouble for years."

"She has had trouble for years and here she is." It probably sounds uncaring but it was the answer I clung to. They had not counted on Paula's extraordinary resilience and, as we came up the Bay of Biscay in perfect August weather, the cleansing sea air and proper food began their work. Soon she was running about on deck and even in the noise and crowding of that cabin, mercifully sleeping, she who hardly ever slept. Soon in my own mind some little seed of wisdom woke; 'One step at a time. For the moment don't think any further than Darrynane.'

"Tomorrow we shall be in England," Jane had told Paula the night before and Paula, who could walk now, had come up on deck that early morning filled with expectation.

There were, of course, no azaleas, not on the docks of Liverpool, besides it was August, not azalea time, as I should have foreseen.

We waited from early morning to disembark. The Army, for some reason known only to itself, had taken the men off first. Now they took the single officers, leaving no one to help the families, three or four hundred women, some with babies or small children; we had perhaps eight husbands between us.

We were told to leave the ship with what we could carry, making only one trip down the gangway—the rest of our luggage was piled in the customs shed. It was impossible to help one another.

Paula carried my despatch case and Jane's precious doll, Mignonette; Jane the Agra rug which was heavy; I had a basket of provisions which I hung round my neck and our two suitcases, one in either hand. I staggered.

"Claim your baggage," was shouted over the loudspeaker.

The husbands did their best to help but they were too few, we women, too many. The luggage was piled in a mountain of trunks, packing cases, bundles, so high it was dangerous; to pull any piece out could bring an avalanche down.

I saw a young soldier watching the scene with a smile on his face. I thought perhaps he was a Customs guard and only discovered later he was supposed to be there to help. I went up to him and said, "Look, I'm alone with two small children. I have just one trunk. Could you help?"

He looked me up and down, then at the other near frantic women and, "Officers' wives," he jeered with obvious enjoyment.

"An officer's wife is a woman," I said.

"So what?"

Then, "If you won't do it for kindness, will you do it for money?" He was instantly alert. "If you'll get that trunk out for me, carry it and our suitcases and put us on the train, I'll give you five pounds." It was a great deal of money for those days and, "Done," he said.

I described the trunk, he got it out easily—he was strong—picked up our suitcases and, immensely relieved, we followed him.

The train was waiting—we had been told which one to catch—but at the barrier he stopped, put the luggage down and held out his hand.

"Put us *on* the train, that was the bargain."

"I'm not allowed on the platform, see," which was a lie; there were soldiers on the platform. "Gimme my money!" He began to bluster; he was so big he could easily have snatched my bag.

"I will put the lady on the train." It was a porter, a real British porter. I had been told they were almost extinct or, if to be had, charged exorbitant prices, a pound for every piece of luggage but there was nothing else to do. I gave the lout his money. "You be off, my lad," the porter said and picked up our luggage. He found us a carriage—there were no classes on that train. "It'll be crowded," he warned us. When he had stored the trunk under the seats, suitcases and rug up on the rack, hesitantly I brought out a ten shilling note, hoping it would do; the last time I had given a tip to a porter it had been half-a-crown and that was generous.

He looked at it, then said, "Lady, do you know the value of that note?"

"Yes. Yes I do, and know what you have done for us."

"I couldn't think of taking it. Two bob will be fine." I gave him the old half-a-crown—and shall not forget him.

In those days, Liverpool to Bodmin was a long journey. "Cross-country," the porter had said. "They would have done better," he told us, "to send you to London and take a train direct."

The army had given us each a paper bag of rations, bully beef sandwiches, a fruit pie, but the beef had gone off. Fortunately I had a bottle of orange squash in my basket, and at some station, it seemed to me in the middle of nowhere, a young soldier sprinted along the platform and bought the children some buns.

It was seven o'clock when we reached Exeter, to find there was no further train to Bodmin Road—our halt for Darrynane—that night.

Another myth I had heard of England, was that people had hardly any petrol; I had no idea it could be applied for if there were a special need. If I had telephoned Mam from Liverpool she would have met us at Exeter—intrepid Mam! When, after a cataract operation on his eyes, Fa had been forbidden to drive, "We must give up the car," he had said.

"We won't," Mam had answered. "I'll drive it," and, at sixty-three, had passed her driving test, first time. "Charmed the examiner," said Fa. She had driven for the hospitals through the rest of the war.

It never occurred to me—or the R.T.O., the Railway Transport Officer—at the station that she could have driven that fifty miles and, as the Army was still responsible for us, he had to find us somewhere to spend the night. Hotels and lodging houses were full; he telephoned and telephoned while we waited forlornly on the platform. At last, past eight o'clock, we were driven in a truck to what seemed a mission hostel run by a maiden lady who was gentle and kind but could only give us each two slices of bread and margarine, a little tea. "In the evening we're not usually asked to feed people," which made me feel we were trespassing on her rations.

Breakfast was porridge, after a night spent in a cellar with some twenty camp beds, each with one folded army blanket. "You see, it's mainly for WRAC drivers," she explained. "They come in and out, all day and all night." They did.

When the porridge was ladled out I remembered my first sight of it, long, long ago when Jon and I were sent to school, we had peered at the grey, lumpy—to us slimy—mass with horrified disbelief. "Do we *eat* it?" To my amazement both children ate it; for me, the tea was saving.

We were finished and were getting up—there was a train to catch—when, "Please sit still," said the lady, and began to pray.

She prayed and prayed, "For this poor mother, may she be able to guide and help her children." "For this dear girl"—a young woman driver.

At first we sat with bowed heads but it went on and on. I had begun to think we would have to interrupt when Paula used the age-old nursery request, "Please may I get down? I *must*," said Paula clutching herself. "I must go to the bathroom."

The train from Exeter to Bodmin Road meandered. Once again it was full, and to my surprise with holiday-makers. I had forgotten it was August and holidays seemed out of my sphere. As with the porter, I can never forget the kindness of the people.

It was a broilingly hot day. Stupidly, perhaps going back to that long ago landing in nineteen twenty at Plymouth, I had thought England would strike cold and had dressed the children in what was their best—skirts and jackets of blue tweed, woven and made in Kashmir with yellow jerseys and knee socks of hand-spun wool. "They prickle," and soon both children were sweltering. Our luggage had now been put in the guard's van so that they could not change but, "Poor lambs," said the women and when I had explained how we came to be there, "Poor *poor* lambs," and they opened their own cases. I knew clothes were on coupons but they still produced a cotton frock for Jane, far too big and gaudy but it was cool. For Paula a sleeveless shirt and a pair of little boy's shorts—which suited her.

By luck I had the remains of the Turkish Delight which was handed round, exclaimed about, particularly when Jane told how she had been given it.

Bodmin Road station—the halt for Darrynane's village St. Breward—was only a platform high above the trees in the wood below. Fa and Mam were waiting for us; as we saw one another there was a gasp and an immediate barricade of silence.

That moment brought the war closer than it had ever been.

When you have been away from anyone for a long time you are apt to conjure up a picture of them from memory; now I saw what the war had done to Fa and Mam; I had always thought of Mam as pretty—as she was to be again—but she was bent, her face weather-beaten and wrinkled while Fa, who had been to me magnificent, was an old man, over-thin, one eye practically gone; their clothes were out of shape and shabby. What they in their turn saw of us was plain on their faces; we must have looked three vagabonds, dirty—there had been no water on the train—dressed in a medley of clothes—on Jane the cotton dress hung to her knees—and with a small heap of battered luggage.

There was no hiding it, the shock was there until Jane rescued it when she rushed to Mam with shouts of joy. "I remember you —I remember you both." Then Paula emerged from behind me. Just as Fa had made my younger sister, Nancy, his especial pet because she, like Paula, had been born almost too delicate to live, he had made a pet of Paula. She could not have remembered it but, as if she had, she went straight up to Fa and held out her hand. Fa knew better than to kiss her but, as he bent down to shake the hand, for the first time in all the years I had known him, he had tears in his eyes.

"Are those azaleas?"

As we had turned in at Darrynane's gate, all down the drive the hydrangeas were out, a bank of deep blue. Paula's eyes were wide.

"The azaleas are over," said Mam, "but come and see." The hillside garden had run riot; Mam had had no gardener since the war and her careful planting had turned into a drift of flowers— Michaelmas daisies, mauve, purple, pink among yellow black-eyed Susans; marguerites were in clumps against the grey granite rocks which were climbed over by saxifrage and pansies. There were the Japanese anemones I love, late roses and clematis, honeysuckle. Hundreds of underplanting flowers had seeded themselves, rioting onto the paths and over the rocks. Paula stood and stared, drinking in the colours and scents. Then, "I don't mind about the azaleas," she said.

In the house it was reassuring to find practically everything un-changed; the furniture that had come from my grandmother's house, especially the big black and gold buhl cabinet that held among other treasures a miniature teaset I had been allowed to play with when I was five years old; Mam's Dresden lamps that had been her mother's, the table laid for lunch with the Georgian silver worn thin by the use of everyday, the family portraits much prized by Fa—but Jane wanted to explore. "Is Harlequin here?"

"Well, Harlequin's son is here," said Mam and, "Eggs," said Paula suddenly. Soon Jane was in the fruit cage below the garden, "We used to have strawberries," and there, though half tumbled down, was the donkey hut in which I had revised *Black Narcissus*. At the gate was the lodge, our cottage. Jane rushed in and, "I've found my jug," she cried.

It was a red jug with white spots bought long ago in France on our momentous trip* as school children to Château-Thierry with Mam to see the battlefields of France. "That jug is the first thing I remember," Jane had said to me often. Now it made a still life: the jug with white spots filled with roses, the small tapestry bag Jane had carried all the way from Kashmir flung down in its woven blue, green and purple colours with a few family toys Mam had kept; a jack-in-the-box, a set of two-centuries-old plain wooden bricks, a Noah's ark with some of the animals set out two by two. Paula picked up an elephant.

"I've found my jug," exulted Jane.

*The trip that would give rise to my novel *The Greengage Summer*; it was to have a notable film.

In the Potting Shed

With all Fa and Mam's love and planning, and my real need, it failed, had to fail. The lodge was ready but not for us, which was the first shock. "Nancy is coming on leave," said Mam her face aglow. "She and the little boys will be arriving any day. Dick is following."

Dick was my younger sister's husband; their elder son, Simon, was now five, to Paula's six years—they had been like brother and sister when I looked after Simon in Kashmir and were only separated in age by a year and a day; Richard, Nancy's baby, was almost two. Of course they had to go into the cottage, there was nowhere else for them to go. "I'm sure you, Jane and Paula can manage in the spare room and, for your writing," said Mam with pride. "Look," and opened the door to her own bedroom.

Mam loved her bedroom that looked far down the valley and had a balcony hung with a clematis that had clambered up onto the roof but she had turned out of it into the smaller spare room, a dark little bedroom off the kitchen originally intended, I think, for a maid. "I shall be perfectly happy," she insisted. Fa had given up his desk, a heavy rolltop desk. How could I explain that it would hem me in—I should far rather have had a kitchen table? How, explain that, for writing, a cell is better than a large light room, especially as, in summer, the family liked to gather on the balcony?* 'I knew I couldn't work there,' I wrote to Jon. 'I couldn't.'

*I know Jane Austen—to me peerless as a novelist—wrote in the family sitting-room but I need to be a little apart, though I did write a novel at my desk in my dancing school with classes going on all round me.

Jon, still in Calcutta, was the eldest of us four sisters: Jon, Rumer, Nancy and Rose. Jon was born in India, I in England, with fourteen months between us, but we were so inseparable that we might have been Siamese twins and until, at the late ages of fourteen and twelve, we went to the first of our abhorred English schools, we had always slept together, done everything together, shared everything. Though since we had married we had been apart most of the time, our sharing still held.

Of the donkey hut where I had finished my first successful novel, *Black Narcissus*—and written another—only a shell was left in the field but part of Darrynane's large garden was on the other side of the lane, a walled space where a waterfall fell into a pool by plots of vegetables and flowers for cutting. It had a potting shed with a sturdy table and a wooden chair; before the war Mam's old gardener used to sit in it to eat his pasty and read his newspaper. There was no gardener now and,

It's ideal!, I wrote to Jon, away from everyone with only the sound of the waterfall. The shed smells of moist earth, Mam's geraniums, heliotrope and lemon verbena. A perfect place for work. The family, of course, think I am mad!

"There are letters waiting for you," Fa had told me. "Mostly from America."

Fa had been dealing with my affairs so long now that he had come to think them important but when we first grew up, the idea that any of his daughters could become a professional amazed him and when I, the first, broke away to teach dancing, he was appalled. All the same he had backed me and now, "Letters," he said firmly.

The first I opened was from my London agent, Spencer Curtis Brown. Faithful Spencer. I had come to know him well in the first year of the war which we had called the cold war because life seemed almost normal and *Black Narcissus* had been published with real excitement; but in nineteen forty I had had to take the children out to India. There, in my long lonely exile in Kashmir, every three or four months, Spencer used to send me a cable, not about anything in particular, but to show me I was not forgotten as so often I had felt I was. Now, in this autumn of nineteen forty-five he wrote, 'When am I going to see you? There are things to tell you.'

There were. Before we left Calcutta I had had a telephone call from New York, the first that had come to me in India from America. It had been from Curtis Brown, New York, in particular from their representative for British books, Edith Haggard, a redoubtable small lady who was to become a touchstone to me and a precious friend. The call was about the novel I had written in Kashmir, *A Fugue in Time*; that much I could make out but, as with most overseas calls to India then, the line was so bad I had only heard a few words: *'Ladies' Home Journal'* which sounded like a magazine and conveyed little to me. Now, with his letter, Spencer enclosed a copy of a cable which explained Edith's telephone call but that had never reached me:

SOLD FUGUE LADIES HOME JOURNAL SEVENTY FIVE HUNDRED DOLLARS

Seventy-five hundred dollars! Seven thousand five hundred. . . . The geraniums, heliotrope and lemon verbena seemed to swim together.

It was, though, a fact as a letter from Curtis Brown's American President, Alan Collins, head of the New York office, confirmed. He wrote:

I feel certain that to have your name appear in the *Ladies' Home Journal*, a magazine of some four million circulation, will do much to establish your name with a wider audience and can only have an extremely beneficial effect in the long run.

Perhaps he sensed that I still had in my head the literary British attitude of disdain for women's magazines—the 'glossies' as we called them—and had no idea of their power and prestige in America. *The Ladies' Home Journal* published authors of the rank of Hemingway, Rebecca West, Karen Blixen, Eudora Welty and had the lead over other quality magazines such as *McCall's* and *American Good Housekeeping*. As I was to discover, American magazine editors were kings and queens.

Another of the letters came from Robert Lusty of Michael Joseph, my new publishers. Much as I had liked my first publishers, Peter Davies and his brother Nico, their distribution was limited —they had found it difficult to cope with *Black Narcissus*—so that, "You must go to someone bigger," Spencer had said and that April

Michael Joseph had published *A Fugue in Time*. Robert Lusty's letter was dated 12 June, more than two months ago. It ended:

> We have rarely published a book with greater pleasure than we have *A Fugue in Time* . . . it has, despite the very real difficulties of the paper situation, achieved a considerable success and sales at the moment are in the neighbourhood of 14,000 copies.

It had not appeared in America yet—my publisher of those days, Little, Brown of Boston wrote:

> We received a few days ago "Take Three Tenses" [*A Fugue in Time*] and I just finished with it last night. The overtones and undertones you give to such a short story ring on and on. While some readers may think your technique is difficult, I think that once they get through a few pages and understand how you deal with the time elements, they will rather cheer than complain. Sincere congratulations.

A Fugue in Time had been written in those long solitary evenings in Dove House in winter, under an oil lamp—we had had no electricity. It had been bitterly cold; I had a 'kangri,' the Kashmiri firepot, filled with hot coals, a wicker shield round it to keep me warm; I wrote again in the dawn hours when I got up at half past four to write before the children were awake. Trying to weave the three generations of characters together, telling of them not consecutively but interwoven, I wrote the book over and over again and thought I should never succeed. It was not until I tried putting the past into the present tense, the present into the past that I had found the key. This sounds improbable but worked so smoothly that most readers—even editors—never noticed.

A Fugue in Time though had been written a long time ago. I had shown nothing to anyone since. There is a saying of Chekhov's, written to a young writer he had tried to help:

> What is needed is constant work day and night, constant reading, study, will. Every hour is precious for it . . . it is time.

I had, I had to get to work, my work.

It seemed, though, that it had been growing without me. Another letter from Alan Collins bore that out:

New York
25 March 1945

I am sorry to hear your personal affairs have been difficult of recent date and I hope they are now beginning to get back in orderly form. I cannot urge on you too strongly the advisability of getting to New York for a visit if you possibly can. I believe a meeting would be helpful all around for you could judge for yourself then as to whether or not you will want to continue permanently on the Little Brown list. More important than that, however, is that such a trip would give you a chance to meet the magazine editors and in particular some play producers.

Aside from all this, it would be a great pleasure for us at Curtis Brown at last to meet you after all this time. I cannot urge you too strongly to come.

As I laid the letters down on the potting shed table, I found I was trembling with excitement.

For the moment I said nothing to anyone; even had I wanted to, there was no chance. Nancy and her family had flown from Calcutta to London.

The contrast with us three vagabonds, could not help biting; Dick, though still young, had risen high in his firm, the powerful Imperial Chemical Industries, and was to go higher. During the war, he and Nancy had been given a luxurious flat in the Turf Club, an enclave of big houses in a private park, this because, owing to the war, there was an acute shortage of paid racecourse officials and Dick was acting as Starter, one of the few amateur starters on a major racecourse anywhere in the world—he was brilliant at everything he did. Nancy arrived, well dressed and groomed; there was a young nanny waiting for her who took immediate charge of Richard. Nancy brought too, an array of presents, shirts for Fa, blouses and little embroidered coats for Mam.

There were nine of us now in Darrynane, not a large house— the cottage was kept for the Nursery.

We all began to flourish, as people always did round Mam. The children, even Paula, began to lose their Indian pallidness, to fill out in energy and life as they had in the mountain healthiness of Dove House. It meant, of course, that they were noisy. Fa, after long years of being alone with Mam, often found it unendurable; Dick, too found it hard on his nerves and said so.

We were outside as much as we could be. Best I liked the long days on the moor, going to Mam's beloved Alex Tor* away from the village, and further to Brown Willie and Rough Tor.

'There is a magical tinge to Cornwall,' I had written years ago when Paula was born there—the villagers had insisted she was a changeling, she was so small.

It is faerie in the old sense of the word, not little creatures with wings but wild, elfin, eerie, as is the faerie quality of La Belle Dame Sans Merci and Goblin Market.

We went to Dozemary Pool where Excalibur, King Arthur's sword was thrown when the Lady of the Lake and her attendants came to fetch him as he died. The sword had magic powers too; the lake seemed always still as if it were waiting for Excalibur to appear, but the wind only brought ripples. Often we picked up bits of amber on its shores.

I was not as happy when we went to the sea—I have always disliked beaches, the sand that gets into everything, the hard salt wind, glaring sun, but sometimes, if Betty the Nanny, Mam or Nancy were there I could stay on the headlands where the heather was coming into bloom with wild scabious and there were butter-flies. Sometimes I would walk, looking far down the coast's curious rock funnels to the sea, unbelievably blue, sending spray leaping high. I could look down to the beach too and see Jane drawing on the sand with her spade, Paula and Simon shrimping in, I was sure, secret places, Richard sitting in warm pools while Betty placidly knitted.

It was not always as halcyon—"What *have* you been doing?" Spencer's impatient voice asked me on the telephone.

"Living," would have been the answer or, "Trying to live."

This new life was beginning to declare itself; I had been far less daunted by the remote primitive life in Dove House. Here we seemed hemmed in by inhibitions; we had collected our necessities, some of which we had not heard of, like identity cards; though we had known about ration books, coupons seemed needed for every-thing, clothes, house linen—we had none—furnishing, even pots and pans. More and more I began to see how difficult it was going

*A tor is one of the strange outcrop hills of granite rock and earth found on the moors.

to be to establish ourselves and make a home. I soon knew, too, how ill-equipped I was to run a house in post-war England.

Over and over again, people who have read my account of our life in Kashmir with its peasant simplicity, have said, "But you had servants. You couldn't have been poor." It does seem an anomaly but, in those days, even the poorest family, Indian or English, shared a sweeper* and had at least one servant—the Eurasians called them, no matter what their age, 'Boy'. With Fa and Mam in Narayangunj we had had sixteen servants, not counting the dhobie or washermen; in Calcutta, Laurence and I, a newly married young couple, had eight. Servants were cheap, also each, because of his religion, could only do certain things.

A Hindu could not serve at table; only untouchables could sweep the floors or wash them; they looked after and fed the dogs, cleared the commodes, but were not allowed to lay a hand, for instance, on a washbasin. In Dove House we had had a cook bearer and a sweeper boy who came twice a day from the village to empty the cess pots; the gardener was paid by our landlord; the dhobie, who in summer served all the Indian villas on the lakeside, came once a week and took our laundry.

I had never washed or ironed a dress or shirt in my life, let alone a sheet; there seemed to be no laundries. If I sewed on a button, it immediately fell off; seams came apart. My darning looked like cobbling. Even thirty years later, my grand-daughter Charlotte, then ten, watched me trying to help Jane—I was darning grey school socks—and said, "Grandmother, that looks like porridge."

It was not all my fault; my hands, though small, are unbelievably clumsy. I have always known this; when I am given flowers, though I love them more than anything else, I go into a panic because I know I cannot arrange them, except cottage bunches; odd, because Mam, and Jane who is so like her, could make one exquisite bowl or vase or glass after the other whether with a few flowers out of the fields or a vast bouquet.

When Fa and Mam retired to Darrynane, on a modest pension, they had had a cook, a house parlourmaid and gardener; now there

---

*Modern India is different. Wages have become so high, staff so difficult to find, that even top ranking families have had to settle for the same, one general servant, a shared sweeper. The wives usually do the cooking.

was only a cleaning lady who came twice a week. Mam had taught herself to cook; she had an instinct for it, though she could never explain what she did, never used a recipe; even with wartime rationing her dishes were delicious. She made her own bread; Darrynane kitchen was filled with the smell of dough set to rise in front of the Aga or the good smell of warm loaves cooling on racks on the kitchen table.

I had no such instinct but there was, though, one thing I knew Mam was aching for, to go away and see her sister who had always been close to her, as close as Jon and I.

Aunt Mary had lived with us in India but was now in Eastbourne, keeping house for her eldest brother, my gentle solicitor uncle, Alfred Edward Hingley. She and Mam had been separated all the war. "Is your journey really necessary?" had been the slogan. At last, with us arrived, Mam could go.

"Can you manage?" she asked me anxiously.

"Mrs. Treemeer"—our 'lady'—"will help me, and, of course, Nancy."

Mrs. Treemeer baked a batch of scones at home and brought them. Nancy would have done far more but, apart from one visit to Kashmir, Dick had not taken leave all the war years, was desperately tense and tired, and wanted Nancy for long walks, days by the sea, visits to London; also she had no more idea than I as to what cooking and shopping for a family meant. Soon I found I was doing it alone.

It was a fierce baptism. There were nine of us, counting Betty, and I was almost like the woman in Rachel Fields' delicious book, *All This and Heaven Too* who, in a like position, said, "I don't know what is the matter with this egg. The more I boil it, the harder it gets."

There were not even enough eggs; Harlequin's wives could not keep up with this invasion and for the first time I met dried egg as well as powdered milk, margarine—there was no oil—minuscule rations of butter. I had no idea how to make the most of the meagre rations of meat and though, in theory, I knew how vegetables should be cooked, I found it difficult to time them, getting everything together for a meal. I was, too, terrified of spoiling what I could get; anything burnt or curdled could not be replaced.

Fortunately a few things were off ration, vegetables, potatoes—I have never cooked as many potatoes as I did then. There was also rice—the one thing that perhaps I knew how to cook but, "If we have rice and spinach again I shall throw up," said Fa. "Can't you even make a sauce?"

"Get a woman from the village, I'll pay," was Dick's way of solving it. After all he was used to hordes of willing servants.

"A woman in the village won't come." Who after working in munitions or factories wanted to go into domestic service?

There is a tale still told in the family; desperately trying to conjure up something for dinner, I had made—or tried to make—dried egg cutlets. I suppose someone, somewhere, could make cutlets that tasted and were crisp out of dried eggs, but not I, though I had used, as the recipe ordered, precious breadcrumbs—bread was rationed—parsley and thyme. "What's this?" asked Fa looking at the curious, shrivelled yellow objects. The others looked, and did not even taste. "Very well," I snapped. "I'll put them in the dustbin," and did. I do not think it is true but could well have been.

"What a fuss," Jane and her contemporaries would say now—they are so deft, practical and quick. When I was young it was thought there were five things a girl needed to know if she were to take her place in any sort of society: 'to dance, to play the piano, to ride, shoot, and speak French.' I now added 'to cook' and determined there and then that no daughter of mine would grow up to be such a fool as her mother. Both Jane and Paula went to Tante Marie, that famous school of cookery; Giovanna, their Italian-Swiss Nanny—with us for many years—had taught them from their almost baby days to wash, iron and sew. They were competent as are my grand-daughters—and grandson.

"Grandmother," ten-year-old Charlotte had said that day when I tried to darn her socks, "give them to me." I gave them, willingly.

The, I suppose, shocking thing about those weeks of Mam's absence from Darrynane and, afterwards, when I was trying to make a home, was that they gave me no desire to learn or grow more adept: on the contrary, as soon as it was possible to free myself, I evolved a philosophy, disgraceful to most people, but which has stood me in good stead: 'Never do anything that someone else around you can do better than you can.' As almost everyone can do everything better than I, it is wiser to let them and I find they like it; they feel superior which in most cases they are, except for the few odd things for which I do have a gift: teaching children perhaps and amusing them; bringing up pekingese, and writing. That, above all, is what I knew I must cleave to because the worst thing about that cooking at Darrynane was that every nerve in me said I should not be doing it. "You must get that manuscript out of your suitcase," my 'voices' cried. "Revise it and get it to Spencer, *now*."

There is a vast difference between a book that is 'vouchsafed', its idea or theme coming of itself into your mind, and a book that comes from a searching, as with *A Fugue in Time* which arose from my interest in Dunnes' theory of time and the evolving of a technique which could illustrate that theory in the context of three generations of a family.* *The River* was one of these rare books that are given to you.

In our last winter—cold weather as it was called—in India, staying with Jon and Roland in Calcutta, I was asked to do a report for the Women's Voluntary Services on what British women were doing in the way of war work;† derogatory questions had been raised in Parliament. I was told to choose a province, so chose Bengal which allowed me to be in and out of Calcutta where Jon looked after the children. I travelled unobtrusively, wearing every kind of uniform so that people took me for granted; the result was a book, *Bengal Journey*. As part of the journey I had to go from Bengal's capital, Dacca, now called Dhaka, to our childhood river town Narayangunj, eleven miles away, driving along the road that was utterly familiar to me.

My hostess-to-be at Narayangunj had telephoned early that morning; the manager of one of the jute works that spread on both banks of the river had died and was to be buried that morning as is the custom in a hot country—it was April—and, of course, every European in Narayangunj's small community had to drive into Dacca to attend the funeral. As I was booked to leave on the midday steamer for Calcutta it was impossible to postpone my visit and, "Would you mind," she asked, "being received by the Babu‡

---

*More than twenty years later I came back to this technique with the novel *China Court*, set in Cornwall, in which I used five generations. Nothing is ever wasted.

†As told in the Epilogue to the first volume of memoirs—*A Time to Dance, No Time to Weep*.

‡Babu: Indian clerk.

in charge?" Mind! I could not have been more relieved but had no idea of what was waiting for me.

Indians do not change; their clothes and customs are timeless and there was not one Westerner in the little town to disturb this. As I walked through the bazaars and the jute works, along the river, past the Club, the bamboo-built church and school, the houses I had known, it was as if I had gone back thirty or more years and was seven, eight, nine, ten, eleven, twelve, again. Everything was the same: I had lunch on the verandah of one of the houses, waited on by white-clad servants who might have been our own. On the way to the ghāt we passed the gates of our house; I could see the top of my cork tree over the gate; the cork tree with its white blossom stood in a bed of scarlet amaryllis lilies. A short way up the trunk was a hole, my secret hole where I kept the poems I wrote and showed to no-one else but Jon. The tree was in flower. For a moment I hesitated. "Go in. Go in," the Babu urged but I could not bring myself to do that.

Most uncanny of all was the steamer; it was one of Fa's double-decked paddle-wheeled steamers with the first class forward on the upper deck, where I was the only passenger. As the paddle wheels began to turn I stood at the front rail.

Usually, as I knew well, the steamers draw away from the ghāt, then turn in a wide circle to go upstream but now, for some reason, the steamer backed. She backed further and further so that I, looking at the town, its banks along the river, its houses, mosques, temples and bathing steps, saw it grow smaller and smaller until it was like looking at it down a telescope, smaller but more and more clear until it was out of sight.

As the steamer turned I went to my cabin and began to write *The River*.

Spencer Curtis Brown could be a remarkable agent, sometimes so much in tune with me that, as with my first publisher, Peter Davies, we hardly needed words.

When Spencer had read *The River* he wrote:

> You need have no doubts that Robert Lusty will publish this. I particularly like the names* of the four frog children.

which told me he had read the book down to the smallest details.

*Their names were Olive, Bice, Emerald and Spinach.

*   *   *

In September, "Mam, could you manage if I went for a short while to London? Betty has said she'll help with the children."

"Of course," said Mam. "There must be people you should see."

"Yes. The Simons have asked me to stay."

A look that I knew came on Mam's face. Long long ago, as it seemed to me now in Darrynane, when I was young in Calcutta and carefree, except for my School of Dancing, I had been the Simons' lodger. They were then just married and impecunious although Gilbert—Jay as we called him—was the only son of Sir John Simon, later Lord Simon and Chancellor of the Exchequer. Jay's wife, Jimmie, had been a dancer and we had had—and have kept—such an affinity that she has become for me, another sister. To Mam, sisters are born not made and I knew she felt the Simons had influenced me away from the family—in which she was quite right. Jon felt the same.

Jay now worked in London, being Deputy Chairman of Cunard, the Peninsular and Oriental line. He and Jimmie had an elegant little house in Pont Street Mews and a country house in Buckinghamshire—I quickly became almost a lodger again in both; we had picked up exactly where we had left off.

A greater contrast to my solitary, frugal life in Kashmir cannot be imagined. Jimmie loves parties; in the aftermath of the war, her London and country houses were 'at home' to every sort of people; she cheerfully mixed them all, from high ruling generals and admirals to refugees and ordinary seamen and their wives. There were famous conductors, Malcolm Sargent was one, dancers, actors, consorting, as was Jimmie's way, with her cleaning lady's children. There were many Americans who to my astonishment—and delight—already knew of me; people of many nationalities came, many Indians.

No-one could forget of course, the sadnesses; few of us had escaped the suffering of the war years. Jimmie herself was not well; there were men who had been in Japanese prisoner-of-war camps, and were terribly scarred, mentally and physically; all the same life had something of the old ease and gaiety. Nor did it cost a great deal; 'You can go to the Ritz,' wrote Fa; Lord Woolton, in charge of food during the war, had brought in his edict against restaurant profiteering so that no restaurant, not even in the Ritz Hotel, could charge more than five shillings for a meal.

More important, for me, than the fun was that I was a good deal with Spencer and his wife, Jean in the tide of a writer's life. Lady Rhondha of the, then influential, weekly *Time and Tide* asked me to write for it; *Vogue* asked for a series of articles on any theme I chose. I was, too, constantly asked out—which was a problem because of my dearth of clothes.

It was all the breath of life to me; the place where, I was sure, I belonged; it was hard to tear myself away and go back to Darrynane:

To Jon.   October 1945

Oh Jon, I feel such a brute.......

On the night after we had arrived at Darrynane, before Nancy came on leave and before I had opened my letters, Fa and Mam had revealed a plan they had made for us; it was for me to have the lodge cottage as my own—"Without paying rent," said Fa—and do with it exactly as I liked. "It needs a proper fireplace," it had only an old-fashioned cooking stove, "Which you won't need," said Mam. "I'll do the cooking so as to leave you free. We might try to get a girl from the village later on when you can run to it...."

> They have even, I had written to Jon, found a school for Jane now, Paula when she is stronger. It is at Bude. Fa and Mam have both been over to see it. It's near enough for the children to come home at weekends.

Schools, I had known would be a problem; St. Breward village school was too rough for Paula, Jane was too old for it and had not been taught thoroughly enough to get into Camelford's Grammar School—in any case eight miles away. To be weekly boarders would have solved everything.

> It was such a wonderful generous plan.
>   You should have seen Mam's face when she said, "You'll all get well," which I am sure would be true at any rate for the children.
>   For myself, as you know, I have somehow been able not to take much notice of being ill.

Now, when I came back from London, Fa and Mam spoke of the plan again. "I can see the cottage idea isn't possible," said

Mam. "The others . . ." meaning Jon and Roland, Nancy, Dick, the little boys, as well as Rose, "will be coming and going, but we could find you a little house near, perhaps in Blisland." They knew I loved Blisland with its village green, great trees, white cottages grey slated, its age-old church. "I can raise a mortgage on Darrynane to put down the money," said Fa.

I was silent, had to be silent I had such a lump in my throat, but at last I had to say it.

I knew in my very bones, as I had known before, that I had to go. That I should never amount to anything if I stayed—the very contentment and protection would undo me. "It's dear of you," I said. "Most dear, but Fa and Mam, I need to live in London."

"In *London*!" Fa said it as if nobody lived in London.

"For a while I must."

"But how?" asked Mam. "How will you be able to?"

"I don't know yet. Somehow." I had not shown them the letters and, "If you go to London," said Fa, "you go on your own."

The Red Spotted
Handkerchief

Dick Whittington came to London to seek his fortune, carrying all his worldly goods in a red spotted handkerchief. Our worldly goods did not amount to much more than that.

I have an inner ear, 'voices' that, if I listen to them, save me from going wrong; if I listen I do right and, in fact, as I listen, an awareness comes of something in myself larger than myself, a feeling of being allied, that I am guided.

In those years of nineteen forty-five to forty-six everyone on every side said, "You must get a job."

"Only writing."

Spencer offered to take me into Curtis Brown. He was hurt when I refused. "Then what are you going to do?"

"Write."

Later, the Judge, when my divorce at last came up in court, was to look at me over his spectacles, "I will make a maintenance order."

"Please no, my Lord." What in any case would have been the use? Laurence, even if he could, would not have paid it.

"You don't look very strong. Are you sure you can support these children?"

"Yes, my Lord."

He did not ask me how; if he had, the answer would have been the same. "By writing."

What would have happened to us if I had followed Fa and Mam's plan? There is of course no knowing, but I took a risk, and made it riskier, by not stopping really to think.

To Jon   November 1945

I have found a house in London, not I suppose a proper house, but
I can pay for it.

Everything had been far beyond my reach; even with the com-
parative success of *Fugue in Time* and the near publication of *The
River*, I knew I had to be careful, and had almost decided to go
back to Cornwall when I saw an advertisement in an estate agent's
window. I was attracted at once by the price, 'Eleven hundred
pounds for thirteen years leasehold.'

It was in a mews* off Eaton Square, squeezed between two other
houses, with only one sitting room, a miniature kitchen, one fair-
sized bedroom—Jane's and Paula's I thought—a smaller one, mine
and a little telephone room off the stairs which would hold a bed
for Simon, who was with us once again as Nancy and Dick had
gone back to Calcutta taking Richard. There was also a resident
mouse with which we made friends; it always came out when the
telephone rang.

In front, the little house gave directly onto the cobbled yard; at
the back it was against a wall, but it had a garage—"I'll make that
into a playroom one day." It seemed possible, but when I came
with the key to take possession, it all looked so small, dirty and
shabby that I sat down on the doorstep and wept.

At first the tears seemed justified. "It's hopeless trying to get
electricians or painters," I was told. I was lucky in that the invaluable Simons knew a painter of the old school, too old to have
been in the war, who was prevailed on to come; lucky too, in that
people gave me coupons to buy essentials like kitchen things. Jon
sent, from Calcutta, some handwoven cream cotton material for
curtains. I painted the walls all in the same palest blue that I like,
so pale it was almost white, which perfectly sets off all other colours or paintings—or would have had we had any.

The house was so small it needed little furniture; fortunately it
had built-in cupboards and I had bought beds, some chintzes and the
upstairs carpeting from the former owner; for the rest we had
nothing and, at once I came up against a problem; the only furniture

---

*Mews were not fashionable then. They had their name from the old days when
hunting falcons were kept behind the big houses; falcons 'mew' or shed their
feathers. Later the low buildings were used for horses and carriages—in our time
for cars.

available on coupons was 'utility,' hastily made furniture replacements for bombed or blasted houses, cheap and badly finished. The alternative seemed to be antiques. I found that prices of these were not exorbitant, perhaps because people were still so numbed by loss and by restrictions that they had not woken up to true values, indeed most antique shops were still shut. Here I evolved another small philosophy which again has stood me in good stead, 'If you haven't the money to buy the quality you want, go without, don't compromise.' I decided to buy what I could—better to sit on packing cases than squander precious money on utility.

I found a sofa table large enough for me to work on or to use as a dining table, a set of chairs in Dutch marquetry: the stuffing was coming out of their seats but I loved their inlay of flowers and leaves. Best of all, I bought a Persian carpet for the sitting room; tutored by Ghulam Rasool, I knew I could not go wrong as this was a Kerman, to me the only feminine Persian carpets with their patterns of flowers and garlands; this one had a turquoise background, exceedingly rare. I remember too, our first set of porcelain; on my prowls through London I saw it, an almost complete small set in blue and white china, laid out in the window of a just-reopened shop. Any china then was as rare and precious as gold; I knew I had to make up my mind quickly, shut my eyes and bought it. Temptation lay on every side and I succumbed; I wish now I had succumbed more often.

Nobody approved of the house. "It's rather bijou," said Spencer which meant he did not like it. To me it was bijou, a little jewel of a house but, "Totally unsuitable for children," Laurence's father, my father-in-law, Doctor Percy Foster, whom I loved said reproachfully while his wife kept a disapproving silence. I did not tell them the children would not often be there.

Coming back to England I had never imagined Jane and Paula as anything else but at a day school, had never thought of our being separated, but that first summer at Darrynane had shown me that Jane needed to go away to school out of the worries and the work. Misguidedly I did not try and send her to my own last school, Moira House in Eastbourne, the only school I have liked where the Vice-President, Mona Swann had rescued me from complete educational failure besides giving me invaluable help with writing. Instead I was persuaded to send Jane to a school in Oxford; it shall be nameless.

A more powerful factor was Paula. Soon after landing in England, she had had to be rushed into Truro hospital for an operation—she had had what seemed, at first, another abscess on her thumb. It was a whitlow, dangerous in those days before penicillin because of septicaemia. The surgeon had been a Miss May, one of the most understanding and wise doctors I have known. She had seen, almost at once, that unlike most ill children, Paula was far more tractable with me than with the nurses. She even allowed me to go with her into the operating theatre though of course, I left as soon as she was under the anaesthetic —and let me be there beside her in the ward when she came round; mothers then were not encouraged to be with their children in hospital.

When it was all over, Miss May talked to me; "You must separate yourself from that child," she said. "Every time she sneezes, you tremble and that's not good for either of you. Find a small, old-fashioned unambitious school in the country, the more humdrum the better, and send her there."

Again it was the Simons who solved it. Jimmie Simon took me to a small home school in the quiet of the Malvern Hills where her own small son, Jan, had been evacuated when he was two. The big country house had been the prototype of Jalna, in the Mazo de la Roche Whiteoaks novels, only Mazo de la Roche removed it to Canada. It looked a children's paradise; the children built houses up in the trees, there were picnics, rambles; the curriculum was plain, untaxing, not much more than the three R's with singing, painting, needlework. It was kept by two ex-missionaries who looked like buns with rosy faces. It was ideal but, "Send that mite to boarding school!" Fa was furious and, "How can you pay for it?" Mam asked bewildered.

"Somehow." The educational policies I had taken out long ago had vanished with Laurence but I was working steadily and, "Somehow," I said.

I did not take Paula to St. Nicholas until the following April, she had not been well enough. The uniform was hideous, brown and yellow. She had to have a brown felt hat; the only one I could find to fit her was in Harrod's baby boy department at enormous expense. One of the 'buns' took the small brown-clad figure—it had never looked smaller—away to a classroom.

I saw her look back, crying, dragging at the kind firm hand.

To Jon.   April 1946

I had to walk away into the woods in tears myself. There were
sheets of bluebells, birds singing, slowly I recovered. Before I left
I stole up to the classroom window and saw Paula sitting at a desk;
she had been given a drawing book and coloured pencils; as I
watched she looked up at the teacher with a watery smile and began
to draw.

Going back to London in the train I was suddenly filled with a
new and extraordinary sensation—freedom.

For the first time for years, really since Jane was born, no before
that, since I married, I am free. I can get up when I want, go to
bed when I want, eat or not eat when I want and what I want; stay
out at night, work all hours and not be interrupted.

Most mothers are left desolate when their children go to school;
they face emptiness. Though indeed I would miss Jane and Paula
acutely and perhaps loved them more than ever, it was a strange
mingling of triumph and achievement; the schools could give them
what I could not and now, at last, I could, I thought, come into
the literary world where I belonged and, too, find London.

Dick Whittington had a wise cat to guide him. I had no one.

That early spring and summer of nineteen forty-six was a grat-
ifying time; it was not only *Vogue* and *Time and Tide* magazines
who wanted my work—offers came too from America. Dame Una
Pope Henessy, who was then the doyenne or the matriarch among
writers asked me to tea; her sons John and James were there to
meet me—James was the only one who eventually did not find me
impossibly farouche. That first tea was in March, a bitterly cold day;
unable, even after Kashmir's winter, to stand the cold, I had bought a
Persian lamb coat from a friend though I hated it, because it was
heavy and was fur—skins taken from an animal, I thought shudder-
ing and soon found an excuse to get rid of it—a delightful excuse.

In my wanderings about London—something I have always
loved to do—I came across an antique shop in the Brompton
Road. Peering inside, I saw it was full of packing cases and
shrouded objects—its windows were still half-shuttered—but in
the centre was a doll's house, a strange big doll's house, with
beautifully painted red brick walls, a slated roof. On the roof a

railing ran round a fitting for a telescope. When I went in I found the house was labelled, 'Observatory House 1868.' "Must've been the model of an astronomer's own house," said the shop-keeper. "How much?" I asked. "Sixty pounds." To me that was a large sum of money—in those days it would have paid half a term's school fees but I went to a second-hand shop and sold the coat. "After all summer is coming," I justified myself to myself, "never mind if you're cold now." I got sixty-five pounds but it cost five pounds to get the doll's house to the Mews; the 'contents unseen,' though, included every kind of Victorian furniture down to a tiny plate-rack in the kitchen, and a minuscule mouse in a mousetrap. There was also a two-and-a-half-inch occasional table—one of Sheraton's 'samples' worth, even then, forty pounds; while the drawing-room had a miniature Waterford glass chandelier.

That tea at Dame Una's was the last time I wore the Persian lamb coat; the tea, like it, was not a success. Rose Macaulay the novelist was there. "She has come," said Dame Una, "especially to meet you." Like all shy people I must have seemed arrogant, indeed heard myself lecturing Miss Macaulay on Indian music, about which she probably knew more than I. She did not make any move to see me again which was a pity as I had not only admired her books but revelled in them; altogether, not a promising foray into London's literary life.

And why did I think literary drinks parties would be different from the Calcutta ones from which I used to shrink? At which I always became what E. M. Forster called an 'ice-palace'—palace because, once again, shyness seemed arrogance? Of course much of London was enjoyable; there were luncheons, dinners, theatres, exhibitions—and I went to my first night-club.

I had fallen for an evening dress of rose-coloured pleated chiffon, hand embroidered in glittering silver; it was far too expensive but I had been starved of clothes. The first time I wore it was to a dance at the Piccadilly Hotel which had a famous band. When we came out into the street, well after midnight, a prostitute who had her beat there called out to me, "What a loverly dress," which was a real compliment. Prostitutes were allowed in Piccadilly then; I was told that, in the blackout, they carried small red-ended torches. That evening ended with my walking—or rather lilting—down a deserted Regent Street after the night-club, at three in the morning, hand in hand with my escort in the middle of the road.

*   *   *

To complete my home—also, incidentally putting myself back in bondage—I bought another pekingese.

> It's not that I am being unfaithful to Candytuft, I wrote to Jon. He will be in his place with me for ever, but I don't feel complete without a pekingese, besides this one is a bitch. Why I bought a bitch when it is the males that I like, I do not know. She is palest gold, with white paws, white on the ruff, dark mask and great appealing eyes which she knows how to use.

Silk spent a great deal of her first year in the cloakroom of restaurants, cinemas or theatres in charge of cloakroom ladies— London had them then.

Spring in London has its special quality, a stirring, waking more exciting than in the country because it is of humans, not the more steady wakening of trees, crops, insects, animals, birds and flowers; though London has plenty of flowers almost all are cultivated.

The particular square to which our mews was joined had, like all London squares in the war, given up its railings—every scrap of metal that could be spared had been requisitioned; in nineteen forty-six they had not been put back. I spent as much time as I could in the square garden, taking Silk, sometimes my lunch, picnicking while she ran free on the grass. We had no idea we were trespassing.

Children used to come there from the poorer streets and play cricket until a grown-up from one of the impressive square's houses came out to chase them away. One leggy small girl with a fuzz of red hair, pale face, pale eyes had a fixture on me—or on Silk. Her conversation was ghoulish:

"Do you like gravy?"

"Sometimes," I said. "Why?"

"It's *blood*!" Her eyes dilated with excitement. She was the origin of the child in a horrific short story I was to write long afterwards, *Lily and the Sparrows*. Instinctively I would not let her pick Silk up or take her out of my sight.

As spring turned into summer the pace of my life seemed to increase. *The River* had been published by Michael Joseph in London,

Little, Brown in Boston and had attracted quite some notice, "From the right people," Dame Una had said with satisfaction.

To Jon.

Last Thursday I gave a party at the Simons' house—and had several people including Judith Furse with whom I have become great friends. She was to be Sister Briony in the film of *Black Narcissus*. Also had the man who is adapting *The River* for the BBC, the editors of *Vogue* and so on. Next day I gave a woman's luncheon for Dame Una Pope Henessy to try and repay her kindness. It has all left me more exhausted than days of hard work. Why?

I had felt justified in launching out a little. School fees were, for the moment, safe.

Sam Goldwyn had bought the film rights of *Fugue in Time* the winter before but I had heard nothing more about it until one evening, Jimmie Simon and I went, on the spur of the moment, to the cinema where a film called *Enchantment* was being shown set in a London house that was vaguely familiar. The names of the characters were mine; there all resemblance to *Fugue in Time* ended, not even the concept was kept. 'Why did Goldwyn bother to buy it?' I wrote to Spencer.

'It was like buying a bottle of wine, using only a spoonful and filling it up with sticky lemonade.' 'It often happens,' Spencer wrote back. 'Forget it and think of the beautiful money.'

Almost straight after *Enchantment*—anything but enchanting—came the film of *Black Narcissus*.

Michael Powell who directed it, has told me since he saw the book as a fairy tale, while for me it was utterly true as the critic, Maurice Collis, wrote when he had reviewed the book:

'In these days of fiction we tend to forget that the novel can be, and at its best is, a medium in which the artist is able to catch the will-o'-the-wisp of truth, the wandering light which so many poets, philosophers and mystics have followed.'

There is not an atom of truth in the film of *Black Narcissus*—famous as it has become.

The book was set in Northern Bengal, India, in an old palace, the 'House of Women' near the imaginary village of Mopu. The Maharajah Prince—or General as princes were called in Nepal—

who owned all the land, gave the palace to an Order of nuns so that they could establish a clinic and school for his people but, "It's an impossible place to put a nunnery," says the Maharajah's agent, Mr. Dean the book's hero.

> "Straight across from here are the Himalayas, the Snows. You think that if you look level you'll see them but you find that you have to look up, far above your head. Right over you here, is Kanchenjungha. I have never liked anything better than that mountain, Sister."
> "Look at the eagles," he said.
> In the gulf eagles were flying, circling round one small spot in the air. Higher and higher they flew, but still they could not reach the head of cloud that hid the mountain in the North; they could not reach its foot; always they were beaten down to be lost in the colours of the valley and they always came up to circle dizzily again.
> Sister Laura spoke. "Look at that blue and pearl colour and the light in the sky," she cried. "It might be Heaven and feels like it too, the wind's so pure and cool. It's an inspiration just to stand here. Who could live here and not feel close to God?"

In the film the snows were white muslin blown up on bamboo poles; the remote Himalayan valley was a garden in Surrey; the palace looked a ramshackle imitation of the Pavilion in Brighton. It was, almost magically, redeemed by Jack Cardiff's marvellous photography—he even managed to get a sense of altitude and I have never had a more marvellous cast with the exception of Sabu of 'Elephant Boy' fame; he had charm but to cast a thick-set, snub-nosed South Indian coolie boy as a young Rajput prince seemed deliberately blind. David Farrar was Mr. Dean, Deborah Kerr, the Sister Superior. Jean Simmons at sixteen, perfectly fulfilled my description of Kanchi, the young Nepalese girl—'like a basket of fruit piled high, luscious and ready to eat.' Among the nuns, besides Judith Furse and Kathleen Byron was Flora Robson for whom I came to have a lasting affection.

I did not realise how counterfeit the film was until the première to which Queen Mary came. I took Mam and Fa who had come up especially from Cornwall; Mam, of course was bewitched but Fa's comments were wry. "Why are those fellows dressed up in those pantomine clothes?" he asked of Esmond Knight's and Sabu's brocaded coats, turbans and glittering aigrettes. A rajah or Maharajah only wore such things for a durbar, a wedding or a State ball; their usual dress was a dark cloth achkan, or long coat, buttoned up to a high collar and with it fine white pantaloons cut like jodhpurs. It was as ridiculous as were the troops in the film, Bengal Lancers, who rode into battle wearing full mess dress.

"Who gave that poor man a Shetland pony to ride?" Fa watched David Farrar's long legs trailing, his feet on the ground.

"Ssh! It's supposed to be a Tibetan palfrey." Fa snorted.

I suppose I was so unhappy because I knew what the film could have been; it must be remembered that in the forties, no film, as far as I know, had been shot in India for the Western market; it had not entered Michael Powell's, or the producer Emeric Pressburger's, minds that a film could be.

Black Narcissus has become a classic; it has been shown again and again on television and at film festivals. In nineteen eighty-six—almost forty years after it was made—it was given a new 'print' with a six-week season in London. 'The most beautiful, and sensitive film I have ever seen,' has been the theme of dozens and dozens of letters; if you have never seen the Himalayas I am sure it has a Shangri-la magic.

Next day I was the guest of honour at a luncheon at Grosvenor House given by the News and Theatrical Association and had to make a speech on writing for films. I was naive enough to think I could do it from a few notes scribbled on postcards while I waited in the National Gallery and I am sure it was a fiasco but I remember the silence that fell when Rodney Ackland asked me what I felt about the film. "Only that I have taken a vow," I said, "never to allow a book of mine to be made into a film again."

"Keep to books," was another resolution but that, too, was not altogether smooth.

"Robert Lusty is longing to meet you," Spencer had said over and over again. Mr. Lusty himself had written almost as soon as I arrived in London to say how delighted he was with, 'What we are all anticipating will be a long and extremely successful association,' and it seemed that no-one could be happier with a publisher and perhaps a publisher with an author, until Mr. Lusty and I met.

Though I would not claim to be psychic, now and again I have been subjected to an 'interference' which transcends the ordinary; it has always been difficult to know whether it should be fought or taken as a warning.

Mr. Lusty asked me to lunch with him at the Jardin des Gourmets. I had been all morning with Jimmie Simon at the House of Lords where Lord Simon was presiding over the Court of Appeal. I had to leave before the end, needing to wash and go to the lavatory before my lunch date but the Peeress's cloakroom was closed so that I arrived at the Jardin des Gourmets in rather dire need, only to be told that the cistern in the ladies' room had suddenly exploded and the room was out of action. I was too shy to insist I must be taken somewhere else and went through the lunch in agony.

Mr. Lusty—he is now Sir Robert—was a great editor who did much for writers, especially the young or new; he became Jon's publisher too. He was more than kind and understanding to me but the poltergeist manifestation persisted; after that luncheon he suggested that next time we needed to see each other I should come to 26 Bloomsbury Street which, as he says in his autobiography, 'should have been safe but as she (RG) arrived the ancient lavatory cistern of the house shattered into small pieces.'

It was not only explosions; Michael Joseph published a long poem of mine, *In Noah's Ark*. I read proof; Jon read proof; Mr. Lusty read proof as did his copy editor yet, when the book was printed, words had been left out or distorted, lines had been reversed, paragraphs were missing. The whole edition had to be withdrawn.

In an effort to end this 'nonsense' as I tried to call it, the following summer I gave a small luncheon for Mr. Lusty at the Colony asking an Indian friend and his wife who, I thought, would particularly charm him. It was a hot day, hot as only a city can be and I had ordered an iced fruit cup—white wine with fruit, cucumber and watercress in it. Mr. Lusty was talking happily to glamorous Cuckoo Chaudhuri, when the big glass jug with its silver top was placed on the table. As he laughed with her, there was a loud crack, a bang and the jug exploded over the table, festooning them both with pieces of ice, watercress, pineapple and cherries.

After that we decided, perhaps with mutual relief, to part.

Since February of that year I had been what Spencer called 'with book', but it grew slowly; everything else took up so much time and, "You must, you must," I told myself as spring came on, "must get some sort of help in the house, particularly before the children come for the holidays."

I applied to an agency called Proxy Parents and engaged a 'parent' to come from two in the afternoon until half-past five and take the children out, then give them tea, while I worked. Her name was Mrs. Errington Condé.

As soon as she arrived, "This is a very small house for children," she said looking it, and me, up and down.

Paula as usual—and as usual inadvertently—rescued me. "We don't live here," she said. "We live in Cornwall."

"Oh!" That obviously raised us a little in Mrs. Errington Condé's eyes though not a great deal. She looked at the children with hostility; with even more hostility the little girls looked back, but Simon, as always with strange ladies, was charming. "How do you do?" he said with a winning smile—Simon could be most winning. "Are you going to take us to London?"

"Yes, dear," said Mrs. Errington Condé. I think she meant the 'dear' but, "This is London, silly," Jane hissed.

"No. London's out there," said Simon, waving his hand beyond the mews.

"What a beautiful little boy you have," said Mrs. Errington Condé.

"Unfortunately he isn't mine." Her look said, "I'm not surprised."

Mrs. Errington Condé was tall, too thin, with a back like a ramrod, invincibly upright; I could not visualise her bending to put on a child's shoe.

She had a fur coat—"She smells of mothballs," whispered Jane. Her felt hat had a feather which gave an impression of elegance for which I respected her; she was hatted and gloved, her umbrella neatly rolled. I was in a jersey, slacks and an apron as I was washing up lunch; my hair untidy, my hands red from hot water, I am sure, too, I was obviously tired but, looking at the sink, the piled up dishes, "I'm afraid I cannot help you," she said—was it with a small titter? "On my terms I am not expected to wash up, nor as much as lay a spoon, fork or knife on the table. As specified, I will give the children their tea, but I expect that to be prepared and laid. I am here for the children."

"In that case, please help them to put on their outdoor things and shoes."

"School coats!" and Mrs. Errington Condé asked, "Have they no London coats?"

"These are our coats," said Jane fiercely.

Mrs. Errington Condé was not, of course, a success except with Simon—she even bought him some chocolate out of her ration but I desperately needed those three hours respite. "I can look after Paula and Simon better than that," said Jane. I was sure she could but eleven years old was not quite old enough to brave a totally unknown London and I had to harden my heart, trying not to see those two pairs of eyes, aquamarine and blue, demanding, "How can you do this to us?" Jane's worry frown had come back. "Suppose Paula runs away?"

"She's got plenty of sense," I said. "She would probably get in a taxi and come home."

For all my seeming nonchalance I knew it could not last long; that ramrod back never bent.

On the seventh afternoon when Mrs. Errington Condé arrived, an interviewer was there with a photographer. The children, accustomed now, had gone quietly upstairs; the luncheon washing up was stacked in the kitchen, while I, properly dressed and groomed, sat answering questions while the photographer set up his lights and his camera near the window.

Mrs. Errington Condé hovered in the doorway amazed, then came in so that I had to introduce her. "This is Mr. . . . ."—I will call him Mr. Brown—of, was it *Vogue* or the *Tatler?* "This is Roy Hatton, his photographer."

"The *Tatler* . . ." Her surprise was unflatteringly genuine. "Then you are???"

"Rumer Godden, the writer," said Mr. Brown.

When she brought the children back, Mr. Brown and the photographer had long gone; I, wearily, was getting tea—as specified—before I tackled the washing up.

Mrs. Errington Condé came straight to the kitchen her face aglow. "Let me do that," she said taking off her gloves. "Now that I know who you are I will gladly wash up."

That, for us, was the end of Mrs. Errington Condé.

Soon after came Arthur.

In the London of nineteen forty-six for any newcomer, domestic help was almost impossible to get; again I applied to an Agency, imaginatively called Clean Doorsteps, who had, I was told, excellent men. Men? I had thought of the modern equivalent of a charwoman.

Arthur was a small dapper man, going a little bald; his face had the greyness of city people who do not have enough to eat; he was though—'spry' is the adjective that seemed to suit him—'spry and deft' making no noise, except that now and then he used to hum—a contented hum. His eyes were grey too, with the unexpectedly long lashes that sensitive and delicate people often have. They used to light up when he saw anything he liked—he liked passionately. He wore black trousers, a striped steward's cotton jacket, black highly polished shoes. Though he only came three times a week—he was though, always dropping in—he transformed the house and me; my clothes were cleaned, pressed, folded and hung immaculately. If I dropped my coat on a chair, "Tchk! Tchk!" went Arthur. "That's a nice coat. You shouldn't treat it like that," and he took it away to be brushed and hung up.

He had been, he told me, a private valet. "A gentleman's gentleman?" I brought out the old cliché and, "Yes," he said with a curious wistfulness.

"Then, Arthur, why are you working for Clean Doorsteps doing work like this when you could get a post anywhere as a valet or butler? You would be a godsend."

"I know," said Arthur.

Soon I knew too.

"Arthur, have you seen my little silver horse paperweight?" The paperweight was precious to me; one of the few possessions I had taken everywhere I went. Of no special value it had once been the brass holder on the lid of a Chinese incense burner, a little horse lying down, its hooves curled beside it, its tail flowing round it; on its back sat a monkey scratching its head as if it were thinking; on the underside a cloud was engraved. It seemed to me most suitable for a writer's table but, in Kashmir, my perfectionist friend, Ghulam Rasool had taken exception to it. "Why brass?" he had asked, "when you have a silver inkstand?" The inkstand had been Fa's and it, too, went with me everywhere. "Give it to me," Ghulam Rasool had said of the paperweight. He took it away and it had come back silver. "Where is it?" I asked Arthur.

Not a flicker of response. Then it was, "Arthur, I can't find my scarf. The magenta silk one my sister brought me from India." "There doesn't seem to be enough teaspoons, those little ones I bought with enamel handles. I'm sure there were six." It culminated with an ivory netsuke*—a baby boy lying on his stomach playing with a ball, the whole two inches long, exquisitely carved. I had only had it three days and had put it on the shelf over the fireplace. "Arthur where is it?"

---

*Netsuke—a small wood or ivory carving worn by the Japanese as a bob or button.

Arthur broke down. "It's kleptomania," he said. "I can't help it, Madam, I can't. I love beautiful things, especially fine little things," he wept. "To hold a silver teaspoon, to feel silk like your scarf . . ."

The Agency was alarmed. "Please, don't prosecute."

"Prosecute *Arthur*?" I almost said, "Don't be silly."

"He's such a nice little man," they said. "Such a good worker. Usually we keep him to offices or factories where there's nothing to tempt him, nothing he likes." It sounded like a death knell to me—as it did to Arthur.

"Oh, Madam," he pleaded, "can't we come to some arrangement?" He had brought everything back in impeccable order. "I . . ." he swallowed, "I've been happier here than I've been all these years. Couldn't you just let me take something every now and then? You'll know where it is. You'll know I'll bring it back."

With deep apologies, the Agency was obdurate. "We'll send you Mr. Barty, ex-navy, completely reliable." I did not want Mr. Barty. "You'll know I'll bring them back." I can still hear Arthur's voice. "Please. Just let me take the things for a little while."

If only I could have.

September 1946.

A new factor has come into our lives—I have to acknowledge it— factor in the sense of one who does things, who makes them happen, a partisan, adherent, approver—sometimes a disapprover, James Haynes-Dixon.

The autumn before when I had been house-hunting, I had again stayed with the Simons and Jimmie had announced one evening that she and Jay were taking me out to the Mayfair for dinner and dancing.

"Dancing?" I said as if I had never heard of it.

"You can still dance, you know," said Jimmie and told me it was to be a foursome with, "A colleague of Jay's. One of those nice ugly men and a beautiful dancer."

I almost said, "But I've nothing to wear." It was true that then I had few clothes, certainly not London ones; the first time Jimmie had taken me to the Court of Appeal in the House of Lords, in the taxi she had suddenly remembered that hats were obligatory; I had none so she took the veil off hers, then fastened it over my hair with a rose; I must have looked like an imitation Carmen. All I had for the Mayfair was a long skirt, made out of a velvet curtain and a jacket that Ghulam Rasool had had embroidered for me in Kashmir with roses in shaded silks, not exactly suitable for dancing but I had no choice.

It was an evening of a kind I had thought I would never have again. James Haynes-Dixon was all that Jimmie had said; a nice ugly man, he could have been an amateur champion of ballroom dancing had he cared to. I had forgotten what bliss it was really to dance.

An unexpected thing happened, something James said had not happened to him before: dancing with me, he fell prone on the dance floor—perhaps it was symbolic. Next day he rang up Jimmie to thank her and asked her if I would go with him to see the film of *Henry V* and have dinner. Jimmie gave me the message. "Say no," was my immediate instinct.

It was strange, after only one encounter, every hair of me told me that James was serious—and I did not want to be involved. I would not have minded a passing affair—after all I was still flesh and blood—but, "Say no," I told myself sternly and said, "Yes."

James was constant in the lightest possible way; it was with him that I lilted down Regent Street in the early hours of the morning, yet it was not all fun; soon I began to have an inkling of what he was really like; for an uncommon thing, he really understood about writing.

One evening he called to take me out to dinner and, alert as it seemed to every shade or mood of mine, "What are you worrying about?" he asked at once.

It was an article for *Time and Tide*. "And it won't come," I moaned. "It's not right."

Then, "Never mind. I'll do it again tomorrow."

"When is it due?"

"Tomorrow," I said miserably.

"Then you must do it tonight. Now."

"James, I'm tired—and hungry."

Any other man in love—I knew he was in love—would have sympathised but, "You won't relax until it's done," said James. "Go and do it. I'll wait," and he picked up the newspaper.

It was half past ten before we had dinner but the article was done.

After that night he wrote to me:

> You were tired when I came, tired with the house and its difficul-
> ties: people, bills, arrangements, even Silk but, when the article was
> done you were less tired—refreshed.

How right he was! It is always work that restores me—and in
which, no matter how recalcitrant, I find my sanity.

I did not really guess James's true calibre of unselfishness until
that Christmas. The children had come to the mews; Jane and
Simon broken up from school, Paula who had been staying with
the Fosters. I had arranged to take them down to Cornwall and
Darrynane for Christmas and the holidays; we had acquired a car;
second-hand cars were almost unobtainable but James had found
one that had belonged to the head waiter at Dolphin Square—
James seemed to know all the head waiters in London. He was
reluctant for me to have it, "Too powerful for you," which was
true as it was an S. S. Jaguar sports car, painted turquoise blue. I
loved it but was terrified of it, so much so that I did not think I
could drive it some two hundred and thirty miles to Cornwall over
wintry roads with three children, so that I had booked to go by
train. Taxis were unreliable and I asked James if he would drive
us to the station in the Jaguar, bring it back and put it in the
garage; he had volunteered to keep an eye on the house.

We were booked to go on the day before Christmas Eve, the
23rd of December, and woke to a blizzard. Snow soon hid the
cobbles of the mews; it was difficult to see across it. James arrived
early. "Conditions are bad," he said. "People will try not to travel
by road. There'll be a mob at the station. Come along."

"I've booked our seats," I protested. It made no difference in
the pushing fighting crowd on the platform. James found a porter
and offered him ten pounds to put us on the train but we could
not get near it, and, as it pulled out, "All further trains to the West
country are cancelled," said the porter.

Silently we went back to the car. "What am I to do?" I thought
frantically. All our Christmas things had been sent on by post to
Darrynane, as had our ration books; there was no food in the
house, how was I to get any, let alone Christmas fare? What could
Christmas be like for children cooped up in a mews house without
presents, a tree, decorations—it was probably too late to get them,
besides the cost. All this was going through my mind as James
started the car, with three subdued children in the back, Silk in the

passenger seat with me. Then I realised that, instead of going back across the Park to our square, he was heading west. "James, where are you taking us?"

"To Cornwall," said James.

There was a cheer from the back. "But—you have an important meeting tomorrow," I whispered. "You told me."

"I'll come back on the night train or if they are not running, hitch a lorry."

We got as far as Exeter where, at the Duke of Clarence, Exeter's old traditional hotel, James prevailed on the manager to take us in—there were other stranded guests—and give us a late supper which the children ate voraciously. There was wine jelly; "Will I be drunk if I eat this?" Simon asked hopefully. I think we were all a little drunk with tiredness and cold. When the children were in bed—at half past ten—I drove James to the station. One train was running, but it had no heating or sleepers; he would have to sit up all night. He looked exhausted but all he said was, "I'm worried about your driving that monster over the moors. If it's bad in the morning promise me you'll get a taxi or someone to drive you. I wish I could . . ."

"You can't," I said. "I'll be careful." Next morning was clear, even sunny, though the snow was deep; two or three times the car waltzed almost off the road; on a humped bridge it skidded and hit the wall but all the way I was conscious of not being alone.

James had a magnetic quality with people of all kinds—except my family. He was strangely nervous of Fa; made terms with Jon when she arrived from India. How could he not, he was so good to her? Mam he adored and she appreciated him but, from the beginning I, who had learned not to trust anyone or be surprised at their behavior, trusted James, even though in those early days I hardly knew him. That January he was told by the Ministry and his doctor that he must take a holiday—he had had hardly a day off since the beginning of the war. "A holiday for myself?" he said as if that were unheard of, and hit upon the idea of taking two small girls skiing. Jill, the ten-year-old daughter of a surgeon friend was one, Jane was the other.

To Jon   January 3 1947

I woke in the night. 'I must be mad' I thought. Letting my child go out of the country, abroad with a man of whom I really only know that he is likeable and a man about town, and Jon, just *now*. As you know my divorce is, at last, pending. What if Laurence hears? He might make trouble, even challenge custody—though that's not likely.

James knew Switzerland as it seemed he knew almost everywhere—except I do not think he had been to mainland China or Siberia. He brought back a rosy sun-tanned Jane loaded with presents of Swiss chocolate for everyone, and sporting a gold watch. "James didn't give Jill one!" Jill's mother said next time I met her, said it with a certain look that made me want to say, "I'm sorry to disappoint you." Instead, "He's a very good friend," I said emphasising the friend.

There is an uncomfortable small poem by W. H. Auden:

> Everywhere I go, I go too
> and spoil everything.

I no longer felt like adventurous Dick Whittington.

Long before that Christmas I had begun to feel the chill of disapproval; was it that the book people did not like the films? That film people do not read many books? But I think I had disappointed everyone. Dame Una no longer bothered with me which hurt more than I would admit even to myself. It had started so well; she had been immensely kind and interested. "You should have had the Hawthornden Prize for *The River*," she told me, balm especially as one reviewer had just said, 'There is not enough meat on this book for the library cat.' If only I could have been lighter, less intense; as it was, I am sure she saw it was no use trying to mould me into a writer about town. *Vogue* quietly dropped me though I was still to write articles for them and, "When are you going to do some *writing*?" Spencer asked while, 'We are looking forward to news of your next book,' Mr. Lusty had written before we parted but the novel still lay unfinished on my table.

Then I found I had not as much money as I thought. "I'm not surprised," said Spencer. "You've been running about looking for pennies when you might have been earning pounds." The pennies were for the articles. The paradox was that I hated writing them

—I had never had any talent for facts and, like Emily Eden* in her delicious Indian Diary *Up the Country* I detest information, so that writing an article is a strain; it also means a great deal of checking and rechecking because I do not trust myself. Spencer was right; my only hope lay in my real writing—books.

I did not dare confess to him that I had almost forgotten about tax. When Curtis Brown in London or America told me of some, to me, wonderful sale, what stayed in my head was the original figure, like that payment from *The Ladies' Home Journal* for *Fugue in Time*, seven thousand, five hundred dollars; it would have been at least ten times that today. No wonder I was dazzled but what eventually came was this.

Curtis Brown, Ltd. LONDON NEW YORK

```
Received from -LADIES HOME JOURNAL                    $7500.00
For all American and Canadian Serial
rights on A FUGUE IN TIME by Rumer Godden.

       Less: 10% Commission        $ 750.00
             30% Alien Tax          2250.00
             Typing Fugue-play        23.48          3023.48

   Transferred via cable thru the Bank of Manhattan-    $4476.52
   New York City. , to the above address.
```

Now I looked at the little slip more carefully with mounting dismay.

Alien tax? That meant it would have to be paid on all my American royalties, worse on the Goldwyn money for *Fugue in Time*, which I had spent. Michael Powell and Emeric Pressburger must have made millions from *Black Narcissus*; I was paid only eighteen hundred pounds without a percentage. "Surely you must have known it was a poor deal," said James.

"They told me it was a poor struggling company."

"Poor struggling company, my foot!" said James in wrath.

He found me a new accountant. Murray Duncan of a prestigious firm in London was to become almost a guardian to me and the children but the first thing he had to do was break it to me that I owed the Inland Revenue nine thousand pounds, equivalent to ninety-nine thousand today.

"You have squandered, wasted and muddled everything," I told

*Emily Eden was the sister of Lord Auckland. She came out to India when he was Governor-General.

myself miserably. "Wasted everything from opportunity to money."

There I was wrong; from that time in the mews 'seeds' came, like the child in the square gardens that led to the short story *Lily and the Sparrows* in the old mysterious way.

That summer I had had my window boxes filled by a jobbing gardener; they were my only garden and looked fresh, as pretty as the house in that rather squalid mews. A few days later I had a call from two ladies who lived in the square, "Not a social call," they told me because, did I know, that the earth in my window boxes had been stolen from the gardens in the square? It was the first time I knew that earth could be stolen. The elder of the two ladies, she wore a hat with blue feather wings, spoke those, to me, memorable words: "If you want earth you can buy it from the Army and Navy Stores, seven shillings and sixpence the carton."

Ten years later, this turned into the London novel—*An Episode of Sparrows*—which begins:

> The Garden Committee had met to discuss the earth; not the whole earth, the terrestrial globe, but the bit of it that had been stolen from the gardens in the square.

I have come to believe that nothing is ever quite wasted; looking back I know that space of gaiety, even luxury was what I needed though it could not, of course, go on. I had to stop it but how?

In the end it was settled for me as things so often have been.

The mews between the tall houses of the squares was a cul-de-sac from which no fumes could escape; most of its narrowness was taken up by garages belonging to the houses; there was also a car hire firm where the chauffeurs often ran the engines when the cars were stationary so that the air was full of exhaust fumes and the smell of petrol. I kept getting ill; twice Mam had come up from Cornwall to look after me.

Finally, "You have had pneumonia three times this summer," said dear Doctor Foster. "You have a patch on your lungs. If you don't want to have to go into a sanatorium you must get out of London *now*."

"Say goodbye to the mews," I told Jane, Paula and Simon at the end of the holidays.

"We're always saying goodbye," said Jane, which was true.

Domestic Interior

To Jon.

Why does it seem that I always have to move house in January? And such a January!

The vans could hardly get up to the house for snow. It was said that the winter of nineteen forty-seven was the coldest for a hundred years.

Never have I been as cold, not even in the winters in Kashmir.

There Dove House, being made chiefly of wood could, in spite of its primitiveness, quickly be made warm. This Sussex house was built of stone and stucco. Though the rooms were not large the sitting room and dining-room had French doors opening straight onto the garden, letting the draughts in; all the windows were big and I had no curtains. The floors downstairs were stone-flagged, added to which there was a curious dankness or dampness that seemed to be in the walls. This was no wonder; I found out afterwards that the cellars were full of water.

I have had no running water all this time which means, of course, no baths, not even a pull plug. In the morning I take two buckets to the gamekeeper's cottage which is warmer so that their water is not frozen, half-fill them—filled they are too heavy—and stagger back up the hill with them; by the evening I have to break the ice.

Of course the beauty is such that you cannot imagine it with the snow on these beech trees outside my window and the pheasants picking in the snow, their feathers glistening, but I feel what one can only call 'seized' up with cold.

That too was no wonder; there were no radiators—I had only one small electric fire—though there were good fireplaces I had not understood about applying for coal so that the only fuel I had were sticks and fallen branches I picked up in the woods.

Silk loves it. She is stuffed inside with rabbit stew and plays in the snow until all her mask is white.

Nancy had found the house for me; friends of hers had lived there before the war. It was the small Dower House of Dale Park in Sussex, an estate that adjoined Arundel Park with its castle and old walled town that belonged to the Duke of Norfolk. Dale Park's Big House was occupied by a Mr. and Mrs. Pike—his name was Ebenezer but mercifully, he was called Ebon. He ran part of the park as a market garden but the Dower House had been empty since Nancy's friends had left. "I meant to put it into repair but can't get the labour," my landlord, a Mr. Green had said. "You can have it until I succeed—or until it falls down." The rent was only four pounds a week.

It was not, of course, practical; it was two miles from the lodge gates, even quite far from the gamekeeper's cottage and stood high on the edge of the Downs which stretched away beyond woods that I knew would presently be filled with anemones, violets, primroses, then bluebells. On clear days you could look far across to Chanctonbury Ring.

There is so much space and air, fresh downland air, that I ought to get well, I wrote to Jon.

It was though, lonely; in Dove House, remote as it was, I had had the children; here I was quite alone. There was not, as yet, even a telephone. I could not get the car out of the garage. London now seemed like another planet, my friends vanished into ghosts.

To Jon.   February 3rd 1947

A great adventure. The gamekeeper actually drove me to Arundel. I don't think he liked doing it. He and his wife are curiously surly,

I don't know why—perhaps they disapprove of a woman living alone—but I had to get provisions, had almost run out though the grocer nobly trudged through the snow with some emergency rations. Arundel looked like a toy town with burghers, a castle, in deep glossy hush, like a scene inside one of those crystal balls with snow. I gave myself a cup of coffee in one of the endless oldie worldie cafés. This winter is really kill or cure. I am well—only tired, chilled and missing my loved ones.

One person, though, would not be a ghost. I had resolved to hold out against James. When I leave London, I thought, it will all fizzle out, but he must have heard from Jimmie Simon of my plight and wrote, 'I am collecting bits of coal and as soon as a sizeable parcel is possible, will post it to you.' Who else would have thought of parcels of coal? The sizeable parcels soon came regularly—I do not know where he got the coal from, and that was not all he sent:

To James Haynes-Dixon   February 1947

When you said you would write to Naples and get me some really small and soft gloves it sounded like one of those magic geography stories* we had when we were young when it was nothing to fly to Smyrna—on a carpet—and buy some raisins. Of course I did not believe you and now here they are! Not raisins but gloves. What can I say? Only that they are small, soft, *lovely*, and thank you. They are laid away, literally in lavender, until I emerge into gloved circles again—here it is two pairs of woolly mitts.

The book grew slowly until there came a night when my mind, and fingers were too stiff with cold to go on. 'If only I could *speak* to someone,' I said, 'hear a voice.' There was still no telephone and the wind had blown itself out; there was ice bound stillness. If the stillness broke, it was only the crack of a branch snapping, the thud of snow shaken down. I did not know it was Saturday, when people could get off from work—only that it had been another frozen day; I had spent most of it gathering wood and was tired out. At last I gave up, left my table to crouch with Silk as close to the small fire as I could get. "I must open a tin of soup,

*I was to discover that James had never been told stories or been read to; indeed he was taken away from school when he was twelve and sent out to work.

break the ice in the bucket to get some water to warm and, I suppose, wash," I told her. "Put you out and go to bed."

Suddenly she got up, listened, rushed to the door and whined, scratching frantically to get out. There was a tap at the window. Startled I saw a man's face looking in; then, more startling still, a great bunch of mimosa.

It was James. Somehow he had got his car up the long hilly road and with him, what had he brought? Or what had he not brought? Besides the mimosa—its golden fluffy yellowness lit up the house—there was a load of peat and logs, he piled them on the fire; a chicken, paté, a big basket of fruit; new potatoes—in February—meat for Silk; Fortnum and Mason honey; Fortnum and Mason soup; wine, whisky. "But I'm so dirty James," I said near to tears. "I'm not fit to have dinner."

"We'll see to that," said James.

He went outside, filled two buckets with snow, they would have been too heavy for me to lift and put them on the electric cooker.

In one of my moments of silliness before I left the mews, I had bought an antique wooden cradle; it was supposed to be for flowers—I had thought I would put it in the Dower House hall. It had a zinc container; James lifted that out, stood it on the kitchen floor and poured in hot water while I collected towels, soap, powder and had a bath. I could just fit in the container. You have only to go without a bath for days on end to know how like heaven it is to be cleansed—and warm. I put on clean trousers and a jersey, cooked supper or, rather warmed it—everything was ready—laid a small table by the leaping, flaming fire, while James sat, getting warm himself, sipping whisky, with Silk on his knee and, "It's no use you asking me not to stay the night," said James. "I'm staying."

The first thing I try to do anywhere, in any house is to make it into a home; slowly the deserted house began to come alive.

Again furniture had been a problem: what I had had in the mews could not begin to furnish the Dower House which had four rooms, a kitchen and a bathroom downstairs, two bedrooms above. James took me down the Old Kent Road to a junk shop where I found two chests of drawers, a few chairs and a kitchen table which we used for meals. I did not attempt to furnish the dining-room. A carpenter put up book shelves but I was forced to buy a utility sofa and armchairs. I had no coupons, there was nothing to cover them with until I saw some mattress ticking which did not need them; it was striped pale grey and blue; a dressmaker in Arundel made loose covers of them piped with blue; they went well with the walls Mr. Green had had painted for me, the same palest blue of the mews, my hallmark in a house. The turquoise Kerman carpet did not even cover the floor but its colours shone in the space; the Agra rug was hung on the wall—it was too precious to be trodden on and, with the sofa tables from London —I could now use the large one entirely for writing and had bought a miniature one as an occasional table—the sitting room looked well even if the rest of the house was bare.

To Jon   March 1st 1947

My house sends its love to yours.

Jon and Roland had a house and garden at Tollygunj outside Calcutta.

I think of East Lodge over and over again, shut my eyes and see a shimmer of colour, hibiscus and the verandah and the fish, and the quisqualis and smell of sun and a great wave comes over me ... I cannot write about it. Of late it has been heart tearing, simply an overwhelming yearning, a bodily one, for sun and for the India that is, and always will be, ours.

I was content though.

This whole place is so lovely now that I ache; there are drifts of violets so that the woods are blue in great patches, why do violets look mauve near to and blue far away? There are cowslips and primroses everywhere. The garden has been sweet with narcissi and daffodils and grape hyacinths; it has lilac in it and a pear tree and a laburnum.

I had finished the novel begun in London. This was my long cherished idea for a book about the ballet, started long ago in Darrynane after Paula was born. Everything had seemed favourable; I had even made contact with Ninette de Valois at Sadlers Wells and she had said I could watch her classes, rehearsals, even be backstage during performances but the war had put a stop to that idea, I had thought for ever; yet, as soon as I was back in London six years later, in the mysterious way of writing, the theme had sprung to life again; the same setting but a different story. *A*

Candle for St. Jude is the story of a prima ballerina known world-wide, now living in London where she has her own theatre, small company and school. The book opens when she is on the brink of the autumn season, an uniquely special season as the opening coincides with her eightieth birthday and is to be a gala. The novel tells how she is first outwitted, later rescued, by her own pupils, in particular the brilliant seventeen-year-old girl Hilda whom she detests. "Because she is you," says madame's companion and sister-in-law Miss Ilse.

As always, when a book told me clearly there was no more to be said, I wrote 'The End' and signed my name. Then, handwritten as it was I sent it by air to Jon just in time; the Easter holidays were on us. Somehow I got ready.

No matter where we have been or if we never went to church, we have kept Easter. It is the feeling of newness and, I suppose, resurrection.

We kept it with family tradition; at teatime an Easter table decorated with flowers—in this case primroses—an Easter cake; boiled eggs coloured red for tea and after it an Easter Egg Hunt all over the garden—I had managed to save up our sweet rations—but this year I asked James who was spending the holiday with us, to take the children to church while I made everything ready. Children's service was at three o'clock.

"Church?" asked Jane. "*We* don't go to church."

"You do at school."

"Do I have to go?"

"Yes."

More and more, over these years I had come to feel I must have something; something, far beyond myself to hold to. For a long time I had thought it would be Hinduism but since I came to England it was as if that long long ago childhood time in London with our grandmother and the Godden Aunts' passionate involvement with the church, woke echoes in me now. Christianity? I had begun to wonder and perhaps, naturally, turned to the church I knew and went to see our vicar. "Easter is resurrection," I told Jane, "so we should think of Jesus. When you are older you can decide for yourself how or even if you want to do that, but now I think you should go to church. You'll like it," I said. "It will be all decorated with flowers." When they had gone, as I put our best new cloth on the table and began our decorations, I felt I had been tolerant, wise and—quite new for me—virtuous, even a little uplifted.

They did not come back till nearly five.

"That was a long service," I said and looking at their faces, "Was it so wonderful?"

"Yes," shouted Simon. "I've been on the ghost train."

"So have I," said Paula. "We had candyfloss."

"I won a goldfish," said Jane.

"Goldfish? Candyfloss? In church?"

"Oh we didn't go to *church*," said Jane. "James took us on the pier."

Late in April when the children had reluctantly gone back to school, Jon sent the novel back, and with it her report.

To Jon.

Your letter came as complete manna as did the cable. I did not dream you would like the book as much. I go about with Christina Rossetti's singing bird and watered shoot inside me. It is being typed at present and then I am sending it to Curtis Brown, the next hoop it must go through.

Of course I was on tenterhooks. Was Jon right—she usually was—but would, could, Spencer in London, Alan Collins in New York like it as much? Would Mr. Lusty?—under my contract with Michael Joseph I owed them one more novel. Would Little, Brown? Or the new publisher Alan had talked of?

Alan could not get on with Spencer but who could? Only a very few. Alan asked me to lunch at the Caprice and when I arrived, it was to find him walking up and down the little foyer, up and down. "Rumer," he had exploded, "I cannot deal with that man. I can *not* and certainly not through him for you."

Alan had made it clear he was not happy with Little, Brown's publishing of my books which echoed my own disappointment but, "Spencer thinks they are what I should expect," I told Alan.

"That's belittling you. How does he dare!"

"Little, Brown's Raymond Everitt writes charming letters . . ."

"And does nothing. Look how he treated *Breakfast with the Nikolides*."

That had been a disappointment still rankling as *Breakfast with the Nikolides* is the novel that, though it is faulty, comes closest to what I have always tried to do, truthful writing. The war had made it miss out in Britain—which I understood, there were many of us writer casualties—but I had had hopes for it in America but Little Brown published it with no attempt at promotion so that it passed unheeded and, "That was bitter," I had to acknowledge. "All you say is true, I don't want to stay at Little, Brown but where can I go?"

"You are going," said Alan, "to the Viking Press."

"But Spencer said . . ."

"Confound Spencer!" said Alan, and did exactly that.

Meanwhile Spencer had read Jon's new book, *The House by the Sea*, and sent it straight to Michael Joseph. Mr. Lusty wrote to me.

> Reading the novel, I was aware right from the start of a new and very real talent, of a born novelist who was giving one the authentic new frisson, presenting an original world, as though a world seen and expressed for the first time. All of which means that the author has something beyond the normal competence. . . .

I knew that, knew too that Jon's talent far exceeded my own.

The House by the Sea is the story of a middle-aged, lonely unmarried woman who is left a little money with which she buys a house on the Cornish coast. Here she will start a new life but her house—and herself and her life—are taken possession of by an American soldier, a fugitive deserter on the run. As she learns his secret, between the solitary woman who has always fled from pain and danger, and the hunted, evil man, there develops a strange understanding and link.

At Jon's request, Mr. Lusty sent the proofs to me.

Jon had always had the power to terrify. She had a strange dark macabre streak in her that at times made her another person. As a child she could terrify, particularly me; other children used to beg their mothers, "*Please* need we go to tea with the Goddens?"

We used to make them play a game called Iurki in our big nursery, dark when its shutters were closed. The luckless children were compelled to build a tower putting a chair on our sturdy table, a stool on the chair and then climbed up to the top of a massive wardrobe. The guest children would be induced to climb up, the stool, chair and table were taken away so that none could get down; the lights were turned off and one of us who had stayed behind would come in as a ghost.

When it was Jon it was blood-curdling; something soft with moving ends would brush our cheeks; "Spider," crooned Jon—cut wool on the end of a fishing rod, "Big spider. Black Widow spider. Poison. Poison." A hooka pipe wet and sinuous would come with a hiss. "Cobra. Cobra," and a white shrouded faceless ghost would moan, "I've got no nose. No nose." Some of the children had hysterics. "*Please* need we go to the Goddens?"

I had to correct those proofs, usually at night when I was alone in the Dower House and have seldom been more frightened. The very opening had a menace though it was deceptively happy and peaceful.

The house was a firm white shape on the changing colours of the field. Under the canopy of cloud the light was very clean and pure; every detail of cliff and field and house stood out sharply; the pales of the fence, an oblong of red earth where the front garden was going to be, even the aerial on the roof. She [Edwina] put her parcels on the step and sat down on the stile to rest.

She stood up, stretched out her arms as if they could draw the house across the fields and up against her breast. 'I love it already,' she thought, 'as if I had made it myself out of my own mind and body and heart.'

But, being Jon, the menace was drawing nearer. That night as Edwina listened to the wind she knew that the house was not as safe as it had been.

'There is something out there,' she thought suddenly. She waited. Yes, something was knocking at her front door. The knocking drew her from the room into the hall.

The dog ran before her with waving tail and a low growl in his throat and that did not seem to her to be strange or contradictory. She only knew that something was knocking at her door and that she must cross the hall, push back the bolt, undo the chain, and let that something in.

'Something out there.' For a moment I thought of forsaking the house and running with Silk to the Pikes at the Big House. Never mind the dark woods—but if something were there I should have to meet that 'something' first, worse if it were a 'someone.' Like Edwina in the book I raised my head and listened, like her heard only the wind yet I was in a cold sweat. 'It's only a book,' I told myself but I stopped correcting those proofs at night!

Once or twice at the Dower House there was a reason to be afraid. Near us was a prisoner of war camp from which the prisoners worked on farms round about or in Dale Park's Big House market garden. Most were content; in fact when their repatriation papers came some, especially the Italians, chose to stay in Britain but a few, especially the older Germans, convinced Nazis, tried to escape.

One early Monday morning, James, who had been staying the weekend, rang me from the station—we at last had a telephone. "I don't want to scare you," he said, "but coming down through the Park"—he had taken a taxi—"I saw police cars massed at the gates and managed to see the Chief Inspector. Four Germans have escaped and are somewhere in the woods. They have been gone three days and must be hungry and getting desperate. Don't go out. Get Mrs. Gatsford." She was an old lady living in one of the cottages who helped me with the housework. "Take the keys out of the car and hide them. Lock what you can. There are things I must attend to in the Office but I'll be down as soon as I can." Fortunately I was able to telephone James at three o'clock to say the men had given themselves up. James came all the same; he picked up a locksmith in Arundel and saw to it that all our doors and locks were repaired.

"Things are no different, no different at all with James," I told Jon, but it was difficult to resist him. There was almost no way in which he did not protect and help me, telephoning, meeting my trains, doing errands in London:

> Have sent off the card for Family Allowances. I get quite a kick out of this. I wonder how many people would, if they could, steal families? Perhaps many more than you'd think at first.

We telephoned or wrote almost every day.

The House by the Sea was a Book Society Choice which in those days brought real prestige for Jon, long reviews, requests for in-

For Brother James,

From my Cell to your Cell.

At seven o'clock, first meditation;

at eight o'clock, first breaking bread;

then humble tasks, and, like St Francis,

the birds, our brothers, to be fed.

At nine o'clock begin inditing,

travail of spirit, sweat of brow;

at one o'clock prepare refection,

lentils andpotatoes   now.

More humble tasks, more meditation,

then business and letter writing;

a silent walk in woods or forest,

or garden toil, then more inditing.;

a break, perhaps, to hear a chorale

or elevating sermon read;

more lentils and more meditation

and so, with halo bright, to be .

Mineis a contemplative order,* I like my work
(for lentils please read mutton-
chop.)
My halo fits me far too tightly,
I think this monkliness should
stop)*?

terviews, radio interviews and letters which often came care of me. People seemed to think she was my younger brother. Soon there began to be Jon Godden Clubs which she found difficult to believe; over writing Jon was always to disparage herself, which was paradoxical; she was innately proud.

She must have been heartened though because she had started another novel.

All this time, too—and as always—books, poems, articles, reviews cut from newspapers went between Arundel and Calcutta.

To Jon.

Nine letters today, three for you. One of mine was from an American asking me to trace the Foster family ancestry as she says she is descended from them too. There are only perhaps fifty thousand Fosters in Britain but her Foster, she says, is the only family in America that has a coat of arms of 'three bucks heads embossed.' —she does not say what kind of buck ... As she claims kinship I shall have to tell her we have no coat of arms. Do you think she would settle for a crest?

Fa had at last prised Mam out of Darrynane. 'Prise' was the right word because she had settled into it, taken root, deep root. She understood the villagers and, something rare among the Cornish with English outsiders, they understood and liked her. She loved her odd semi-basement kitchen that seemed set in the garden; she liked the roomy living-room where, in summer, the white rhododendrons behind the house seemed to press up to the window sills. She loved every view from every window. Mam loved the garden even more than the house and she had fiercely resisted Fa. Then he had had another eye operation which was not a success; this was the end of his shooting and fishing—he could no longer see well enough. For years he had not been able to drive; and the steep hill from Darrynane to the village was too much for him as it was, though she would not admit it, too much for Mam; she had developed a troublesome heart. In May nineteen forty-seven they had bought a house, more accessible, away—to her distress—from the moors, nearer the coast; Fa, through his telescope could watch the ships he loved, see the lighthouse rays at night.

Windmill was what he called a 'real house', built of Cornish granite, with granite curbed fireplaces, wide planked oak floors, deep window sills, a well laid out garden which Mam never liked.

I had to go down to help them move. Any move is dreadful—at least disturbing but this was poignant. After the long distressing day I went to my room in the hotel where we had gone for the night and, unable to sleep, picked up a book from a pile I had salvaged and brought from the house, a small book, rubbed with age, *The Meditations of the Emperor Marcus Aurelius Antonius*. I opened it at the words: 'Time is a stream in which there is no abiding,' and at once a story began in my mind, a story called *Time Is a Stream*. In it Mrs. Throckmorton is Mam.

Twice she gave way, went under: once when a man she had not seen before, a little man in a pepper and salt suit, busy taking a magnifying glass out of his pocket and holding it over chair arms and table legs and frames and china; he put it down on the mantel and rang one of her blue and white bowls with his finger and thumb. 'But—I understood it was for sale, Madam,' said the little man furiously. 'Not today. Today it is a private bowl.' 'Oh Mother! Come away.' Once was when she came on the spice cabinet standing outside on the white sand of the kitchen path. For a moment she failed to understand. She stood looking at it, holding to a piece of ivy from the wall. 'But you said it should go with you, Mother.' 'It shouldn't go anywhere,' said Mrs Throckmorton in an ugly loud voice. 'It belongs. It belongs on the wall in the kitchen between the clock and the dresser. You know that very well. It is not an ornament. It is for spice. Where else should it go?' 'Mother, listen.' 'I will not listen. These are facts,' and as she said that, a dark young man in a green apron, green and dark as the ivy, came up and gave her a look of pity and picked up the spice cabinet and carried it away.

How the children longed to come home.

Jane had come for half term, now the long summer holiday brought them all.

I had begun to make friends round about which surprised me as, in the nineteen forties, it was unusual to be a single parent unless you were a widow when you had everyone's sympathy but, with a soon-to-be divorcée and one who earned her own living, it was surprising. The Pikes at the Big House had been kind, she especially seemed intrigued by my work and I suppose they set the pattern. Jane and Paula were asked out to tea and to riding picnics—Jon had given them riding lessons. Soon they had quite a circle of friends.

Jan, Jimmie and Jay's small son came to stay while they went abroad; they took Gemma, their daughter with them. She, though slightly older than Jane was her especial friend—they were both redheads—and Jane was a little wistful but, "You went to Switzerland," I told her, "Gemma didn't," which cheered her. Now Simon trotted after Jane, a faithful slave, while Paula and Jan decided to live up a tree and asked for their food to be served there; obediently we handed up plates and cups. I would have done anything for Jan who was a quiet thoughtful little boy, small and contained. One night I found him writing poems in bed by moonlight and, "I can't show them to you until they stop being secret," he said. How well I understood.

To complete the happiness, Giovanna, our loved Nanny, came from Switzerland to stay and immediately—as it was to be always—she seemed never to have been away. Washing, ironing, mending was done, the children doing their own as she had always made them do. Mounds of spaghetti and risottos were cooked as well as a speciality from her region—she was Italian Swiss—potato cubes, rice and onion boiled together, drained, served with a tomato sauce, then topped with grated cheese. I have not met it anywhere else. She and the children made a wigwam in the woods, built a camp fire and cooked nettle soup, one of Giovanna's health rules, "You should always eat nettles in the spring."

I was more than glad to have her as Silk had the puppies the children had so longed for. She screamed like a banshee, would not let me leave her for a moment, even when Giovanna stood guard and slowly but, it seemed to me, with the utmost ease, produced four puppies, one gold like herself, one apricot, two white —she had been mated to a white stud dog—and all male.

Pekingese puppies with their oversize wrinkled heads, shut eyes and tadpole tails look like miniature seals though they are so small you can hold them in one hand. It is an odd fact that, when they are newborn, you can tell the quality; these looked to me extremely good. For three days Silk fussed over them, would hardly be separated, except to eat—quantities—fiercely attacked anyone who came close to them, went into hysterics when I picked one up to see if she had cleaned them; having such flat faces a pekingese mother often cannot clean a puppy under its tail. She had a look of ecstasy on her face when they fed, cuddled them, made crooning noises, then after three days, like the prima donna she was, abandoned them.

I tried to feed them with a fountain pen filler; only one survived, a perfect white but I had to surrender him, as agreed, to Miss Ashton Cross, breeder of the famous Alderbourne Pekingese. He became Jack Frost, a champion.

To Jon.   August 1947

About work, there is little to tell. *Vogue* have done the *Meditations** quite well except that they put Grace last. Why? I don't know. I

*"Meditations on the Qualities of Women."

have since done *A Cup of Tea* very badly for the *House and Garden* magazine. It was done when I had no help at all. Now I have Mrs. Gatsford, who very unfortunately is leaving. A Mrs. Phelps wants to come but has a child. I am seeing it tomorrow but fear it is awful, or at least so Mrs. Gatsford tells me. I would rather do all the work than house an awful child.

I send you *Horizon*. I am glad you like the Picasso book. Poor Mam was so doubtful. She makes me bleed with her few few shillings and her *enormous* desire to give us every inch of possible pleasure she can wring out of a bookshop. She has learnt to please me now but still not you. . . . Strange when she loves you so much the best.

And again from my diary:

Tonight the house is full of chrysanthemums which makes it look like autumn. Every evening this week, we have made a wood fire in the sitting room—with wood that we have gathered in the woods, please note—and sat round it, marking clothes, which is a pity, and having rolls and bowls of soup, which is our supper, while I read aloud, *The Jungle Book* and *Just So* stories. I think The Butterfly that Stamped must be one of the most beautiful stories there are.

The hypocrisy of girls' schools!

I had known, from the moment she arrived home that something was troubling Jane. I have found it best not to ask immediate questions but to wait hoping that, at the right moment, it would be told. The holidays though were running out and at last, "Is everything all right at school?" I asked her when we were doing more of that dreadful sewing on of nametapes—at least Jane was sewing them while, again, I read aloud. Paula and Simon were in bed. "Is everything all right?"

Silence. Then the needle paused, was held forgotten as, "What is it," Jane asked, "that you mustn't talk about and can only do after you're sixteen. Then you have to if you are asked?" That floored me. "Will I have to do it if I'm asked?" Jane was such a barometer for worry that I telephoned the headmistress.

"It was a case of indecent exposure," she said. "Two of my elder girls had seen it. As they were over sixteen they had to be witnesses in Court. I couldn't prevent it," she said virtuously. "The others were too young to be concerned."

"Concerned enough to be frightened." I hoped my anger

sounded over the telephone. "Little girls are not fools you know. Why didn't you tell them? Why make a mystery?"

"There are some things," she said with haughtiness, "I prefer they do not know." This from a school where twelve year old Jane had, in biology, to draw diagrams of the male and female organs.

Not that she needed to. At her play school in Cornwall run by the artist wife of Michael Cardew, that genius of a potter, a five year old girl, Teresa, had announced she had a new baby sister. "The Doctor brought her in his black bag."

"Nonsense," said four year old Seth Cardew who was painting.

"He did. The doctor did."

"He couldn't have," said Seth. "Babies don't come like that."

"Then how do they come?" But Seth was bored. He waved his paintbrush at Jane, "Jane you tell her."

Jane knew because she had asked me about the advent of Paula and I had explained. After a pause, "I see," said Jane. "She grew inside you from a tiny little seed. As she grew your tummy swelled to let her be comfortable in the water." Jane obviously thought this a good arrangement. "When she was ready, you made the hole in your bottom big enough—and she came out. It's like a flower in a flower pot." Then she looked at me, a penetrating look. "Where did you get the seed?" asked Jane. She was three years old.

I could not get that school contradiction over sex out of my mind. "Jane must be a *very* forward little girl," the headmistress had said. I was coming to detest and fear her—for Jane; there was something impure in this "very forward".

"She is normal," I said trying to be steady and not say, "You are the one who is abnormal." "Jane has always had animals," I explained. "She has seen them born, and has lived in India where the lingam—the phallus, in erection—is holy; it and the yoni, the hole in the ground, symbol of the female organ, are sacred and worshipped."

The woman put the telephone down.

I took Jane away and wrote to Mona Swann who answered by return asking me to go over to Moira House, 'if I would'—'would', as if it were a privilege for *her* not me. I went the next day, borrowing the petrol from my garage man and was more than glad I went. Soon it was decided; both girls were to go to Moira House, Jane next term, Paula as soon as she could be moved, maybe in a year or two, maybe sooner. It was a huge relief. I could feel the school would be behind me, they had made that plain. There were bursaries—Mona had told me that with especial emphasis. We should not be as separated. Arundel was only forty miles from Eastbourne so that we should see one another often. The fees were not much more than I was paying now and the uniform was simple; it would not be too hard to find the coupons as mostly the girls wore, as we had done, their own clothes.

It would be strange being at the same time a parent and a pupil; I was a pupil again as Mona and I had decided I should go back to her to try and correct all the ways in which I had grown lax.

I had a long discussion with Mona about the idea of a day school. With whom else could I discuss it? Who else would see, without bias, both sides? "They want it so badly," I told her, "but there is the writing. I feel cruel."

Mona was silent, then gave me the answer, the only answer, "If you give in, would either job be done properly?"

I knew they would not.

But sometimes I wonder, was it all a mistake? The night before the children went I heard them talking in bed. "I do wish," said Paula, "that man's wife had never picked that apple."

"Why?" asked Jane.

"Without it," said Paula, "there wouldn't have been any schools."

There was no chance of buying the Dower House. We had been there just over a year when one night, as I sat by the fire in the sitting room, the ceiling over my head which was the floor of the children's bedroom, began to sag; thank God they were at school. Hastily I evacuated everything though the ceiling did not quite come down. "Dry rot", said the gamekeeper. "I'll ring Mr. Green —you'd better get out of here." Two days afterwards, the chimney breast in the empty dining room fell forward, its bricks and plaster rumbling to the floor.

As if it were linked to the collapse of the house the hearing of my divorce case came on.

To Jon.   February 1948

I managed to go through the case without disgracing myself. It took four minutes precisely, was undefended as Laurence did not appear but to me it was unspeakably dreadful. Everyone is sympathetic, kind and wonderful but I only want to be rather dry and astringent and by myself.

If I had known then what I know now I should not have done it, no matter how sensible it was—I have learned the meaning of 'sacrament'—but then even Fa who was always shocked by divorce had said, "You will never be able to bring up the children if you don't," while Mam had pointed out what was true. "It isn't as if you loved him." She and Fa were hurt that I did not go to stay with them afterwards.

To Mam   March 1948

I feel so ungrateful for not coming and for worrying you. I am afraid you have been getting in a panic over me and *that* you must not do or else I shall stop telling you things and you know we agreed that we should always tell one another in full. I have been very unwell and, I think, on the verge of a real breakdown but I have strength in me and I *know* I shall not break down. What I must do, however, is to be away for a bit from everyone close to me, and any kind of emotion.

Jimmie Simon understood. She would have come with me to Court—as Fa would have done—but I had chosen to be alone; instead she waited in the car then took me to lunch. She did not mention the case, nor that I could not eat but over coffee she said, "I think it's time you bought some dining-room furniture. I have seen a dear little table, the right size for you, with mahogany chairs to match. They have tie-on blue cushion seats. Come and see."

It was exactly what I needed; the thrill of buying and another step towards a complete home—one with a furnished dining-room.

Small scenes of that year still come back to me: watching Jane riding by the Arundel Castle lake on a grey pony under the beech trees, her red hair blowing, the riding mistress with her on a huge chestnut cob, the Duke's shaggy black cattle all round them, and all reflected in the lake with swans sailing over the reflections.

Paula was, of course, the real rider in true Godden tradition.

To Jon.

Apparently Paula is the best child rider they have ever had in the stables; she is absolutely delightful on her pony, upright, firm and so far utterly fearless. She rides a tiny pony called Thistle, a grey flecked with white.

I remember Christmas at the Dower House, the only one we spent there. I had asked two of the German prisoners from the Camp to supper on Christmas Day, Josef and Hans who had sometimes worked for us in the garden at weekends but, "Ask bloody Germans!" said Mrs. Phelps.

Mrs. Phelps and her 'awful child' had come to us. I had tried to avoid anyone living in; one person in the house with you has to become too close, particularly in a far away place like the Dower House, added to which you spend your days chauffeuring, but Mrs. Phelps badly needed a place; her husband had been killed in the war, leaving her with a little boy Patrick, not awful at all, a handsome well set up four year old, but she was bitter. "Ask bloody *Germans!*" she said.

"Mrs. Phelps it's Christmas. Germans think a great deal of Christmas."

"Let them."

"They have nothing for Christmas in that Camp, just army rations."

"Serves them right. They're prisoners. I'd starve them. Nazis!"

"Hans was only sixteen when he was conscripted. He doesn't know what Nazism is about. Josef was a peaceful farm worker."

"All right ask them. I'll stay in my room, so will Patrick."

"You can understand it," said James. He was of course with us for Christmas.

"Of course I understand but . . ."

Josef and Hans arrived spruce and clean. They had carved, with their pen-knives a little wooden angel for each child, including Patrick.

We were able to give them soup, hot sausages, Christmas pudding—James had done a little black marketing—and mince pies sent by Mam which I had kept. Afterwards we sang carols—Hans had a beautiful voice. I saw Mrs. Phelps steal in; Patrick had broken away from her and came far earlier.

Josef was due to go home to Germany. He had a son—"More big than Patrick," Josef told us—whom he had never seen. I was able to give him some of Simon's grown-out-of clothes, at which Josef burst into tears. He had had nothing to take back to his unknown boy.

Mrs. Phelps went out. She came back and silently laid something on Josef's lap, something for which I knew she had saved her coupons and scant money for a long time, Patrick's new pair of shoes.

Perhaps that is the best remembrance of all.

Renoir, Ben,
Macmillan, Renoir

"Are you sitting down?" asked Spencer over the telephone one morning in May nineteen forty-nine. "You had better hold on to your chair. There is a film offer in for, of all your books, *The River*."

"Spencer, I told you, no more films."

"Yes but this is Jean Renoir."

Jean Renoir? Few foreign films had ever come to Calcutta. During my brief times in London, even when I had had the mews, I had gone to the ballet and theatres rather than films so that, though I knew of course of the painter, Auguste Renoir, I had not heard of a Jean. Did Auguste Renoir have a son? and I began "Jean Renoir must be . . ."

"Simply the finest film director in the world," said Spencer.

Jean was the second son of Auguste. The eldest son, Pierre, was an actor at the Comédie Française in Paris; the youngest Claude, or Coco, had been the loveable little clowns in Renoir's paintings as had Jean but it was Jean who inherited the genius, though in films not paintings. He had made the famous *Grand Illusion* and *La Règle du Jeu*. In the war he and his Brazilian wife Dido had escaped from France and gone via Morocco to America arriving almost penniless, but to immediate welcome.

Renoir was not the only French film director who took refuge in America; his great contemporaries, Duvivier and René Claire were there but as soon as the war was over they went back to France. Jean stayed, built himself a house in Beverly Hills and, with Dido, took American citizenship for which France found it hard to forgive him. He made at least one successful film in America, *The Southerner*, but could not stand the ways of the big studios and ended by walking out of RKO in the middle of a film which cost the Company at least a million dollars and Renoir his reputation among the film moguls. He was unrepentant and afterwards wrote:

> At that time, the idea of Hollywood producers was to make me do again the same type of pictures I had done in Europe. I was very flattered to know that they liked those pictures but, being a new person and being anxious to express sincerely in my work what I am ... I had to find a new style which would fit with the new person I had become and with the new life I had found. The day I read Rumer Godden's novel, 'The River', I knew I had found it.

This was largely because *The River* was set in India.

> Today the new person I am feels that there is no more time for sarcasm and that the only thing I can bring to this illogical, irresponsible, cruel world is my love. Of course, in my attitude there is the selfish hope that I will be paid in return.
>
> Rumer Godden's book is an act of love toward childhood. It is also an act of love toward India.

I suppose that was true. *The River* was based on my own childhood though I did not have a little brother who was killed by a cobra; why Nancy became a boy I do not know but she, too had that uncanny power over animals and was once found playing in a flower bed with a cobra. I must, too, have unconsciously anticipated her gifted small son, Richard who has inherited the same power, as is shown in the nature films he makes today: *Amati*, the life in a wild fig tree in Belize; *The Fragile Earth*, *The Rain Forest*, *The Jewel of the Kalahari*. Again Richard's career in films may have been foreshadowed by his playing, at five years old, the part of Bogey in the film.

This, though was to be in the near future. At the time of Spencer's telephone call I had almost forgotten *The River*. Two books had been published since, *A Candle for St. Jude* and a long poem *In Noah's Ark*—the story of how Pegasus got into the ark—and I was now immersed in finishing my new novel.

We had, too, moved to Buckinghamshire where a cottage had come up for sale in the village next to the Simons; Jimmie, knowing we had to leave the Dower House told me of it at once.

To Jon

I have bought a cottage, St. Peter's Hill, in Speen which is in the real Buckinghamshire country; it is seventeenth century, red brick and white paint, tiled roof and high chimneys, while the garden has small green lawns and roses. There is another tangled garden behind with an old espaliered pear, cherry and apple trees, syringas and a vast herbaceous border; it has an orchard, and about an acre and a half of ground.

Its brick is mellowed as it should be—after all it is some three hundred years old. The rooms are low, their ceilings not beamed, of which I am glad, except the hall which has the original deep brick fireplace—you can stand in it and look up the chimney to the stars; originally it must have been one large room, now divided into sitting room, hall which will be our dining room, a small study and, built on, a kitchen that has a steep walled staircase. There are three and a half bedrooms upstairs; one is tiny as it shares the space with a bathroom.

The children are pleased; from their point of view it will make a big difference; they can get about independently of me—the bus goes outside the door—and they have a great many friends near, including of course Gemma and Jan Simon. Later on they can even get up to London by themselves.

It is also a place in which one could be really poor without much minding, still have a darling house even without a car or electric light. I will write more about its arrangements when I have had time to think and work it all out. I do do do hope you are not shocked at me; I feel I need a little quiet cell so desperately.

Certain things had to be done.

The house progresses but like a snail, I wrote to Jon. I don't mind snails, do you?

It was the first house we had ever had which was completely ours, that was not rented or leased but I could not have bought it with the tax debt still looming over me if it had not been for the kindness of the owner.

On reflection and looking back, I do not altogether blame myself for these arrears of tax, because the financial happenings in a writer's—or any artist's—life are so extraordinary that very few even trained accountants can deal with them. Most people know more or less what their income for the year and the next year will be; a writer cannot even predict, let alone know, from one year to another what he or she will earn. It can change dramatically in a way not even a publisher or agent with all their experience can foresee, not only in a year but in a month, even a week. When I open a 'money letter' as our family calls them, the cheque inside may be for thirty thousand pounds or three pence as happened with my first novel *Chinese Puzzle*.

Added to this, tax itself may change; not long after Murray Duncan's dismal assessment, an agreement was reached between Britain and the United States by which alien tax disappeared—with advantage to me as a dollar earner. On the other hand, during what could be called my peak earning time, British tax could reach, in the highest band, eighty three per cent so that of every hundred pounds I earned I got seventeen. Even in nineteen forty-nine tax conditioned everything I did.

Mrs. Vivyan had lived in St. Peter's Hill with her daughter, who, though only in her twenties, had been dying of leukaemia. When finally she died Mrs. Vivyan could not bear to stay in the cottage. "But I want it to go to someone who will make it alive again. I feel you could."

"I think I could but . . ." The price was three thousand pounds and I had to tell her, "I'm afraid I can't rise to that."

"Could you if I let you pay me a thousand a year?"

The overwhelming kindness of people! St. Peter's Hill was only half-detached; its other half being the village bakery. Its great brick oven, still stoked with wood, filled the back garden with the good smell, reminding me of Darrynane, of bread put to cool on great slatted shelves. Many of the village Sunday joints and Christmas turkeys were baked there too.

My first night at St. Peter's I was in the kitchen trying to get things straight when there was a tap on the window. A hand opened it and a man's face appeared, lit with a smile. His hair and his cheeks were patched with white flour; one hand held a cake, the other a loaf—by its smell freshly baked.

"I'm Mr. Martin your baker," said the face. "Mrs. Martin sends the cake. Welcome. We're only next door so don't feel afraid all on your own. One good scream and we'll be out."

*   *   *

The house seemed beneficent. Things were sorting themselves out; I had my decree absolute, and now that the divorce was irrevocable I felt better; we could get on with our lives though Jane was torn —she had such a loyal heart. Paula was not concerned; she had hardly known Laurence. Above all I was free. Slowly, I was reducing the tax debt; I had arranged things amicably with James who remained the support of my life but had agreed to stay on the edge of it—I thought. I had reliable help; the Simons' gardener for six hours a week, while Mrs. Vivyan's daily maid had agreed to stay.

This was Freda, first of the long line of daily helpers who have made such a difference to my life. Freda lived in the village with her mother, Mrs. Bowler with whom she did not get on. They seemed totally without love. Freda was against everyone—except Mrs. Vivyan—and at first resented me as having usurped St. Peter's Hill.

"It is good of you to stay and help me," I said trying to mollify her.

"I couldn't find anywhere else to go to," was the blunt reply.

For weeks she was taciturn. "I don't get on with children," she warned me but she changed; Jane and Paula became her children and the only time in our quite long time together Freda spoke harshly to me was when, driving too fast, I hit a bird. The children loved her, especially when she made lace on a lace cushion with beautiful bobbins. I still have the exquisite small hand-made lace edged handkerchiefs she made for me.

I also had what I had not had before, a secretary—part-time. Beatrice Eugenia Hulton sounded as if she might be a second Mrs. Errington Condé; added to which she was the only child of Speen's biggest house, brought up in almost Edwardian shibboleths, but Bee, as we called her, a honey bee, asked at once, if she might help with the children in the holidays.

Her mother particularly charmed us; tall, stately and unbending—the children called her Aunt Hollyhock—I never saw her without a hat. Her husband was Honest Tom because, "He never says silly pretending things to children," said Jane. They were aristocrats; sometimes Bee and I would go away for the weekend —I usually to Monk's Hall, the house Curtis Brown kept for entertaining and which Spencer ran; on the way I would drop Bee at some aunt or cousin's manor house or stately home. She seemed to have no friends which worried Aunt Hollyhock and Honest Tom and, I think, was partly why they encouraged us. "Bee mustn't *always* be with her family. You make her feel less shy." She had, too, never met children and was almost pathetically entranced by them.

Every holiday the Hultons invited us to tea. "Grown-up tea— in the drawing room," said Jane with satisfaction. The table was spread with an embroidered cloth, silver tray, teapot and jug; a vast bowl to rinse the cups in before each fresh pouring, brown bread and butter—wafer thin; strawberry jam and clotted cream while on a cake stand was always a dark rich plum cake, another cake, often coffee cake, small rock buns, all the work of Bee.

Aunt Hollyhock dispensed tea wearing her hat. Honest Tom waited gravely on us including two small girls—not a word was said about crumbs on the carpet.

Aunt Hollyhock and Honest Tom were our endorsement in that caste-bound village, where it seemed that even with tea there were niceties of behaviour. "They're milk-firsters," I heard one county lady say to another, condemning a newly-arrived household. I did not know what she meant but apparently, when pouring tea, to put the milk in first was, "middle class," they said in derision. I had never done that simply because, having lived on a tea-garden, I knew that the chill impact of milk in the cup before it was filled, would spoil the aroma—the cup, of course, should have been warmed. I expect we did numberless things that would have put us beyond the pale—"But if the *Hultons* are friends," was said. "The Simons in the next village are in and out all the time. He *is* a Viscount," and we were 'accepted', a fact that did not dawn on me until I was enlightened by Bee and which made not the slightest difference because, though liking our first taste of English village life, our real life, even the children's went far beyond it which I suppose was why the advent of Renoir was not really a surprise.

It was not, though, his world reputation that made me change my mind about films of my books; I had known other great film men, Goldwyn, Pressburger and Powell. It was the fact that, as Spencer told me, after Renoir had read *The River* and before he approached me he, Jean Renoir, had gone to Bengal, to Narayangunj to find our old house and had even slept the night in our nursery.

I still laugh when I remember my first meeting with Jean Renoir.

He and Dido had arrived in England and he had telephoned asking if they could come to dinner at St. Peter's Hill, "Chez vous," he said. "Chez moi," I tried to keep the dismay out of my voice. "I hear you are the mother" ... only it was "I 'ear you are ze mozzer," and he lapsed into French, "de deux petite filles charmante, et j'espère—if eet is possible d'être en famille." "Which means no-one else," said Spencer. I had immediately thought of asking Jimmie and Jay, not having learnt that it is not wise to mix business—and after all this was business—with friends or those not concerned. "He wants to see you as you are," said Spencer. "Heaven help him."

"But we have no wineglasses," I said and, as usual, in panic consulted James.

"Give them toothglasses," said James which Jean and Dido would not have minded in the least but I felt I had to go out and buy the only glasses I could get without coupons, cut glass antiques. From the days of *The Greengage Summer* I knew French people always expected wine and perhaps with the memory of that vintage summer, I rang up Harrod's wine department and asked their man to recommend me a really fine champagne. "Whatever the cost?" he asked.

"Well, no." That would have been showing off. "What would you choose to give your guests yourself if you had an especial party?" "There's pink champagne," Jane whispered. "Do have that." But I knew that would not do. "Veuve Clicquot or Pommery," I ventured but he told me a vintage I had not heard of. "Very choice." Then, "How many bottles?" he asked. There was a surprised silence when I said, "One."

I was to find that, in Beverly Hills, when Jean and Dido gave a dinner at home for every guest there was a bottle of wine. As a true Burgundian, Jean with every bottle could not only tell you the vintage but from which vineyard it came.

"And what can I give them to eat?" I had asked. "I shall have to *cook*!" The idea brought another panic.

"Something perfectly plain," said James.

"But I think Renoir is a great gourmand."

"Which is why I said 'plain'," said James. "He'll like that best. I'll send you some smoked salmon which you'll serve with thin brown bread and butter—nothing else but a slice of lemon. Have you any cayenne pepper?" I thought not. "I'll send that too."

I do not remember what our main course could have been—probably Bee came to the rescue, but I had made what I hoped was a trifle.

They came in a chauffeur driven car. "*What* a big car," exclaimed Paula peeping and a moment later, "What a big man!"

Jean was so enormous he hardly fitted into our cottage—the children called him Babar the elephant. Almost bald, his small shrewd eyes were hidden in rolls of fat which shook gently when he laughed; he had the most genial disarming face and voice and spoke the most endearing English—I remember 'come on sense' for 'common sense' but it was usually French, vivid with argot. Dido was a little fiery Brazilian, proud with fine bones, nostrils that could dilate with fury or amusement, almost monkey quick and brilliant dark eyes. I do not know a European language Dido does not speak. I particularly liked to hear her speak Portuguese.

"Why do you laugh?" another film personage was to ask me when we were listening to Dido. "You can't understand." "No," I said, "but it sounds like a little horse trotting!"

Neither she nor Jean betrayed by the least wink or look at one another what they must have thought of our dinner; indeed they seemed to enjoy it—perhaps its very naiveté touched them.

We were waited on reverently by the children. The trifle was a failure. Resourcefully Jane did not serve it but brought in grapes and cheese which was lucky because, "Excellent!" said Jean. "There is one thing I abominate, dessert after a good meal."

He insisted on washing up with the children and tipped them, "A whole pound *each*," Paula marvelled.

Our chairs, even the sofa in the sitting room were too small for Jean who eventually, still talking, lay down on the floor to the children's amazement; ostensibly they had gone to bed but I knew they were fascinated and were still listening and watching.

The film, he explained to me, was to be made entirely in India; but first I was to come out to Beverly Hills and write the script with him. "No-one else," he said, "can write that script."

"You will stay with us", said Dido.

"And of course, be all the time with us in India," said Jean.

"How long will it all take?" I ventured.

"Who can tell?" Jean shrugged. "Two months, perhaps to write the script, then casting. We will cast the principals in America or England, the rest in India. Then we must find locations, et cetera." Jean's rendering of et cetera 'ek-cetté-ra' I was to hear over and over again. "Then will come shooting the film, six months, nine months, who can tell? But first you must come to Beverly Hills."

Nine hundred and ninety nine times out of a thousand Spencer had cautioned me, perhaps ninety nine thousand nine hundred times out of a hundred thousand, when a book or an idea is taken for a film, the film does not happen—many authors live on film options. I had already had two films completed which was more than my share so that I ordered myself sternly to treat that evening as fantasy, nothing more. Fortunately a great deal was happening in my book world. In that year of nineteen forty-nine once again everything was new, the new house, new familiars, and what was to be of lasting importance, new publishers.

In America Alan Collins had succeeded in carrying out his idea of my going to the Viking Press—at that time one of the few privately owned publishing houses in the United States; they had taken me over from Little, Brown who ceded all rights in back books. Viking was especially pleased to have *Black Narcissus* as well as *A Candle for St. Jude*, the last novel owed to Little, Brown under my contract. Viking published it that spring. It seemed like the handing over of footballers from Club to Club except that no money was paid for or to me. Then one evening in April, Spencer announced, "Come up to London. I am taking you to meet Mr. Huebsch, Ben Huebsch, the President of Viking."

I already knew about Ben who had run his own publishing house for twenty years under the sign of a seven branched candlestick because Ben was Jewish of Swedish extraction; his wife Alfhilde was one of three sisters who, together, owned a vast estate near Stockholm. Ben's publishing was pioneer in that it was perhaps the first to bring modern foreign books to America so that it seemed fitting, that when he amalgamated with the rich Harold Guinsberg, also Jewish, they chose the symbol of a Viking ship with its daredevil crew for their joint adventure.

When I met him, Ben was the doyen of New York's literary world, the doyenne being Blanche Knopf, wife of Alfred Knopf, later Jon's publisher. Neither Ben nor Blanche can be replaced, not only because of their flair and style but for their knowledge and the wide net they spread. Until he died, Ben spent three months every summer scouring London or Europe for writers, visiting and revisiting the continental capitals and bringing back authors like James Joyce, Stefan Zweig, Kafka, Roger Martin du Gard, the

French Nobel Prize winner. No wonder I was awed as we waited for the lift at Athenaeum Court in Piccadilly where Ben always stayed.

"Spencer, you won't leave me," I begged, "Promise.'

"I promise."

As he welcomed us in his sitting room, Ben spoke chiefly to Spencer—he had fathomed my shyness at once but I knew he was taking me in as I was taking in him, his height and bulk, fresh clear complexion, silver hair, shrewd grey eyes behind pince-nez. I saw at once the fineness of his dogtooth tweed suit—Ben always had his suits woven for him in Sweden. He had too an aura—to me almost a halo about him—a wise twinkling halo. Irwin Edman, the philosopher once told me that in New York Ben was called "the astute saint." He would have chuckled over that but he could have no better name.

We had been half an hour with him when Spencer looked at his watch and said, "Ben, I'm sorry. I have an appointment. I'll leave Rumer with you," and, perfidious, was gone even before I could get up. It was two hours later that I came down in the lift to find Spencer waiting patiently in the foyer. "Well?" he asked.

"It is *well*," I answered. Ben Huebsch became my literary father, dearer to me than Fa.

In London, with the novel *A Candle for St. Jude*, I had fulfilled my contract with Michael Joseph and Mr. Lusty. "What now?" asked Spencer and suggested Victor Gollancz. "I'm not political," I said, "and I dislike those garish yellow and black jackets." It was the remark of an ignoramus but Spencer, who could not resist a chance to make mischief, repeated it to Victor. I would not be surprised if the result in our village is still talked of today.

Speen had a post office opposite *the* Shop which was kept by Emily who knew every in and out of everybody in the village or if she did not know speedily found out. She was at first shocked by James coming down to see me and spending the night; she always called him The Man. "I see The Man left to catch the eight o'clock at Wycombe," she would say to me. "So he did," I would answer and said no more, though Emily's sharp eyes seemed to be boring holes in me.

The postmaster was ninety-two, a bent frail old man with a Rip Van Winkle beard. The post-office was run by his three daughters but, to keep his title of postmaster, he had to take an active part so, to the houses near enough, he delivered letters and parcels. He carried them in a basket and when, doddering along he came to a gate, he would take the post in—not always the right post—leaving the basket in the middle of the road. "So t'cars know where I be and won't run over I."

There was a heavy parcel for me. As I took it from him, "Why didn't your daughters telephone. I would have come and fetched this," I said.

"They says I mun do it," and, "Books from Lunnon like." I knew they always read postmarks and labels.

It was books, a dozen of them; another dozen came next day, the day after that and the next two days. With the last parcel I had to pick up the basket and help the old man home. The parcels had my address on them, nothing else but every book was a Gollancz book, none of them was political and none of them had a yellow and black jacket. In the end there must have been fifty of them. It was a perfect gesture and, "I should like to go to Victor Gollancz after all," I told Spencer.

"No, you wouldn't," he said firmly.

"I would."

"You wouldn't like it if, when Victor was writing his own books—and when isn't he?—no notice would be taken of yours. You are going to Macmillan," said Spencer.

"Will they have me?" I said astounded.

Macmillan were then, as I hope they are now, one of the most prestigious of British publishers and, as their name implied, Scottish founded, by two brothers, the first Daniel and the first Alexander in eighteen forty-three so that it was one hundred and six years after, that I became their author.

As a tentative move, under Spencer's guardianship I went to Boulestin's, a restaurant I had come to honour even more than the Ivy—to meet my editor to be, Rache Lovat Dickson. I was at once taken by his charm which was infinite though I had to discover, sometimes painfully—disappointment is painful—that charm does not necessarily mean promises will be kept; you would think I would have learned that from Laurence but perhaps for me the publisher obscured the man and Rache's promises were so golden, he was so good-looking, that to begin with I never questioned. Once I understood, we became friends and were friends until he died.

Macmillan's wheels grind slowly and it was not until two or

three months afterwards that I was invited to one of the famous, and intimate, Wednesday luncheons held by the directors in their boardroom.

In nineteen forty-nine Macmillan were still in their handsomely spacious Victorian house in St. Martin's Street—not as handsome or spacious for the staff who, as I discovered that day, had to work in the cramped back quarters, some of the secretaries in what were little more than cupboards while the directors' rooms in the first floor were roomy; Rache's for instance, with its panelling, wide fireplace for a wood fire, Persian rugs and big desk, overlooked a garden courtyard and was filled with light and air. There were upright leather seated chairs for authors which seemed to spell business—and in spite of Rache's sweet embroideries—business in a plain forthright Scots way, but on that Wednesday I had not sat in one of those chairs—yet.

I was ushered into a large hall, panelled too as were the staircase and the gallery above. All were carpeted so that there seemed a reverent hush, into which the receptionist's "Miss Godden?" seemed to ring over loudly. All round the hall and up the staircases were signed photographs. I recognized some of them; Oscar Wilde, Max Beerbohm, Hugh Walpole, Winston Churchill, the Sitwells, Countess von Arnim—otherwise Elizabeth of *Elizabeth and her German Garden*—Bernard Shaw.

The gallery that led to the boardroom was even more impressive with, all down its length, lifesize paintings of Tennyson, Longfellow, Thomas Hardy, Kipling and as, once again, at the boardroom door the receptionist announced, 'Miss Rumer Godden' I felt an exceedingly new new girl.

Harold Macmillan was host with Daniel Macmillan as his second. The guests were Graham Greene and me, the only woman. Rache who came forward to greet and introduce me, waited on us; the food came up in a lift.

This I can perfectly recall, can still see Rache's hands pulling on the rope of the lift, the light falling on the august heads bent above the white tablecloth but, by one of memory's adverse tricks, of anything else I remember nothing at all, cannot even describe how anybody looked, except that there was an atmosphere of kindliness and wit.

After luncheon, Harold Macmillan took me to meet the staff who seemed to me legion. He came with me to the head of the stairs, calling the receptionist to get me a taxi, then said goodbye with

Rose on the balcony at Darrynane

Deborah Kerr, Emeric Pressburger, Michael Powell, Alfred Junge, and R.G. on the set of
Black Narcissus

The Dower House, Arundel

Jane and Paula with Silk and Smoky

At St. Peter's Hill

Fishing boat in The River

Filming the kite scene in The River, *with Richard Foster as Bogey*

With Jean Primrose at the American Library Association's meeting and book fair in Cleveland

Richard and Kanu, his friend, a fisher boy

Walking in the woods at Pollards with Jane

The Old Hall in snow

R.G.

Jane at her twenty-first birthday dance at the London Zoo

The Greengage Summer: With Mam, Jane Asher, Susannah York, Elizabeth Dear, and Kenneth More

great courtliness. "This I hope will be the first of many many meetings."

I did see him quite often at functions and dinners. Now and then we travelled together for some out of town occasions.

Rache, though, taught me a great deal as we talked over books in his room, he at his desk, I sitting in one of the hard chairs that suited me so much better than the usually offered armchairs.

He taught me the ins and outs of publishing, the hazards and costs involved. "For a publisher every book is a gamble."

"What do you think it is for an author?" I said.

With Macmillan as my publisher I seemed to enter into a new dimension, eventually it was not only lunches at Boulestin's and its like or in the boardroom; it was dinner in private houses or at the Garrick, of having cars sent for me, of escorts to publicity interviews, radio and television, or to provincial functions; of attending sales conferences and addressing the salesmen, none of which had happened to me with Peter Davies or Michael Joseph.

The first sales conference I was asked to attend was almost directly after the boardroom luncheon. Salesmen are enormously important to an author so that I was nervous but, though naturally they were businessmen hard as they were sagacious, they were not at all frightening, and encouraged me, "When are you going to give us another book about a doll's house?" they asked. Macmillan had taken over my first children's book *The Doll's House* from Michael Joseph. "When are you going to let us have a new novel?"

What would they have said, I wondered as I parried the questions, if I had told them that, though deeply appreciative of what Macmillan proposed to do for me their new author, she was not going to give anyone a novel or a children's book for quite a while; Renoir's words about the filming of *The River* had not left me though I had kept them secret: "No-one else," he had said, "must write this script."

"Spencer. International Oriental Films are paying my fare."

"Naturally," said Spencer. "First class everywhere."

"And fifty pounds a week."

"A hundred," said Spencer. "I wouldn't agree to fifty, and you claim every penny you spend. Mind."

America

It had all been arranged with amazing swiftness. Jon had arrived
in England for the summer; she at once offered to come to St.
Peter's Hill and look after the children; Giovanna came from Switzerland to help. I hastily bought clothes, far too elaborate clothes
—thin trousers and one or two cotton skirts and blouses would
have done—and, in mid-June, flew to New York.

I stayed there for four days.

To Jon.

I arrived at three in the afternoon, rather battered, sick and head-
achy as we were fourteen hours late having had to put back to
Shannon with engine trouble. It was also broiling hot but, thankfully, Alan Collins met me and I began to feel a little excited when
I saw the porters putting my cases into his huge Mercedes car.

He took me to what I had not dreamed existed in New York,
not a tall apartment block but his little Georgian brownstone house
with a garden.

I should not have been in Alan's house at all but had immediately run into trouble with International Oriental Films, trouble
not caused by them—by me. They had booked a suite for me at
the Waldorf Astoria. A bouquet from Kenneth McEldowney higher
than my head was standing in its hallway which opened into two
rooms that looked to me the size of ballrooms; in the further one

98

was a little lonely bed. Bell boys in smart uniforms came in and out, all round was the clamour and bustle of a big hotel while the air was suddenly chill from air-conditioning. I shivered, then the whole of me went into revolt and, "Alan, I can't stay here," I said. "I won't."

Alan was a family man and under his rich playboy reputation had the kindest, most tender of hearts. He took me to his own house, a small haven of quiet and coolness where his Japanese manservant brought us iced tea. Then, "I must leave you for a little while," said Alan, "while I try to fix you up. I should love to have you here but I've only one spare room and Richard Llewellyn is in it."

"Richard Llewellyn who write *How Green Was My Valley*?"

"Yes. He's upstairs working on his new novel."

When Alan was gone there happened another of those inexplicable moments that now and again have happened to me—I suppose because I was, in a way, 'out of myself'. Richard appeared, a small, very dark Welshman exactly as I had imagined him.

"I've just come to say hello. I'm Richard Llewellyn."

"Alan told me you were staying here," I said.

"Yes. I'm working on a new novel."

"Yes," and I said dreamily, "*A Few Flowers for Shiner*."

He started, stared at me. "How do you know that?"

"I . . . I suppose Alan told me."

"He couldn't have," said Richard, "because I only thought of it myself a few minutes ago."

It was a long time, getting towards evening, before Alan came back. "I am taking you to stay with Ben Huebsch and his wife." Poor Alan! New York was packed for some great conference; every hotel he had tried was full and he had gone to Ben as a last resource. I soon understood why it was the last resource.

Alfhilde Huebsch herself opened the door. She was then about sixty, handsome in a statuesque Jewish way with dark eyes that now seemed ominously sullen.

Did Sarah feel resentful at having, so late in life, to bear Isaac? Rebecca obviously did when Isaac preferred Esau to Jacob, but did Rachel when her father Laban insisted that Jacob marry her elder sister Leah first and Rachel had to wait another seven years? At any rate Alfhilde's eyes that night—though soon I knew how they could glow with that special Jewish response of enthusiasm or tenderness—were unmistakably resentful, even hostile. "You can stay here if you like," she said, "but you won't like it."

I liked it, came to love it. The Huebsches lived in a vast apartment on Central Park West looking far over the trees and green spaces of the Park. At sunset, when the last rays caught the whiteness, the glittering steel and glass of the skyscrapers on the horizon turning them to rose and opal, I was reminded of the Himalayan sunsets, as the rays too caught the great peaks in what the native people called 'the flowering of the snows'. The apartment had long corridors made narrower by shelves of books on either side—I had not seen as many books in any private home. In the high-ceilinged sitting room—the word drawing room did not fit—was the famous oak table, a heavy refectory table, some fifteen feet long—perhaps it came from some old time Scandinavian baronial hall—and which was always heaped with still more books, old books, rare books, books in multiple languages, new books—Viking books. I am sure there was nowhere else in New York like that apartment but Alfhilde had no idea of what could be called home comforts and cared little about them. I was shown into Ian's—the younger son's bedroom—both sons were grown-up long gone but their rooms were kept for them.

Ian's was a room like a cell with an iron railed bed, a bridge table, an upright chair, a small wardrobe, a rag rug on the floor, and nothing else, but there were more books and a good reading lamp by the bed.

"Well?" asked Alfhilde almost like a challenge.

"It's perfect. Perfect. After the Waldorf! *Thank* you."

"You didn't like the Waldorf! Ah!" and Alfhilde kissed me.

She and Ben were on the point of leaving for Europe as they did every summer, closing the apartment; Ben to make his round of the capitals, while Alfhilde was making her first visit to Greece for which she was immersed in learning modern Greek—she took it for granted that if you went to a foreign country you learned its language first. Ben travelled on the big liners, the *Queen Mary* or *Queen Elizabeth*, the *Rotterdam* or the *France*; he would stay at elite hotels where he was known and welcomed. Alfhilde flew economy class, travelled by third class rail and took buses from village to village. "That's how you get to know the people," in which of course, she was right. To Alfhilde, people were more important

than the Acropolis or Delphi or the beauty of Sunion. She would
end up in Sweden to confer with her sisters about the management
of the estate where Ben would join her for a short stay. They never
travelled together. "We live and let live," said Alfhilde.

Nowhere, anywhere have I heard talk such as I heard at the
Huebsches' when, after dinner, we sat on at the table while the
sunset reached the skyscrapers then faded and soon multitudes of
lights came on across the city so that I used to see Ben's head, as
he sat at the top of the table, silhouetted against the window surrounded by what might have been a tapestry of golden bees as he
talked in his gentle voice. Alfhilde's deeper tone came in, as did
say, Irwin Edman's with his dry humour or it might be a writer, a
professor of Greek, a bibliophile. I could have listened every night
but there were meetings I had to go to, interviews, besides I had
friends to see, especially the Harlans, John a barrister, later to become a Judge at the Supreme Court in Washington, and his beautiful wife Ethel whom I had come to know at the Simons' and who
became my first American family.

To Jon, Jane, Paula and Giovanna.

It would have been lovely to be here and be able to wander about
and look and stare. The streets are so full of foreigners that you
seem to see no Americans until you remember they are all Americans; it is one huge melting pot and people tell me that by the time
the children are grown up they are true Americans even if their
parents can't speak a word of English. The flower shops seem kept
by Greeks and Japanese, the laundries by Chinese, the fruit shops
and greengrocers and ice-cream bars by Italians; the mixture of
names is incredible.

I seem to lunch and dine in restaurants almost every day. They
call shrimps and lobsters sea-food here and cook them marvellously. As soon as you go into a restaurant they fill your glasses
with iced water and few people drink anything but water with a
meal. They serve wonderful cold soups in a little cup in a vast silver
bowl of ice and the puddings, what they call dessert, are more
wonderful, children, than anything you can imagine. I can just see
your eyes! With coffee or anything else, they bring bowls of
whipped cream.

Most of the time I was under the tutelage of Edith Haggard who
looked as if she were made of porcelain, fragile but well tended.

She had exquisite hands, a delectable nose—which could snort—and eyes that made you think, if there could be such things, of blue diamonds; they could be as hard and had their cutting strength. Edith loved hats; I remember one made of frill upon frill of black lace which set off the fineness of her skin: she smoked cigarettes through a holder with a tiny gold ring that fitted her finger so that she did not have to hold them and so risk a stain of nicotine. Her office had walls of palest pink; on one of them was a Marie Laurencin.

It seemed as if a rough wind would blow Edith away, but the moment she opened her mouth, there would come out a forceful forthright voice with a trace of a southern accent. It could be harsh, unashamedly harsh. Edith was a powerful agent in New York and she fought doughty battles, many of them for me but all the while niceties had to be preserved. "Manners," Edith would say reprovingly to young men and women; but if you succeeded in becoming Edith's friend you were her friend for life.

Among other things she took me to a privileged table at the Algonquin where I sat next to Harold Ross the *New Yorker*'s editor, but, to Edith's chagrin, he could not hear a word I said. "A soft voice is all very well," said Edith in reproach, "but . . ."

In spite of my dumbness, I suppose that luncheon was more important than anything else I did but in my typical twists of memory I can remember it only hazily while the things that are still vivid from those packed days are inconsequential things, like the cherrystones.

The Harlans gave a dinner party for me at the St. Regis; looking at the enormous menu trying to find something I, as a vegetarian, could eat without causing a nuisance, I saw cherrystones.

"What are they?"

"You've never eaten cherrystones?" John exclaimed. "One of America's great specialities. You must try them. Waiter!"

I had imagined cherries skewered on little sticks like a kebab, dipped in a sauce perhaps, until the waiter put down in front of me a silver platter of ice and small unmistakable shells. "But—they're oysters!" I said.

"Well, no. They're clams but first-rate. Now sprinkle on a little red pepper and a squeeze of lemon."

Once when James had had oysters, when he had squeezed the lemon, I had seen the oyster shrink—I was to write a short story about that which went to the *New Yorker*. The clams shrank now.

"I can't eat them. I can't. They're alive. I *can't*!" But I had to—everyone round the table was looking expectantly at me. An American speciality, I could not insult that and somehow, making myself like steel, I got those cherrystones down, all dozen of them, but my forehead, neck and back were wet with revulsion. The Harlans never knew.

The four days respite in New York ended all too quickly and I left for Los Angeles on the midnight flight.

It was beautiful flying over New York at night, clear moonlight and all the spread and network of coloured lights below. We flew through the night, sleeping a little—though it was a sitting up plane the seats tilted back and were quite comfortable. We came down at Chicago at four o'clock in the morning for half-an-hour and then flew on. I must have dropped asleep because when I woke up we were flying over the Rocky Mountains which were pale blue and snowy in the early dawn light. It was like flying over a landscape in a dream. From there on it was a most beautiful flight. They told us where we were and what we were seeing; first we flew over the Arizona desert that turned from pink to grey to purple to deep rose in the sunrise, finally to a curious hot pink colour. Then we came to the Canyon country; here the land was dark rose but where the sun struck the fissures it was gold. We flew right round the Grand Canyon and over some strange pools that the Indians called Green Water because of their colour which was, from the air, emerald. We could see waterfalls tumbling into them and little patches of Indian villages on the floor of the Canyon and tiny fields. Then we came to Lake Mead which supplies all that part of America with water and the enormous Hoover Dam which spreads like a harbour of water and concrete.

I have always two moments of dread when flying; first when, in that tremendous revving rush the aeroplane lifts off the ground—"Will it, can it fly?" The other, coming down when you feel the engines slow, the wheels of the undercarriage come down and you wait, wait for the bump—nowadays only a jar as you come back to earth.

That first time at Los Angeles, as the huge machine slowly taxied, waited, taxied to the terminal there was such additional apprehension I could hear my heart beating. Would I, could I, be able to measure up to Renoir? Work, actually work not for him, but with him? I had forgotten Jean's magnetism and power.

"We thought you were never coming," were the first words Jean said to me when I landed at Los Angeles where he, Dido and the McEldowneys met me—Dido told me Jean had been rampaging with impatience whereas I think the McEldowneys were filled with some suspicion and dismay; "Keep authors away from the films of their books," was Hollywood's slogan.

"Only someone quite out of his mind would have financed *The River*," Renoir said often but there was, in Hollywood, a man with a dream.

Kenneth McEldowney had made a fortune as a florist, the first to start 'drive-in' florists where 'shapely girls in Scots kilts,' as he described them to me, carrying baskets and bunches of flowers, darted out as soon as a car drove up, darted in and out again with samples, so that the customers could make their choice without moving from the car, which seemed to be thought a great advantage—in California I began to think that, except on the beaches, no-one had the use of their legs. Kenny soon had a chain of drive-in florists across the States but he ached to be more than a businessman, a film impresario, as it turned out a visionary one, ready to explore new ideas. He had tried once before in India and failed—it must be remembered how alone he was, a pioneer for the Western market; Kenny had courage and was so adroit that his very failure brought him valuable contacts, some unique, and he was able to start again with his small company, International Oriental Films never dreaming he could attract a giant like Jean Renoir—nor had he any inkling of what that could mean.

"We will put the book up on the shelf," said Jean. "Then we can keep the flavour while we recreate it in another medium."

We worked in the studio of the house in Beverly Hills to which Jean and Dido had moved only three months before I came.

"But shouldn't we," I asked, "make an outline of the shape to know where we are going?"

"No," said Jean. "We must build. The shape will declare itself," and, from the opening, an old fisherman in his boat on the wide river, Jean made me recreate—for once that presumptuous word seemed fitting—recreate the written book in visual terms; writing in shots; long distance, close up, middle—always keeping to sight-vision.

Changes were inevitable—I had considerably to unstiffen my

mind. Some of my characters disappeared; new ones came in. We changed, unchanged, but not the idea, the flavour.

"Was there a Valentine in the book?" Soon I hardly knew—it had all merged except, the girl Harriet—myself—the father and mother, the small boy, Bogey, friend of the cobra that killed him and the youngest, Victoria with Nan, the Anglo-Indian nurse, remained the same. They were intrinsic, but Bea—Jon—became two characters, Valerie, the outsider—she was in the book—and Melanie the half-caste, necessary as an interpreter between the Western and Indian worlds. Renoir believed passionately, as I do, that in cinema the only authenticity is truth so that he would not have a Bengali peasant, field worker or boatman singing or talking in English as they did in *Black Narcissus*. Nowhere in the film of *The River* is there anything artificial that should be real, nowhere does anyone speak words they could not in real life have said, and with this reality I believe we achieved the quality we wanted, the timelessness of a spell that held the most discerning of the critics and seems to have held them ever since.

'With everything that happens to you, with everyone you meet who is important to you, you either die a little or are born.' Renoir had quoted that from *The River* to the newspapers. That year several people had become important to me, especially Ben Huebsch, but in those weeks in Beverly Hills I seemed to be born again—recreated. It was partly, I am sure, from Renoir's respect, almost reverence, for me. Others had been kindly, interested, heartening yet not in this way; and that a sophisticated—Jean was sophisticated, though like many great men he was intrinsically simple—a sophisticated world renowned genius of a Frenchman should rate me so highly gave me a new confidence and broke for good the shell we Goddens so easily retreat into—all except Nancy—and that makes us seem so reserved, worse, arrogant and unapproachable. I was sure I would not be afraid ever again of meeting anyone, no matter how eminent.

Jean knew *The River* even more deeply than I yet, as we worked, he would wait for minutes, half-an-hour, perhaps an hour while I searched for a word—though we kept what we could of the original dialogue there had to be more. New words were needed and, as the text was sparse—both Jean and I agreed on that—each word was important; also, as usual, I needed time to know the new characters—how they would speak, sound, originate. "No.

Melanie would never have thought of that, done that." "No. I don't feel Harriet would cry. She's not that sort of girl. She would be angry." Jean never hurried or harried me.

Charlie Chaplin, one night after dinner, did an impromptu sketch of Jean and me working together, the ebullient explosive Frenchman and the over-reserved Englishwoman. It was hilarious, but even Chaplin did not know how far from ebullient Jean was with me nor that I was not in the least reserved with him. I was as at home as in my own study.

Beverly Hills
California.

To Jane.   Friday 17 June 1949

This is the first long letter to go to Jane herself but as you know it is meant for all of you. I think about you all so much as, in spite of the lovely place and the utter kindness of everyone, I am often a little homesick.

I loved the letter and especially the four-leafed clover that Paula sent me; I have put it very carefully in my notebook; it will bring us luck, though I am very very lucky already. I am writing this in my bedroom where a new typewriter has been set up for me which I won't use especially as I also have a wonderful secretary called Miss Wolquitt who types so fast I can't keep up with her! In the house there are the Renoirs, me, and their housekeeper, Bessie who is English, dear and faithful but pernickety, and a coloured daily woman, Helen, who sings in a deep lovely voice. There are also two dachshunds, Ninette and Tambour who only speak French; they make me homesick for Silk.

I must go and get ready for dinner. We all wear trousers in the evening. Paulette Goddard is coming. She is the delightful witty and very very pretty actress who was in Jean's film, *The Diary of a Chambermaid*. She has to make a speech in Chicago for the Fourteenth Army which fought in Burma; I am writing part of it for her. They are sending a bomber to fetch her.

There was also Gabrielle, the dark girl of so many of Auguste Renoir's paintings. She had been Jean's nurse and became Renoir's favourite model. "She would be starting the cooking of lunch," Jean would tell me, "when there would be a bellow from my father, 'Gabrielle, Gabrielle.'" He had thrown out his model and

Gabrielle had to leave her omelette or whatever she was cooking and take off her clothes.

She had followed Jean and Dido to California, had married and now had a son Jeannot who seemed as much Jean and Dido's as hers.

Gabrielle detested me. She called me 'La Dame'. When she came to visit as she did every day, "Où est la dame?" she would say and would hardly set a foot inside unless I was in my room. She did not like the hours I spent alone with Jean in the studio, suspecting me of stealing him from Dido whom she adored.

There were in fact quarrels. Dido was as fiery as Jean was tempestuous, becoming like an angry bull. He was renowned for his temper.

It was hard on Dido. Always before she had been at the centre of each current film, now for the first time, she was shut out; it was the first time, too, that Jean had taken a film from a book—usually he found an idea and wrote the script himself. Dido tried to rein herself in but would suddenly explode. Jean would bellow back and I would be caught in the crossfire which at first made me wilt with distress. I soon learned, however, that if I kept quite quiet the storm would blow itself out so that we survived into a deep long friendship of love.

What do I remember of that house and its life? Everything, indelibly. A long low house full of sunlight, though out of doors I did not like the hard white Californian glare; chiefly of all the paintings, the whole house had been designed round them. The long open living room that led into the dining and kitchen spaces was dominated by a large Renoir of Jean as a boy; there were smaller ones of him and Coco—many of Gabrielle.

Then there was the phenomenon of the garden. When I arrived, a stone terrace had been laid outside the house but below it was only bare reddish earth cut into terraces falling to a miniature canyon full of scrub at the foot of the steep slope—the house stood on a hill. The next morning I was woken at dawn as a fleet of lorries arrived with a swarm of blue overalled men; three days later, where the raw earth had been, was an olive grove, some of the olive trees fourteen feet high and all interplanted by flowering white gardenias with their glossy deep green leaves while each terrace had a path of smooth green turf. The hummingbirds, about three inches long, moved in at once. When the sprinklers were turned on—the whole garden was plumbed—the hummingbirds played in the spray. There is a description I found in an old bird book of a hummingbird:

> The feathers on its wings and tail were black, those on its body and under its wings were of a greenish brown with a fine red cast or gloss which neither silk, nor velvet could imitate. It had a small crest on its head, green at the bottom and gilded at the top, which sparkled in the sun like a little star in the middle of its forehead. Its black eyes appeared like two shining points and its bill was black and slender and about the length of a small pin.

No wonder I was bewitched.

The whole house, too, was full of colour, paintings, Mexican rugs, flowers, fruit. I remember the sound of Dido's quick steps on the polished wooden floor; her voice, inflected by many languages, talking to the dogs. Dido and I wrangled, and have done every time we meet, half in amusement, half in truth. My vegetarianism incensed her. "*Really* Rumer. You are not a Brahmin." The r's rolled. "*Why* can't you eat steaks?" I did eat the chickens Jean cooked on a spit.

If friends were coming to dinner, at about five o'clock he would break off work and light the huge charcoal fire at the dining end of the living room—there was another fireplace in the sitting room end. When the charcoal was red—it had to be vine charcoal—he would take chickens—sometimes joints of lamb—thread them on the spit and set them slowly turning so that they roasted evenly. He would sit by the fire, basting the birds—the air soon filled with their aroma and the fragrance of hot herbs, while Bessie would lay the table, putting on salads, cheeses, bowls of fruit. As in our pioneer dinner at St. Peter's Hill there was always only one course, after it fruit and cheese. The wine was incomparable; the food, though plain, almost peasant in simplicity matched it. "Ample" was the name for everything in that house—including Jean.

I hardly saw the Hollywood other writers have described though the McEldowneys insisted that I spend a day at Metro Goldwyn Mayer where Malvina McEldowney was in publicity charge of Esther Williams the swimming star. I stood on the side of the set while a sequence was being filmed and found I could anticipate the dialogue as it went along it was so obvious. I was taken to a caravan dressing room to meet the young Elizabeth Taylor; at seventeen she was shy and very sweet, offering me tea because I was English. Bessie, the Renoirs' housekeeper used to do the same, daring even to break into the afternoon's work. "Really Rumer," said Jean, just as Dido had, "tea and cookies between déjeuner and dinner. It's too much!" Far too much. I do not like tea but not to hurt Bessie's feelings had to accept as I accepted a cup from Elizabeth Taylor which she handed me with a flutter of unbelievably long lashes above the famous eyes; the lashes were real and she was stunningly beautiful though not as beautiful as Greta Garbo.

Dido and I were in a five and ten cent store. I was one side of a glassed-in case; on the other was someone wearing a huge straw hat; the hat lifted and I gave an audible gasp—it was Greta Garbo. I have never seen a face of such bone beauty or such eyes. At that moment they were displeased; another wonderstruck gaper, she palpably thought, but when Dido came up and introduced us she warmed. She seemed to enjoy, immeasurably, any professional talk, what we call 'shop'. Every time we met after that we talked about the script.

Staying with Jean and Dido meant that you had a passport to Olympus. They kept away from Tinsel Town—that cliché for Hollywood—Jean said "tonsil town—swollen tonsils?"—they had their own small circle and firmly kept it.

I got used to seeing Charles Laughton. The first time he came to the door he was in disreputable khaki shorts and shirt, wearing an outsize felt hat and carrying a basket of peaches, his own peaches, warm from the tree. Stravinsky often came to dinner with his wife Vera, who was again ample with a calm and sweetness that made you see what an invaluable counterpart she was for the sometimes abrupt then suddenly eloquent nervous man with his overlarge head and troubled dark eyes; Vera always carried a basket holding anything Stravinsky might need from pills to an extra scarf. I was amazed at the matter-of-fact workaday way they lived, their house not large but overflowing with family, even an old governess in a cottage at the end of the garden, the son, young Stravinsky, acted as his father's secretary, amanuensis, even conducting in his place if it were necessary.

Even dearer, I think, to the Renoirs were Charlie Chaplin and his beautiful, perhaps fifty years younger, wife Oona. They came to us but often we went to them in their rambling big almost haphazard house with a stage character Irish butler who joined in every conversation—and what seemed a swarm of small children, though I think there were then only four, Geraldine, Michael, Victoria, and a baby I never saw. The little girls in long party dresses with tangles of hair, ran barefoot and talked happily, even to this stranger. Michael, I seem to remember was more aloof, quiet with something of Oona's dignity.

We saw much of James Mason, his wife Pamela and their baby Porty—she was christened Portland which combined with Mason seemed a heavy name for a girl. She was present everywhere they went including dinner parties, "Which is *too* much!" Dido protested. I thought so too and was distressed for Porty lying on her back in a carrycot at, for instance, a Mason party, blinking at the lights with a shindy of noise, voices, music, cigarette smoke all round her, but she seemed to survive with equanimity.

The Masons were far more like the Hollywood star life we hear of with their mammoth house—I think it had belonged to Buster Keaton—that had its own cinema, a horde of servants, a swimming pool where at five months old Porty was being taught to swim—Pamela always found the latest gimmick and we all had to watch while the woman instructor batted Porty and the other babies of the famous in, out and under the water like helpless pink tadpoles—again it seemed to work.

The one of all the friends I instinctively revered and loved most was the great Greek actress Katina Paxinou, then living with her husband Alexander Minotis in tragic exile and poverty—Katina had not had a part since Hemingway's *For Whom the Bell Tolls*. We went to dinner at their rather pinched little house, which held them, their children and grandchildren—the smaller ones running in and out while we ate because there was nowhere else for them to go. "We have to live altogether to make it possible to exist here," explained Minotis.

Madame Paxinou's presence was still almost royal in its dignity while her voice resonant, deep had the quality of stirring you as does a harp. I could imagine it stirring the vast audience of a Greek open air auditorium in one of the classics which, when they were able to go back to Greece, it did.

Jean and Dido took me to see their closest neighbour—Lillian Gish who lived in a little house below them. Lillian Gish had made her name with her sister in the classic film, *Broken Blossoms* and still had something of the orphan look about her, with wide-set eyes

—young as a child's, and a frailty which was an illusion; even twenty years later when I went backstage to see her in an off-Broadway play, she was full of plans, "For my future," she said. In nineteen eighty-seven she was in the film chosen for Britain's Royal Performance though it was made in the United States; it was Lindsay Anderson's beautiful film *The Whales of August* of which the critics wrote, 'Lillian Gish gives a tour-de-force starring performance.' She was eighty-eight.

It was not only people. Jean and Dido took me for long drives into the desert to show me the old abobe mission churches; we went to vineyards, to Las Vegas which I hated. Sometimes we lunched downtown at a table under a sun umbrella in the Farmers' Market, really a supermarket, eating peaches and nectarines the size of bowling balls. Everything seemed outsize in America; the very pads of paper I was given to write on for the script were mammoth, lined and bright yellow—they made my preferred primary school exercise books seem paltry; the pencils—Jean liked to work with pencils—were large heavy rubber ended which to my hands made them seem out of balance.

I loved the casualness of our Californian life, its easiness; the thin clothes that went into the washing machine and needed no ironing, the light meals, the open doors and windows so that the house came into the garden, the garden into the house, but I still did not like the light and annoyed Dido by refusing to go out without a shady hat.

Beverly Hills
August 10th 1949

(the first letter I have had time
to write this month).

To Jon.

The last few days have been spent winding up the script. I do feel very pleased as it has been read with great warmth by everyone. Charles Laughton says it is the best he has ever seen—that he said 'seen' is interesting as it shows how vivid is Jean's way of working. Jean himself is delighted and wants me to do a play with him in the Spring from the French which I should like to do.

And two days later:

Dudley Nichols and his wife (he is a very famous screenplay writer here) gave a farewell party for me to which the Chaplins came but last night Jean and Dido and I dined alone; they filled the house with flowers and we had a barbecue all on our own and champagne and a great deal of talk and emotion. It was perhaps the best evening of all as Jean told me so many of his plans and I felt I had lived up to their expectations. I leave tomorrow for New York.

"You have come back from a triumph," said Ben, "and you are unhappy."

Ben had postponed leaving for Europe and had met me at the airport. It was a broiling hot August evening and I was glad to get to the cool of the apartment at Central Park West looking down at the greenness of the trees in the Park that looked cool too, so different from the brilliant greens of California.

Alfhilde had gone on her Grecian journey and there was hardly any food in the apartment. "I meant to take you out," said Ben.

"God forbid," I said to his relief, and we had a puritanical supper of scrambled eggs—I never fathomed in America the difference between shirred and scrambled eggs; after them some blueberries I found in the refrigerator with milk as there was no cream. We drank iced white wine and sat by the open windows and talked. I was back in my own world, the writing world but as Ben had fathomed it had a sick hollow feeling I had not faced before.

"What is it?" asked Ben. "Can you tell me?"

Ben never coerced. He did not say "Tell me," but, "Can you tell me?" and I said, "I shall have to tell you—in the morning."

He and the Viking Press were expecting my new novel.

Ten days before I had left for America I had sent it in to Spencer. "Perhaps it is significant," he had said on the telephone—he had not read it, only looked at it, "Significant that in your time of transition"—he meant leaving Dower House for St. Peter's Hill, the children's boarding schools, my divorce, "you should write a book about an imaginary island."

The book, *A Breath of Air*, was a slight echo of *The Tempest* put into modern times, its characters based on Shakespeare's, from Prospero, Mr. Van Loomis—to Caliban, Mario—an ex-Spanish islander—and Ariel, Filipino. It had been a relief to write it after several serious novels and I had meant it simply as an entertainment in the same sense as Graham Greene's occasional light entertainment novels; I should have thought its title would have indicated this, so that it came as a shock the day I left, to have a four-page letter from Spencer written in pencil and in his own hand from Monk's Hall where he usually discarded all business. It was a dear, even moving letter but he had sent the manuscript back.

The letter began: 'I have had a reader's report on the book and I am sorry but it's pretty bad.' I read on amazed: 'Story will not hold anyone's interest, characters not sufficiently vital to attract . . . second hand imagination . . .' Second hand, and I had thought it original! I nearly choked.

Spencer tried to take a tolerant view but it was plain he thought I should withdraw *A Breath of Air*.

> I think the book would harm you. *St. Jude* got a poorish press here and this I think would get worse; the ultimate result might be bad. You don't want to be a 'downhill' author.

His ending completely disarmed me:

> Dearest Rumer, do *think* about letting me know of your books before you write—or finish—them. It's really not difficult, for I'm not stupid, though I know I often appear so, and I am at my best when my help is asked. Other authors can and do do this, and I don't believe all of them are less sensitive or less secretive than you. Why not *try* it and *see* if it's not possible.

There had been no time to answer. Sick and stiff with disappointment—and, at that time, disbelief—I had put the manuscript in one of my cases; on the plane I had wept all night.

It had been easy not to think about it in Beverly Hills but now . . .

Next morning when I had told him, Ben did not say anything for some time then he asked, "When you read Spencer's letter what did you feel?"

"I couldn't believe it."

"So you did not yourself think the book was bad?"

Did I? Could I? *"No!"* That came out more violently than I had meant. "Not one of my best ones—it wasn't meant to be—but not *bad*!"

"Would you feel disloyal to Spencer if you let me read it?"

"Yes." Then I thought again and said, "But I have to be loyal to myself. If you read it Ben, perhaps you could explain where I have been blind. Make me see."

*   *   *

I did not go straight home to England from Central Park West but, on Alan Collins' advice, spent a little time in New England where Ben wrote his reactions to me.

I opened the letter with trepidation.

19 August 1949

I would have written you a few days ago, as soon as I finished your book, to tell you of my admiration and delight, but in view of the weight which you seemed to attach to SCB's opinion I decided to defer comment. Besides, just as with music I feel more sure of my judgment after a period of reflection.

I found the story first-rate entertainment with its fantasy, color and humor; I found it profound and wise in its presentation of a variety of interesting characters ingeniously assembled and integrated; and of course I was very much aware of the irony of your criticism of our society. To top it all, as a *Tempest* in modern dress it is a literary tour-de-force.

What was the ground for his, Spencer's, negative counsel? (I must say that I am baffled.) A view so contrary to my own spontaneous response to all that you have poured into this book.

Today I read through *The Tempest* to refresh myself as to the parallelism, and it was plain to me that you feel that work in your bones, that it is part of yourself and that you gave it rebirth in your image. One need not be told that you have communed with yourself much and to good result

and, "Will you let me publish it?" wrote Ben. "We should like to persuade you but you must decide."

Alan Collins had booked me into the MacDowell Colony in New England. "You need a little time to think everything over, reflect on what you have done with Renoir, also about other projects." Alan had several plans. I drove up quietly by car into the peace of Peterborough, a little town in New Hampshire.

The Colony had been founded by Mrs. MacDowell in memory of her husband, Edward, the musician—I had been obliged to play his *To a Wild Rose* and *To a Waterlily* at school. The Colony's purpose was to provide a retreat, a place where work could be done unhindered by daily cares, not only for musicians and composers, but painters, sculptors, writers and poets.

The Colony itself was a series of old frame boarding houses,

shabby with fly screens and porches with rocking chairs on which
we sat in the evenings; it was old fashioned, almost William Morris
in feeling but we only went there to sleep and eat our evening
meal which was at six. Scattered about the woods at a safe distance
from each other were small cabins with rough walls, a verandah,
a rocking chair—in New England it seemed you always have a
rocking chair—large tables for work and large fireplaces with piles
of cut logs; there was also a bathroom, loo and washbasin only,
and a divan for resting. It was the rule that no-one went to anyone's cabin unless by express invitation so that you were completely alone; at twelve o'clock a truck drove round and a man
called George brought a hickory basket with lunch and hot coffee.
You could also walk in the woods for miles without seeing a soul
and I had begun to feel quietened and soothed.

I read Ben's letter sitting on the steps up to the verandah, a high
perch where I liked to sit rather than in the rocking chair and sat
so still that a chipmunk, who always bore me company when I
had lunch, not for love of me but crumbs, came and sat beside me
probably wondering why I sat there when there was no food.

Loyal to Spencer. Loyal to myself?

A Breath of Air was published in London by Michael Joseph—under
my contract with them it seemed I still owed them another novel,
and by the Viking Press in America where it was chosen as a dual
Book of the Month Club Choice.

> Apart from anything else this means about 20,000 dollars to you
> which buys quite a little bread and butter,

wrote magnanimous Spencer.

> Also, it proves again how wrong I was about that book.

Yet I still have an uneasy feeling that Spencer was right.

A Breath of Air was not the only decision I had to make in those
few weeks; there was another, far more important, about which I
could not tell even Ben.

James had driven me to Heathrow when I left St. Peter's Hill
and as we had sat waiting in the V.I.P. lounge—International Oriental Films had seen to it that I was there—he had been unusually
silent. Then, as my flight was announced, he leaned across the

table and said, quietly and firmly, "I cannot bear it any more, Rumer. Either you send me a letter or a cable from America telling me you will marry me or I shan't be here when you come back."

I did not want to marry again. I had thought James was content but had he not said, long ago, "If I keep on coming you'll get so used to me you won't notice I am here and I won't have to go away."

How was it, I thought now, in the MacDowell Colony, that I had not noticed the pathos of that? I saw his face as he had said, "I can't bear it any more." How selfish I had been. How mean!

"But I don't want to marry again. I don't." Again I had been able to stifle all thinking in Beverly Hills but now my time was drawing to a close. "I don't want to marry. What am I to do?" I might have asked the chipmunk as someone from the outside world but this was between James and me, no-one else, not even the children. I began seriously to think what my life would be like without James—and found I could not think of it.

One evening I hitched a lift to the post office and cabled James one word, 'Yes'.

James and I were married on the twenty-sixth of November of that eventful year. Three days later I went to India for six months to do the filming of *The River*.

Interlude for
<u>The River</u>

The picture will start, Renoir wrote to me, with a closeup of a notebook on which the first lines of *The River* will be hand-written.

It will then dissolve to our old fisherman sitting in the stern of his boat and singing one of the haunting Bengali folk songs. I can think of no better opening.

Nor could I.

All September letters had gone back and forth between St. Peter's Hill and Beverly Hills.

From Dido.

Le 8 Septèmbre

Enfin ta première lettre d'Angleterre est arrivée. Le temps semblait long sans nouvelles de toi et c'est avec émotion que j'ai reconnu tes petites pattes de mouche sur l'enveloppe.

My flymark handwriting is small because I am so secretive when I write books that I make it small so that no-one can read it. To me the writing of books should be secretive, the moment it is talked about it loses its virtue which is why all the things that are pressed on authors to make writing easier, quicker—dictaphones, word processors—for me would simply be impediments coming between me and what I hope to achieve. I believe, too, as the Chinese and

Japanese calligraphers believe, that there is a mystique between the brain, the hand and the tool, pen, brush or scalpel; sometimes a flow is established between them, bringing a strange power. I acknowledge that you can have a flow with a typewriter—at times it seems to run away with you—but I distrust it because it is too quick and can you love a typewriter as you can a pen?

It could be imagined, then, what it was like for this believer in quiet and slowness to have to work, often produce instantly, extra dialogue or script changes on set among lights, cameras and sound boom crews, continuity girl, make-up and wardrobe people, property-men, green-men, actors. I found it violently interesting and violently exhausting.

I had hoped to stay in the peace of Jon and Roland's house but the fact that almost every day we had to drive some miles outside Calcutta to the house in Barrackpore, which was our main location, made that impossible; also after the long day I was needed for evening conferences so that I had to accept, like the others, the polyglot and noisy atmosphere of Calcutta's Great Eastern Hotel, sternly removed from any quiet nostalgias; the air hummed with all the schemes, discussions, conferences, with Jean, Dido, Lourié the designer, and the cameraman who was Jean's nephew, Claude Renoir, son of the eldest Renoir, Pierre of the Comédie Française. Kenneth McEldowney was usually excluded and sent long 'memos' which nobody read.

Poor Kenny! He had quickly found out the cost of a Renoir directed film. "I am a detailist," said Jean. "A film's quality is in its detail," which echoed my own feeling over books but drove Kenny to frenzy. I remember one scene where, during the film household's afternoon siesta—the siesta that had such dire consequences—the youngest child, Victoria, had rolled off her bed and was asleep on the floor, the bed being occupied by the family's pet rabbit, Hoppity—if any director caught the feeling of a real family, Jean did. He wanted Hoppity to hop across the bed and peer over its edge at Victoria as if to ask how and why they had changed places. There was, of course, no animal trainer in Calcutta; Hoppity belonged to Nancy and was not accustomed to obedience.

Again and again the shot was set up; either Hoppity grew lazy under the lights and would not hop or he hopped in the wrong direction; or Victoria, who was only three years old, would suddenly open her eyes or sit up. Jean got his shot but, "Three *days*," protested Kenny. "Three days wasted."

"Not wasted," said Jean. "We got it."

"But think of the *cost*."

"When you are act-u-ally filming you must not think of the cost. You can always get money," said Jean, "you cannot always get truth."

The River was largely financed by the Ward of Princes, chiefly Prince Fatehsingh of Limbi. Prince Fatehsingh, known to us as Fatty, was a constant visitor and lent his dazzling huge Buick car to the McEldowneys. I remember it being sent, at Jean's behest, to fetch a tiny coolie girl who is shown crossing a bridge with an equally tiny waterpot on her head—another detail. This one though was out of truth as the father in the film, Esmond Knight, presents her with a paper kite which, as he was supposed to know India, he would never in real life have done—kites are for boys. It was my duty to keep Jean, at his special plea, from "anything, any *least* thing," he would insist, "that is not ab-so-lute-ly true," but that day I had been in the garden coaching the children.

There were none of the supports taken for granted in Western film making as, for instance, 'stand-ins' for the principal actors, usually dwarfs/midgets for children. For some reason Jean had added three more children, all girls, to the four in my book, why I do not know unless it was to make it more of a 'house of women' as the father says in the script. When I incorporated that remark, the continuity girl protested, "That has been in a film already, you can't use it."

"I can," I said. "It was in my own film, *Black Narcissus*."

Two of the children were five year old twins which led to problems as no-one could tell them apart; if a line was given to one the other promptly said it too: in the end we had to let them which, in a minuscule way, added to the humour of the film. I found myself in the position of child minder or trainer—more difficult than it sounds because for a small child to have to stand, perhaps for half-an-hour, probably under the lights while the shot is set up was punitive, especially as the make-up man and hairdresser were continually dabbing, brushing and combing. The difficulty was to keep the child fresh when the actual moment of filming came, but I was soon adept at snatching them off the set, giving them a whirl around of play and putting them back in time.

I could not do that with the little boy Bogey—Richard. In the sequence when he was discovered dead he had to be motionless on hard ground—in usual film-making a wax model would have been used. Jean wanted Bogey's eyes looking left, open but still. Richard had also to hold his breath. Fortunately he was passionately interested in insects and had a lively sense of drama, slightly macabre like Jon. There was a deep drain beside him and I crouched there holding a bamboo leaf that scraped against the cement. "Richard," I whispered, "I am a scarab beetle from Egypt coming to bite you. Lie still and pretend you are not there. I'm coming. I'm coming." It worked, though the shot took a long time, panning slowly in; Richard's eyes rolled alarmingly sideways, watching for the horrific scarab beetle. He held his breath but anyone watching that sequence closely can see where suddenly the small stomach moves; he had to take a breath.

I also had to work on the diction, teach the children and most of the Indian characters their lines added to which I became a sanitary inspector of the house in Barrackpore which was our studio. I suppose, remembering Mam in Narayangunj, I knew that the care of kitchens, plumbing—or lack of it—above all, water had to be supervised and inspected every day.

> She even, Kenny told the journalists, insisted on visiting the remotest part of the grounds where the lowest-caste workmen lived —to check the latrines and sewage disposal pits, much to the astonishment of our Indian supervisors who would not have been caught dead near such a place.

I had to, as I was horrified at the Company's ignorance of even rudimentary rules; I saw water and milk boiled, fruit and vegetables washed in what was called 'pinky pani'—water made pink by permanganate—inspected saucepans, saw hands were washed, nails clean, installed flyproof meatsafes, and made sure that any ice-cubes were made with boiled water. Most people forget how dangerous ice can be; as it was, Claude got typhoid.

When we, Jean, Dido, Lourié, Claude, Eleanor and I, the advance party arrived and spent days at Barrackpore training the Indian crew, we ate with them, sharing their meals, but as soon as the American-English contingent joined us that was stopped; they would not eat the excellent Indian food. If they had, I should have had little difficulty, as it is the transition to Western food that brings perils. It ended in separate dining rooms, we, the originals eating apart in the Director's room.

All this, though, did not happen quickly. Jean and Dido, with the McEldowneys and Eleanor Wolquitt who was now the film secretary, had that October followed me to England; Eleanor of the dark hair and almost Irish blue eyes had not been abroad before and was in a euphoria of excitement and happiness. Jean had already found actors for two of the chief male parts both American: Arthur Shields as the father of the half-caste girl—neither was in the book—and most important of all, Captain John, centre of both film and book; by an extraordinary coincidence, good looking Thomas Breen had been in the war, been wounded and like Captain John had lost a leg. "Captain John was *so* brave," croons the children's nurse in the film; she, too, was Eurasian. "He stayed there in the battle until his leg was shot off."

"Why didn't he stay there until the other leg was shot off?" asks little Victoria—a line that in book and film, rescued them from sentimentality though, to my mind, Jean sometimes came dangerously near that. "I am not afraid of sent-i-ment-al-ity," he used to say, "when it is needed."

In London, Norah Swinburne, that gracious actress and Esmond Knight her husband, were engaged as the mother and father; I shrank from meeting Esmond, he had been the exaggerated Rajah in *Black Narcissus*. Adrienne Corri auditioned for the older girl, Valerie, on the roof of Claridge's on the roof so that photographs could be taken. I remember the wonderful auburn hair blowing against the background of grey London and grey cloud: it was to be Adrienne's first major part.

Those overseas actors flew to Calcutta as they were needed. The rest of the casting was done in India.

Wanted: an English boy between the ages of five and seven; also three English girls, three to eight, to play roles in an American film —Kenny had written 'movie' which Jean struck out—to be made near Calcutta during the next four months. Report, Great Eastern Hotel, Banqueting Room. 5 p.m. December 1st.

It has always mystified me why parents seem willing, even eager, in fact will do anything, make any sacrifice, to have their children appear in films for cinema or television, subjecting them to the tediums, the necessary, quite onerous, discipline of film making. As I knew Calcutta, I was inundated with personal calls from acquaintances beseeching me to get Martin, Andrew, Luke, Janet, Joanna and their like into the film.

That evening of December 1st we must have seen more than

five hundred children. The Great Eastern Hotel suffered an invasion. Little boys escaped, rushing up and down the corridors, sliding down its marble staircase; every cloakroom and foyer was filled with mothers prinking up their little girls; if only they had known how much better Jean would have liked them unprinked.

The girls were easy—we could have picked any of a dozen or more suitable children—but for Bogey, of the two or three hundred little boys we saw not one was taken for the necessary preliminary tests yet, right under our noses, was Richard. Nancy had helped us from the beginning, acting as interpreter, finding locations, properties, and Richard not only had the perfect face he was, in real life, the counterpart of Bogey, living in his own world of animals, birds, insects and reptiles as he has done ever since.

On the night of the film's première in Calcutta at the New Empire Cinema in the presence of President Nehru, a motorcade came to fetch Richard; he had to stand on the seat of an open car, waving to the crowd. During the performance he was in a box with his mother and father. At the end he was due to go on stage and garland Nehru but when the lights came up, Richard had disappeared.

There was consternation. Had he been kidnapped? Kidnapping children had been known in India long before it became a threat in Europe. Police were called, guards searched, men sent to comb the streets until Nancy suddenly said, "I know where he is."

In the small private theatre of the cinema where the rushes of *The River* had been shown, there was a tank of tropical fish and goldfish set into a wall. Richard had seen it when he was brought to see the rushes and been fascinated by it. Sure enough, there he was, glued to the fish tank, oblivious of anything else.

One role was difficult to cast. As I have told, my original character of the eldest sister, Bea—Jon—had been split in the script, part being added to the older, sexually aware, attractive rich girl, Valerie, come out to India from her expensive English school for the Christmas holidays and much envied by the heroine, Harriet —me; the other part going to Melanie, daughter of the American, almost penniless, philosopher neighbour and his Indian wife who was dead. Melanie, Valerie, Harriet competing, all three, for Captain John's attention—so that the film became that echo of the legend of Paris and the apple.

Melanie, though, was vital to the film; belonging quite naturally to both East and West she was the essential link between their truths, but we could not find her until after endless auditioning of

Eurasian, European and Indian girls, Jean suddenly announced, "We must go to Benares for this."

"Benares *now!*" To Kenny it seemed like madness to take what seemed to him an unreasonable trip, "When you haven't finished casting! We're over our budget already."

The budget was beginning to be a nightmare but there was, in Jean, a sixth sense or divination; a Swiss photographer had sent him a photograph of a young Indian dancer, at present in Benares and there we went. Of Radha Sri Ram, Jean wrote afterwards:

> At first sight she was so small, light boned and unassuming, she looked a mouse, not even prepossessing but when I talked to her and heard that calm resonant voice I knew why we had had to come. That night I watched her dance. She was a goddess.

I watched her too and could hardly believe the transformation of this quiet young girl into such rivetting beauty, power and intensity.

Radha danced in the classical tradition of Bharata Natyam as spiritual as it is difficult. Temples used to keep hereditary dancing girls, far from nautch girls as they are earthly counterparts of the asparas who dance in the celestial courts, always in the presence of the God; the way the dancer advances and retreats in these dances is to make sure she never turns her back on Him.

Radha had trained since she was five years old—her teacher was her guru. Every gesture has a specific meaning, the movements of face and neck have to correspond and the traditional mudras, or hand and finger gestures, and those expressive thumb movements, have names: 'lotus-bud', 'deer's head', 'swan's neck'.

She was, too, versed in theology, was a Doctor of Sanskrit, musical to her fingertips and treated her dancing with the utmost reverence; before she began, she would make a deep obeisance with folded hands from the ground upwards to the four corners of the earth; then she stood still, only her eyes making darting movements from side to side, until the rhythm filled her from her head to the soles of her hennaed feet which began to quiver, then beat to the sound of her anklet bells.

It was dancing of a kind then almost unknown in America; the McEldowneys were astounded.

In Benares, Jean and Dido stayed with the French musician, Daniélou in his house and music school that stood on the high

bank of the Ganges, so close to the river that the water was reflected in ripples of light on the room walls. Daniélou was the
expert of his time in the double interpretation of Indian music to
the West and Western music to the East; there were two schools
in the house—one for Indian, one for Western music. He and his
Swiss photographer friend—who afterwards married Radha—had
become Hindus; as they had no caste they had necessarily to be
untouchables, but had the humility to accept this. Daniélou, especially, was the most humble of men, sweet as any Indian except
for one thing, his detestation of the British Raj. He would not have
anyone English sleeping under his roof and I was exiled to an
hotel. When I was, finally, allowed in I overheard him say to Jean,
"She isn't—she can't be, English."

"Monsieur Daniélou," I had to say, "I am English. My father
was English and worked in India and for India all his working life.
Her people loved and honoured him. I think he has done as much
for her as even you with your music." After that, oddly enough,
Daniélou accepted me.

It was fitting that we found Radha in Benares;* it is the heart of
Hinduism and her dance in honour of the god Krishna is the heart
of the film, a story within the story, and gives it an unique flavour.
It is the dream of every orthodox Hindu that he or she would die
in Benares beside the Ganges, their pyres be lit on its banks, their
ashes thrown into its sacred waters to be washed away, discarded.
All along the banks are the burning ghāts; the chanting of prayers
goes on from earliest dawn till night as thousands of pilgrims
throng the steps on their way to make their ritual washings, as I
was to describe years afterwards in my novel, *The Peacock Spring*.

> It was a private ghāt lit by one small flickering light; its steps of worn
> stone led deep into the water. There was no one else there and, drop-
> ping her veil and chappals on the steps, Una stepped down them until
> she was breast high and took off her bodice to let coolness flow round
> her. She could feel the current eddying; it must be strong farther out;
> even here it lifted her skirt so that it spread in a circle on the water—
> which was probably filthy—and she thought of babies' dead bodies,
> ashes, and the bones Hindus called 'the flowers' and which the priests
> threw into the river, but nothing, at that moment, Una thought, was
> more filthy than she. Something sinuous caught round her waist mak-
> ing her gasp, but it was soft and light, only a soaked garland of mari-

*Now called Varanasi.

golds. The current took it away as the river took everything—no wonder it was sacred: Ganga ma, Mother Ganges: mother of rivers everywhere—cleansing, purifying.

Now that we had found Radha we could have begun filming—the crew had mustered, the actors from overseas were ready to fly in but as this was India, the astrologers had first to find an auspicious day.

What could be more auspicious than the feast of Saraswati, Goddess of Pen and Ink, of Music and all artists, auspicious for me, too, as from a child I had loved Saraswati. In Narayangunj, each December, we children had seen her image being made by the potter in the bazaar, moulded in clay and whitened, her hair braided and crowned. She would be given a sari of brightest gauze, garlanded with flowers and shells.

The symbols of Saraswati are the vina—a stringed instrument rather like a lute but made from a gourd—and the swan. On her feast day throughout Bengal, in every bazaar or city street a 'pandal,' a shrine made of bamboo, banana stems, strings of lucky mango leaves, is set up and students, artists, composers, bring their brushes, paintings, text books, manuscripts, instruments to her for blessing. Our crew had made a pandal in the largest room of the Barrackpore studio house and all of us, from Renoir and Kenneth McEldowney, to the lowest caste of workmen and washers-up— though untouchables were not allowed—gathered to ask Saraswati's blessing for the film. Cameras, the sound boom, all equipments were garlanded and, as the priest waved lights before the goddess, tall and graceful with her vina and her swan, on behalf of all of us I had to lay the book and script of *The River* at her feet. When a scene of the film was shot, no matter if it turned out good or bad, to satisfy Hindu belief, it had to be included in the film, "If it is to prosper," the astrologers said.

A river is the symbol of life: it cannot flow backwards instead of flowing on but, in those few months of filming, for me, it did. We worked far too hard to dream but always, for me, there was this familiarity in colours, sounds, smells, tastes, thoughts. The swing under the brilliant orange flowered gulmohur tree, the feel of the hot sun on the grass, the colour of the hibiscus flowers, the warm brown flesh, the smell of jasmine, cooking oil and coconut hair oil, of dung fuel, and of the bazaar. The sound of the sewing machine as the little dirzee—sewing man—worked it, sitting cross-legged on a mat on the verandah might have been the sound of our sewing machine as he, with needles stuck in the cone of his embroidered hat, might have been our dirzee. The 'Merry Peasant' played—with wrong notes—on the piano, might have been played by seven year old me; as I heard the sound of drums and of oars on the river they were the same, just as I had known the burning jealousy over the young man, Captain John, and those hopelessly inflated dreams of love and fame. They had all been here before, even the poem that the unhappy, gawky, passionate, little Harriet wrote in her exercise book had been my poem.

> The river runs the round world spins.
> Dawn and lamplight. Midnight. Noon.
> Sun follows day. Night stars and moon.
> The day ends. The end begins.

Few pictures have been made under worse difficulties. There was illness, constant illness; when Claude got typhoid all shooting had to stop—he came back far sooner than he should have and suffered relapses. The senior sound man collapsed and had to have an operation; we had to wait while his replacement was flown from England. People went down with dysentery, the children got a rash, then prickly heat.

Then there was the noise; Jean had meant to shoot in the bazaar but had to abandon that; the noise drowned any attempt at dialogue and a bazaar set was built beside the river where it was quieter but all the traders promptly moved in; not only that, they sold all the goods the company had provided. Even the wind seemed against us; a light breeze sounds like a gale on a sound track. Even the river brought problems; the Hoogly is a tidal river. The crew would get a fishing boat or jute carrying barge ready, its owners rehearsed and set to go a certain way on cue but, when the moment came, the tide would change so that the boats made no headway.

The 'extras' were another problem; they were almost all locals, had never seen a film in their lives and were bewildered and mystified by their orders. In the scene at the jute presses when the coolies, carrying great bundles of jute on their heads, passed up and down the jetty from the barge to the press, while the cameras shot them from all angles, they plainly thought, 'These Americans must be mad, paying us to carry the same bundles back and forth all day long without getting them anywhere.'

Not only mad but rich; as fast as Kenny paid bills more came in, many that could not be accounted for; a cow had been hit by one of our cars; no-one could find out when or where but it was, of course, a most valuable cow; also to hit a cow is, in India, far worse than hitting a child—as Kenny found out, the cow is sacred and there are too many children. The owner of the house in Barrackpore claimed twenty thousand rupees' worth of damage though everything had been put back to its original condition. The merchant who provided the rented furniture when paid, asked for another thousand rupees. "But here's a receipt marked 'paid in full.' "

"Ah yes, but this is for furniture polish for polishing the furniture when I got it back," and, of course, in Indian fashion, everyone, merchants and go-betweens claimed their 'tea-money' or extra on what had been agreed.

Some of Kenny's difficulties were of his own making. There was always the Hollywood credo that everything must be a little, sometimes a great deal, bigger or better than in real life; for instance the cobra that killed Bogey. The morning we were due to shoot its scenes among the roots of a huge peepul tree that grew by the garden wall so that its roots were partly in the Barrackpore garden, partly in the lane outside, we gathered first on the garden side; the snake charmer was duly there with his flat snake basket and the pipe on which he would play to charm the snake into obedience and display. The first scene was set up, camera, sound, lights; all the crew, the actors and, as usual, spectators ready. Then on cue the snake was released.

I have never seen a set empty as quickly—and not surprisingly; in their anxiety to excel, the Company had ordered a king cobra which is a hamadryad, three times as long as a common cobra, as deadly poisonous and the only snake that will attack on sight where most snakes have to be trodden on or otherwise provoked before they strike. "Bogey, what were you doing to it?" Harriet asks when, in the film she first discovers him with his cobra. "Only poking it with a little bit of stick," answers Bogey in a trance. He had enticed it with a saucer of milk and his own small reed pipe.

The McEldowneys met defeat in Radha. Kenny and Malvina were determined to turn her—their only hope of glamour in the film—into the conventional Hollywood starlet of the time, beginning by trying to have her front teeth either strengthened or taken out to be replaced by 'television teeth'. At the dentist's Radha firmly clenched her mouth. She refused to make up, not even for an interview or wear the gorgeous saris they bought; she liked her own simple hand-spun cotton ones, went barefoot indoors and had light chappals for outside. "If you want me, you must have me as I am," she said.

To their grief, there was no coquetry in Radha. She treated men and women alike. "Have you never been kissed?" a dazzled reporter asked her when she went to America for the film's promotions. "I expect my mother kissed me when I was a baby," Radha stalled him.

Kenny's difficulties though were as nothing to Jean's.

His principal actors were working in a country foreign to them, of which they were half afraid, half over-fascinated. Adrienne Corri, for instance, came at once into Calcutta's 'season'. What girl at seventeen could resist that? But she had late night after late night which showed in her face. Jean had also to direct dozens, perhaps hundreds of extras, through interpreters which made a barrier between him and them.

He was seldom given the chance to reshoot and, worst of all was working almost blindfold. In most films, the rushes of the day's work are seen the same day or, at worst, the next. Jean had to wait at least ten days for these to be flown to and from Technicolour in London. Often they were held up by customs—Kenny had continued battles with the customs officers—nor, when the rushes arrived could Jean see them in quiet with Claude, Lourié and me; they were shown in a small theatre of the Empire Cinema at the price of including the manager's female family, wife, sisters, sisters-in-law, aunts, cousins and children—often the customs officer's family as well.

Jean was, too, continually exposed to the production side's incomprehension of what he was trying to do—even Kenny had no idea until he saw the finished film. How Jean kept his vision I do not know and I was often reminded of what I had once seen in one of Fa's jungle camps, a great stag hunted by a pack of red dogs; when one dropped out another came to take its place, all doing their best to bring him down.

One of the drawbacks—or boons—was that, as the film was largely Indian financed, seventy-five per cent of the crew had to be Indian. In any case we were polyglot: Jean and Claude French, Dido Brazilian, Lourié Russian, the sound and Technicolour men Londoners, make-up man English, Kenny and most of the production crew American, actors American, English, Indian, Eurasians. The Indians in the crew were inexperienced, many of them then had not seen an arc lamp before, certainly not a Technicolour camera, but in the end this turned out to be an advantage because they were ingenious in contriving and adapting.

Indian film makers owe a great debt to Renoir; one of them who came over and over again to watch him was Satyajit Ray. To our own young Indians, Jean was more than their director, he was their guru. I did not realise how deep was the bond until the night of the riot.

The trouble began in the morning. When our bazaar set had been built there had been an obstacle; a peepul—sacred tree—that had become a shrine, stood in the middle of the proposed site and to film near it would have been sacrilege. The problem was solved by the building of a platform round it, edged by a neat low wall. The priest who attended the tree was delighted, particularly as there was a present of money.

A film is never shot in continuity; as far as possible, every scene set in the same location is shot while the lights and equipment are there so that our present schedule was to film the festival sequences of Diwali, the Hindu Feast of Lights by night while by day we shot innumerable small 'bit' scenes or 'linking' shots that were set in the bazaar—such as the father, Esmond Knight, buying paper kites, including the one for the small girl, from the kite shop; Harriet and Bogey squatting on their heels to watch a snake-charmer, an important scene for Bogey; Captain John wandering through the bazaar, Harriet trailing him. These were shots for which all traces of the night before's Diwali had to be removed or should have been removed.

The camera was ready to roll when Jean's unfailing eye saw one of the ceremonial garlands of mango leaves still hanging on the peepul tree, background now but still noticeable. His bellow of rage put the property men into consternation. Each blamed it on the other until it was the third humble property man who was sent scurrying. In his fright and haste to get the offending garland down, he forgot to take off his shoes before climbing the sacred tree. "Jean stop him. Stop him," I cried but it was too late, the outrage had been committed and, "Heaven help us," I said to the continuity girl.

We were to come back to Diwali that night and, with just time at the hotel to wash, change—we were all dirty—have a quick supper, we drove out to Barrackpore again soon after it was dark.

Work began. I was in my usual place at the side of the set, where I sat watching unless Jean called me. Soon I became aware of a noise like a distant roar that grew nearer, louder. Standing up,

I moved into the shadows off set, some of the Indian crew with me and we saw them, first flares and torches, then hundreds, perhaps a thousand or more of white dressed figures, all chanting in Hindi and Bengali, "Hai! Hai! Filmi bidesi." "Hai! Hai! Bideshider." "Tarao Hai."

What they were chanting was ominous. "Hai. Hai. Foreigner film." "Hai. Hai. Foreigners out." "Bapré Bap," whispered Kalyan, Jean's assistant director.

Kalyan immediately took charge. Everything was stopped and, "Stay where you are," he ordered. "Don't move. Don't speak. Please Mr. Renoir, do as I say until . . ."

He was interrupted. The two Englishmen from Technicolour, in charge of the cameras had whipped them into their boxes and to my dismay and surprise, whipped out revolvers which no-one had dreamed they had. Kalyan almost screamed, "Put those away you fools. Put those *away*." Jean went over to them, patted their shoulders and said one word, "Calm." The revolvers went back into their pockets.

The invaders were students, chiefly from the University of Calcutta. For some time, exaggerated stories had been reaching them as to whom and what we were filming. What was an American company doing anyhow, spoiling India's own film industry, exploiting India's talents for its own ends? Sensational tales began to spread: 'pretending to be princes,' 'filming Hindu women who were forced to appear naked!' I thought of last night's exquisite sequence of women in flowing saris, coming in procession with their lights and humble offerings of rice and flowers to the village shrine and, 'Now, this very morning', ran the tale 'that same shrine had been desecrated at Jean Renoir's orders.'

It was fortunate that, on this night there were no women on the set except for Dido, the continuity girl and me. They might have screamed. Our Indian crew could easily have deserted us, joining the students; instead, beseeching us to stand or sit still, they formed a circle round us, facing outwards and, for the first time, I saw Gandhi's 'passive resistance' in action. They stood shoulder to shoulder, their hands in the traditional namaskar or greeting; they too did not move or speak.

Claude's young assistant cameraman, Ram Sen, had stood by the camera trembling—Bengalis are more sensitive than brave—but now he joined the circle, joined too his hands in namaskar to still their shaking and closed his eyes waiting.

As the students came on, they overturned the flimsy wickerwork of our bazaar and set it alight. Nearer, they began to throw sand. You would think sand was harmless as a weapon but it can sting, eyes, throat and skin; soon it was all over us. Then, the foremost began to hit our crew across the face, over the head and on the feet with lathis, wooden staffs. Still no-one moved or spoke. Slowly the blows ceased—many of our men's faces were bleeding. The roars and shouted slogans began to peter out. The students came to a halt, uncertain and Kalyan spoke through his megaphone.

"Friends, let us be reasonable. You have come here indignant. We do not know why. We have no idea why. Tell us."

There was a violent outbreak of voices.

"I cannot hear. This is all confusing," and, "I will ask Mr. Renoir to make it clear."

The circle made a gap for Jean who came through to face the mob. Never had he appeared bigger, more impressive and, astonishingly, genial as only he could be. His voice would have disarmed the angriest young man. "Please," he said, "sit down. Then I can see you all." That alone was such an extraordinary request to make to rioters that those in front obeyed. Slowly the rest sat too: we could see over the sea of heads.

"When hundreds speak", said Jean, "no-one can hear them, so please ask three of your leaders, any three to come close and tell me what is your trouble—I can see you are troubled." A rumble of thunder answered him as Kalyan interpreted but, "Let us talk," Jean went on. "Then perhaps you will stay and see what our film is all about," and, One glimpse is better than a thousand words, I thought.

Kalyan and the crew insisted that we, the Westerners should go to the Barrackpore house and wait while as much of the set as was possible was rebuilt. Many of the students helped. Jean then restarted the filming. "It does not matter what we film," he told us, "anything, anywhere. But we must go on." I spent the rest of the night going, at Kalyan's request, from group to group of students, sometimes in a boat moored on the river, telling them the story of the book.

Next night we were able to film properly again and with the women. Diwali is the most beautiful of all Hindu festivals, honouring the goddess Durga, consort of the great Shiva, god of death, therefore of resurrection. To help Durga in her fight that night against the powers of darkness and evil, thousands of little 'divas' are lit—traditionally a wick burning in the oil of a small earthenware saucer shaped like a leaf—and placed under trees, at crossroads, at shrines, and, because the goddess might overlook a house, they are set along rooftops, on window ledges, walls, gates so that every building, house and temple, even every boat on the river, is outlined in small twinkling lights. I had seen them in my childhood, Diwali after Diwali; we were always allowed to sit up, were taken on the river, then came back to a party; the Diwali party in the film might have been our party though we had no fireworks.

When a film is over it is over. There seems to be an unwritten code that, when crew and actors part, you let them go. Maybe you will see them again in perhaps another film—as I have several times; then you pick up the threads where you left off but, meanwhile, you do not seek to keep contact. This sounds heartless but it is sense. How can professionals remember everyone they meet on a film?

It is hard though for people outside the stage and film world to understand. They are often hurt by it. "We thought Renoir liked us," said the wife of the manager of the jute press in which we had filmed, and said it in bitterness. She felt they had been 'used' —as they had. "We thought he liked us." They had sent Christmas cards which were not reciprocated.

"We did. He does." Which was true or would have been true if Jean had been reminded of them, but when the cards came he was probably in Italy or Mexico. "*The River?*" he would have said. "That's over long ago."

For me it has never been over. Though I never saw Claude Renoir again or Eugène Lourié, nor Kalyan or any of the Indian crew and though I have had several films since, *The River* will be with me always.

After almost forty years I can still hear that call for quiet; "Quiet please. Everybody quiet." Then Renoir's voice beginning as the scene settles down, the last child coaxed into place and, as I sat there, the press of people, the horn-rimmed glasses and the eye shades, the lights and the cameras, the make-up man dabbing shiny faces with his deep chamois would fade, whole years roll away as for me the river flowed the other way.

PART TWO

With James

Istanbul
My diary April 1950

We are grounded here for at least two days.

This was the second time I had been delayed flying on Pan Am's 'fat boy' as they called their double decker planes, then an innovation. I was on my way back to England, the children and James.

It seemed aeons since that November day when we had been married in a Registry Office in London. Only Jay and Jimmie Simon had been there—Fa and Mam could not come; Jon and Nancy were in India, Rose with the Red Cross in France. We had a small luncheon at Claridge's afterwards, then James and I drove down to Buckinghamshire to the ancient small private church of Little Hampden Park. It was dusk when we arrived and the light from the stained glass windows fell over the grass and stones of the little churchyard as we went in. The vicar blessed us.

Afterwards we went back to St. Peter's Hill and had supper by the fire.

It was a cherished memory but could I pick up our thread exactly where it had been broken, as if it had not been broken at all? When so much had happened since?

For the last weeks in India, the film company had moved from Barrackpore to Calcutta itself for work in a studio and we had spent the whole of March shooting in a vast studio that had a corrugated iron roof, no fans, let alone air-conditioning, so that the heat was intense. We had all been tired, actors temperamental, children fractious, everyone on edge. Still Jean had managed to keep his temper, wheedling, coaxing, making people laugh— though he lost a great deal of weight. It had been relentless; I felt too tired, still too much in the film, to be ready for a new life I had hardly tasted, married life to James. The other passengers were dismayed, even angry; I was thankful for the respite.

> Here it is full spring, the Turkish spring of almond blossom and young wheat. It reminds me of Kashmir. We have been put in a luxurious American run hotel at Pan Am's expense. Our windows overlook the Bosphorous where the ferries come and go among big boats, little boats, rafts. The sea is a sparkling almost turquoise blue; the sun falls warm through the windows.
>
> We women have been allotted two to a room and, most merciful of all, my companion is a little Chinese girl who cannot speak English or any other language the airline can fathom.

The night before we had come down at Delhi at four o'clock in the morning. The 'fat boy' had flown from Australia via Hong Kong and Singapore, so that there was a variety of passengers, all nationalities and as, in the airport dining-room we had been served with breakfast which I could not eat though tea was welcome, I had become aware of a curious little mewing noise which sounded so distressed that I got up to see. It was not a kitten; a young, extremely young, Chinese girl was sitting at the next table. She was wearing full Chinese dress, a tunic of white and gold brocade, light trousers, little slippers—quite inappropriate for travelling. Her hair was short, the eyes large for a Chinese, and terrified. Waiters hovered solicitous and curious as only Indians can be; everything they offered provoked a shudder, more distress. I moved over and tried English, French, with no response until by a process of elimination, I discovered that what she wanted was a glass of milk. After that she clung to me. When we boarded again the stewardess, herself puzzled and full of pity, suggested the girl should share my seat.

Seldom have I seen anyone as airsick or more distressed. All we could do was hold her head, wipe her face and hands, prop the little body; she was small and light as a child. At Istanbul she was almost carried down the gangway. In the hotel bedroom the stewardess and I undressed her and put her to bed; she slept, again like a child, exhausted. I looked at the little black head on the pillow, the cheeks still wet with tears and wondered.

When we had unpacked her things—she had no luggage, only an overnight bag—besides a jersey, a change of underclothes—at least I supposed that was what they were—a pair of white socks, a brush, comb and toothbrush, nothing else, we found a Bible in Chinese. "She must be mission schooled," I had said. That night in one of the hotel drawers I found a Gideon Bible; at once it occurred to me that, by looking up and comparing verses I might learn a little about her and she a few English words. We started next day.

A-Kuie as I will call her, was I discovered sixteen. She came from the mainland of China—I could not make out the place— was an only daughter with two brothers, one of whom had put her on the plane to be shipped to Pennsylvania in America, where she would be married to a man she had never seen, a business associate of her brother who would provide everything for her— she had no clothes except what she wore and a coat given by the brother. The family must have been truly poor.

A-Kuie had no idea where she was. She had thought Delhi, then Istanbul, was New York. Everything was more than strange, frightening; she could not understand a word, nor eat the food. Yet, about her, in the very helplessness there was an acceptance and trust that held no matter how afraid she was nor how she suffered. Sometimes in those four days she was almost merry.

We had to part in London. Alerted by Pan Am, James was waiting at the barrier with Silk; they had been there every evening for the last three days. "Roses, fresh asparagus, salmon. All ready," James used to tell. "Next day had to go out and buy some more. Then some more, lived on the telephone and, when Rumer did arrive, a hasty kiss, 'Sorry I have to see about a little Chinese girl,' and vanished."

It was poignant; the stewardess had, gently but forcibly, to take A-Kuie's hands from me and lead her away.

Three months later I had a letter written in English—I could guess by her husband—from Pennsylvania. A-Kuie was married and was well.

James used to say I married him so that while I was away he could look after the girls in the Christmas holidays—he took them to

Switzerland with Mam, for her the first of her dreams to travel come true; but I used to say he married me so that he could become the owner of Silk.

"I wouldn't have believed I could come to love a pekingese," James said.

"That's because you had never known one," was the answer. Silk had always sensed when James was coming. Now, in the evenings when he was driving down from London to Buckinghamshire, she knew when he was two miles away—we timed it; she would suddenly get up, go to the front door and wait, her plume of a tail wagging. In the morning, as soon as I let her out and she had been in the garden she would rush upstairs, jump from a chair on to James's bed, walk up the length of him and sit on his chest; if he still lay with his eyes closed she would gently dab their lids with her paw, a white paw with soft feathers—pekingese were bred with plentifully feathered paws so that, when they were allowed out in the Imperial courtyards of the Summer Palace in Peking during the afternoons of the siesta, they would not disturb the Empress as she slept.

We were not all as happy as Silk.

Several times in those first two years I found myself regretting that we, James and I, had not stayed as we were, he, ever at hand, he to whom I could say, "I think we need an illicit weekend." Now it was not weekends—or visits, it was for always.

I had not dreamed that he would feel such a responsibility for us. I must have been blind, because what man worth respecting would have felt anything less? But it meant authority and we were not used to being under that, the three of us had been on our own too long.

St. Peter's Hill itself was a cottage for three, not four. "Ours," Jane used to say in satisfaction.

> You should see us paying the bills, I wrote to Jon. I write the cheques; Jane addresses the envelopes; Paula scrutinises them carefully—she is very exact and often I forget to sign them—puts them in the envelope and stamps them. Then we add them all up. "They're paid!" Jane says in triumph. Paid, I think in relief.

Now James paid the bills; with relief again I had handed them over to him—giving him a cheque. Nor did he sympathise with our money manoeuvres and many of them were crushed. For instance, we had a money box at the foot of the stairs; anyone going up or down was supposed to put a penny in, "For a stair carpet," Jane explained. She and Paula had another money box for a chandelier. "A cottage doesn't need a chandelier," said James which was true, and he said, "When I was a child I had to save up to buy a pair of shoes. Make the girls put that ridiculous money box away." The sad part was that, before we were married, he would have been amused by it.

"Is he my stepfather?" Paula asked incredulously and added with Paula plainness, "He was better as James."

If anyone should have understood about stepfathers it was James. Soon after he was born in nineteen hundred—he was as old as the century—his father was killed in the Boer War. Ten years later his mother married again but went to run an hotel in Margate leaving James, his two sisters and a baby brother with their grandmother in one of the mean small houses of a run down London suburb; oddly enough the stepfather stayed there too.

No-one meeting James, even his close friends, could have believed what he had been through in his boyhood.

The grandmother had had a grudge against him; she had been a beauty but one day James, dashing in from his grandfather's garden, had run full tilt into her, knocking her over; she broke her nose which ruined her looks. Though he was only nine at the time she never forgave him. She had too, been used to living in comfort if not luxury. Her husband had been a master builder—he had built the Carlton Hotel in London but died bankrupt which made her even more bitter.

I would have felt sympathy with the grandmother in her old age to look after four children but not for the way she vented her bitterness on James—Jim as she called him.

Sometimes the mother sent money, sometimes not—the stepfather seemed to have been a ne'er-do-well—and so at twelve years old, James was taken away from school and sent out to work in spite of his headmaster's protests; there was a Labour Examination then which exempted children from further schooling if the family were in need.

In his autobiographical book, *Home Made Trousers*, James told of exactly one day in his life, the day he went up to the West End to apply for a place as a messenger boy at an electrical firm. He had

had no long trousers. "I can't wear shorts. I can't," he pleaded to his grandmother; she would not listen and he was in despair until a kindly aunt made him a pair of long trousers out of his uncle's discarded ones.

The firm was an electrical one with a difference. They were By Royal Appointment. James had an innate feeling for beautiful things, for quality and he describes it:

> Number Twenty-one Grafton Street was different from the other houses and shops: it was more brightly lit, more cared for; there were railings outside, and the ornamental porch sheltered four white marble steps which led up to double inner doors of polished wood. Behind the railings and stretching up to a height equal to the top of the porch was a big window, not a shop-window, as there seemed to be nothing marked for sale. It looked like the inside of a room, a very rich room, panelled in light-coloured wood, with a brocaded armchair, a little table, a lamp-standard with a silk shade, and on the table was an open book. On the wall at the back there were ornamental electric bracket-lights, each with two candles and little silken shades, and a rich-looking patterned rug covered the floor; the lights were lit.

The shop and its railings are still there. Every time I go down Grafton Street and pass them I feel a pang for that small boy.

The book has a Dickensian feeling about it but it is not fiction. James was paid six shillings a week which the grandmother took; she also sent him out scrubbing stairs on Saturdays. He does not tell that, nor in full about the beatings he had when Uncle Lou came in drunk each evening—Uncle Lou was his stepfather.

Macmillan, who published the book, made James tone that down. What is left is horrific enough.

> 'Uncle Lou, please don't lam me tonight. I've got a headache.' That had been true. Then he had shrunk away, but there was little room in the scullery; he was caught and one arm was twisted behind his back. 'Ouch!' Jim had cried as his arm was twisted upwards. 'Please don't twist my arm, it'll break.'
>
> 'I'll break your neck, you little bastard.'
>
> And then his arm had been released; Jim knew the pattern and now the real stuff was coming: the box on the one ear, and then the other, the one with the chilblain; the clenched fist deep into his side so that he could not breathe.

The later blows did not hurt so much; they could not hurt him more. Sobbing heavily, twisting and squirming to avoid the full force Jim had screamed out in fear as he was knocked first against the mangle then against the gas stove.

'That'll teach you,' a fist sunk into his ribs, a blow smashed into his cheek. And then, at long last, the neighbours were banging on the wall, and the lamming was over.'

How I wonder did James grow up to be the knowledgeable, tolerant, gentle, even tender man I knew.

At fourteen he had run away. War had been declared and he enlisted in the Army, being so tall that it was several weeks before his age was discovered. At sixteen he tried again and, this time accepted, ended as a pilot in the Fleet Air Arm, was shot down over the North Sea and spent twenty-four hours in the water. After the war he built up a fleet of lorries driving many himself; then, with his perpetual interest in people, he started a successful travel firm with an especial interest in young exchange visits, by which perhaps a hundred Norwegian students came to homes in Britain, a hundred British students went to Norway; they used to send him as little as half-a-crown a week which he banked for them until they had the money needed. These exchanges are commonplace now but then it was a daring innovation. He was, too, one of the founders of the Youth Hostels.

He had worked so hard that his first marriage had been a failure. "My fault," he told me. "I was always travelling." He hardly knew his delicate little son. "But soon I knew what I had lost," he said. He had never been close to a family and found it as difficult as it was intriguing.

One of the complications was that, to begin with, I was not there for his authority to be used on me. My work on *The River* was not over; the picture was being put together and every day of that summer I had to be at Technicolour by nine o'clock in the morning to see the rushes flown first from India, later from America, viewing them with Monsieur Koch, Renoir's collaborator in London, and discussing them with him; Koch shared Jean's eye and knew what he wanted. He was also technically expert while I dealt with effect. Together we would concoct long cables—telephoning to India then was almost useless, there was too much interference on the line and calls had to be booked hours in advance; Telex, of course, was not invented then. Later there were

long calls to America but we still sent written reports—and I wrote
constant long letters.

3 May 1950

Madame Renoir,
c/o Oriental International Films Inc.,
Great Eastern Hotel,
Calcutta,
India.

Dear Dido,
The children went back to school yesterday. My life seems to
have been chopped into two parts: house, children / *The River*, Koch
and Technicolour. It has been wonderful to me to see all the rushes
and watch the film growing, and I do not feel severed from it. Being
with Koch has a little of the flavour of being with Jean, and it is
refreshing to talk with him. All of the film that I have seen is very
beautiful.

Later:

I cabled Jean what I felt about the bathing scene at the holy place;
what I saw was honest, soothing and beautiful, but I had wondered
if it balanced in power with the jute work scene. Maybe it does, as
there is so much of *The River* in the picture, but I felt it best to give
you my feelings.

I have hated to think of all your tribulations of the dreadful heat
and can only hope that the beauty of the film will be an adequate
reward. I think of you both very much and of our evenings together. Please give my love to Radha, Claude, Ram, the little umbrella man and any other favourites.

Then a letter from Jean from America:

Beverly Hills, California.
November 20 1950.

Today I can write to you that my work on *The River* is practically
finished. I had a last projection with a few people, among them
some friends representing an average American taste. They understood each intention, every bit of dialogue, all the gestures and
situations. They were caught by the story, moved by Bogey's death,
and they loved the people on the screen. This verdict coincides
entirely with my very deep impression. I like this version and am
convinced that at least a part of the audience will follow us with
great interest.

Now my work will be purely technical. I have no more to invent.
I am very happy.

The film was a success in America, and broke all records in Paris
and on the Continent. Jympson Harman said, "As the beautiful
Technicolour setting passes on the screen a deep, relaxing sense
of peace steals into the spectator's soul in a way I have never
known in the cinema before." Not until years later did it make any
real impact on London.

It had been a world James could not enter and those first weeks
back home had been for all of us a strain. To be late at Technicolour meant your chance was missed, the studios were heavily
booked and to reach West Drayton in time, driving from St. Peter's Hill in the rush hour, having to organise the house and breakfast first was difficult, especially as this was in the Easter holidays—sometimes the children came with me, sometimes not.
James could not help me; he had to get himself to the office.

When the Second World War came, in typical James fashion,
he had simply closed his travel firm, making no attempt to keep at
least its name extant. Volunteering for service, he was taken for
the duration by the Ministry of Transport and was sent twice on
urgent and important naval missions round the world. "When can
you leave?" his chiefs asked at his first briefing. "When? Tomorrow," said James. As with the firm, he went home, packed a bag,
locked the door of his flat and left. On the first tour he was away
two years; on coming back when he opened the flat door a cloud
of moths flew up; there was hardly a shred of upholstery, carpet
or curtains left. He had not thought to tell anyone—in any case it
was a hush-hush mission. Dolphin Square has a thousand flats and,
in the pressures of war-time no-one noticed he had gone, or if
they did, took it as natural; so many people disappeared and then
reappeared. "It didn't matter," said James. "the work was done."
After the war he had transferred to the Central Office of Information where, as he dealt with personnel, he liked it. He had
though, to leave home as early as I did; it led to tension and
snappishness.

"It is all very difficult," he wrote to Mam in what I can guess
now was near despair.

The one person, then, who seemed able to comfort James—and
guide him—was Mam.

What a lovely handkerchief, she wrote to him. And however did you know today is my birthday. It is dear of you to think of me. It warms my old heart. Very many thanks.

James, James what a silly old juggins you are to spoil things so.

James could never do enough for people, especially my family, especially Mam, more especially the children. What a pity that love, care and utter loyalty should be forgotten in the smart of words spoken in temper or tactlessness, sharp words of which I, too, am often guilty—Goddens have poisonous tongues. I had learned to try and hold mine, knowing that you could not be harsh to Jane—she wilted like a sensitive plant—while Paula retaliated with shrieks and hate and, when Mam showed me another letter James had written to her at that time, I was filled with shame.

Dear Mam

Don't worry about these things. Believe me it isn't always so very bad as it seems to you. We do have fun, we do have happiness. The second year is always the worst I have heard and it is now nearly two years. Jacob served fourteen years: I have only twelve more to go. Perhaps then. . . .

When James and I were alone together everything was right which was a good sign, perhaps the best sign and it did not take another twelve years. Soon our boat seemed to enter into calmer seas—though being ourselves, there were patches of storm—and we grew content.

We had, though, three house moves in those fifteen years.

St. Peter's Hill had a charm, a simplicity and plainness I was not to achieve again. 'When I walk into the kitchen from the garden,' I had written to Jane at school, 'Silk and a tame thrush walk in after me . . .' It was a darling house but it had to go if James was to stay in our lives.

There seems to be in many men—I almost wrote most men— a dream to have a farm. Is it an innate desire to fulfil God's command, 'Be fruitful and multiply'? Fortunately most of them do not nowadays take that as begetting numbers of children, but the desire seems there, innate. Most have to settle for an ordinary garden, but we bought White House Farm in the next village.

As James had come late into the Civil Service, when the government decided to prune it he was certain he would be axed. "I am too old to start a new career," he said, "let's find a place where I can make us self-sufficient with our own vegetables, fruit, maybe some wheat." With dismay I could see in his eye the vision of hand-milled, home-baked bread. "Honey—we'll keep bees, chickens, ducks, *pigs*," said James, his eyes brighter still with a new unaccustomed light.

He began with one pig, a sow; as if she were the only sow in the world, her name was Mrs. Pig.

Mrs. Pig was a 'large white', her skin showing pink through the bristles; her size it seemed to me could be compared to a hippopotamus, she was almost as heavy. I was terrified of her—sows can be fierce—but James was bewitched.

The piggery was on the side of the hill on which the farm was built and behind the sties was a high knoll carefully fenced so that forthcoming litters of piglets could safely run and squeal. Blossom trees grew there too and all that spring, every evening at sunset Mrs. Pig would lumber up to the top of the knoll and stand there silhouetted against the sky. "What a picture!" James would cry, "she and the cherryblossom. Come and look at her."

Standing against the sun, Mrs. Pig's white hide took on a deeper tinge of pink; the sun shone through her ears. "They're like carnations," said besotted James.

Mrs. Pig was taken by lorry to a white boar named Ransom White Cloud. "She'll farrow in three months, three weeks and three days," said James. Every evening when he came home he would go out and watch her slowly swelling form against the sunset or, more often, a rainy sky.

James was not axed and we had to engage a man to run the farm which meant, as it was not much more than a small-holding, that Ern's wages took away any savings we might have made—there was no possibility of profit. One late afternoon Ern came to me as I was working and said, "Mrs. Pig has started."

"Oh, Ern!" I thought of James's excitement and, though I was in mid-sentence, rushed to get the car to go to the village and telephone—our own had still not been put in. "Mr. Haynes-Dixon is in a meeting," the secretary's voice was reproving but, "Get him out," I said.

"An *important* meeting."

"This is important. Get him out."

"What on earth?" said James.

"Mrs. Pig has started."

"Started what?" said James to my unbelieving ears.

"You know quite well. She's pigging—what do you call it?—farrowing. Hurry or it will be over. Hurry!"

"Hurry?"

"Come at once."

"Don't be silly," said James and rang off.

At five o'clock Ern came in again and told me five piglets had been born. "There'll be plenty more to come," he said and then, cheerfully, "Well, I'll be off."

"Ern! You're not going to leave me with Mrs. Pig!"

"S'nothing," said Ern. "All yer have to do is watch. Then when she starts her heaving, go in."

"Into the sty!" I said in horror.

" 'Course. Take up the little pigs and put 'em out of the way—I've made a pen like. When the new ones come out, put 'em back."

"Suppose it doesn't come out. Gets stuck?"

"Use your gumption," said Ern. "Or get the vet."

"Ern!" It was almost a shriek but a few minutes later I heard his motorbike start. "I'll never forgive James. Never!" I told Silk bitterly.

I nerved myself to go to the sty. Mrs. Pig was unmistakably heaving and I had to be so quick that I forgot to be afraid, hastily removing five sticky pink protesting piglets to a strawlined niche at the side of the sty but already what looked like a package in cellophane was on the straw. Mrs. Pig ripped off the film with her snout, revealing a neat little pink parcel. Never could anything have been more perfectly packed; forelegs and backlegs were folded against the chest and stomach, ears folded back against the head, tail tucked in. Mrs. Pig gave the package a thwack; ears, tail, legs were shaken out. Next second a tiny complete piglet was standing upright; at once it trotted round until it found a nipple. I could have stood transfixed in wonder but there was no time.

Mrs. Pig had thirteen piglets—thirteen was our lucky number. James arrived as the last was born. "Hush. Look. *Look*," I whispered, too filled with awe to be cross. This last born, when it was standing, went the wrong way round the mound of Mrs. Pig, to her back as she lay; halfway, it realised, stopped as if it had put brakes on, turned and trotted back.

All thirteen waxed strong, rushing up and down the knoll, squealing, rootling, eating quantities of food. When they were two months old a lorry came for Mrs. Pig, taking her to Ransom White Cloud again; I soon saw the necessity for bacon.

We had a pig fairy tale or near fairy tale.

Our kitchen and breakfast room looked out on the orchard which slanted up the hill; it was pleasant to step outside and pick our own fruit for breakfast or dinner, cherries, apples, greengages, straight off the trees. Among the fruit trees was a walnut tree and one Sunday morning when the walnuts were ripe, "Look," I said to James. There was a small saddle-backed pig, grey and white, sitting under the walnut tree.

We reported it to the police, asked in the village; no-one claimed it. Next Sunday there were two saddleback pigs under the walnut tree; the Sunday after, another, followed by three, all on Sundays.

When there were nine it was serious. We had to feed them, and our own sties were filled with our whites. The police had agreed to take them away when late in the morning next Sunday, a long red sports car drew up, a laconically elegant young man got out and said, in a voice I did not like, "I hear you have my pigs."

"It's about time you heard," said Ern who was there that Sunday. "How come they got out, hey?"

Our part of Buckinghamshire, near the Chiltern Hills had valleys called 'bottoms'. Our bottom was Lily Bottom named after the small pub that stood above its far end, the Pink and Lily, where Rupert Brooke had written many of his poems. Beside it was Lily Farm which had just been bought by a 'crooner', as rock stars were called then, who had made a great deal of money—he of the red car. It seemed he only came down at weekends. "Gentleman farmer," Ern said in scorn. "Gentleman! I don't think." His man did not come in on Sundays, as neither usually, did Ern, but the young man could not or would not get up to feed his pigs. "So they fends for themselves," said Ern. "That's pigs."

The young man's lorry took them away next day. He did not offer to pay, neither did he say 'thank you'.

To begin with it was all a little fairy tale and more than fun, even satisfying.

To Jon   Autumn 1951

Here it is a thin sunlight autumn day, cold and pale; the colours have been wonderful and so have the berries; it is all scarlet and crimson, yellow and russet, gold and green; our winter wheat is just showing. We seem to have entered into a creature's kingdom. We collect trays of brown eggs from the black leghorn pullets that have just come into lay and bigger ones from the ducks, brown and white Campbells. Yesterday I collected our Chinese geese from Princes Risborough station where they were in an enormous open basket with a net over it through which their heads came out, trumpeting. "Thanks be you've come" said the stationmaster, "We couldn't hear ourselves speak." Jon, have you ever seen Chinese geese? They are enchanting, small for geese, grey and brown plumaged, and graceful.

We had four, a gander, Clamour and his three goose wives, Clamorous, Glamorous and Amorous. Clamour was well-named; a gander is the best watchdog anyone could have—people are terrified when he rushes, hissing furiously, wings outspread, neck outstretched. Soon Clamour and his wives were so tame they would come on to the terrace, even into the house if we had let them. They used to sleep standing one one leg, their head and neck tucked under one wing; I never knew how they kept their balance. Their eggs were big, strong tasting but made good cakes. To the girls' delight we raised one brood of goslings, their fluff a curiously greenish yellow.

We were offered a Jersey cow, Christmas Rose. "*Please* have her," coaxed Jane. "I'll do the milking," while Paula went on pleading, as she had always pleaded, "Can't I have a pony?"

One of our neighbours at the Farm was the composer, Edmund Rubbra. He was a good friend to us. Rubbra let me in to his musical world which was a rare privilege, especially when I went with him to some of his rehearsals; we loved Antoinette, his French wife, who made their valley cottage into a place of peace and simplicity.

My diary. August 1952.

Dominic Rubbra has fallen in love with Jane.

"She isn't old enough," I said to James.
"Of course she is. She's sixteen and very, very pretty," said James.
Dominic was the eldest of the two Rubbra boys, brilliant, diffi-

cult, quite unlike his brother Benedict, already an artist who had inherited Antoinette's sweetness, her sturdy country French content.

"Seventeen's a dreadful age for a boy!" said James.

It should have been idyllic. In that balmy July, the lane that ran along the 'bottom' below our house was sweet with the scent of honeysuckle and spirea, white with lady's lace and marguerites; nightingales sang there. James and I used to stroll along it before we went to bed. "I wish I were young in my first love," I said to James.

"You have forgotten how it hurts."

Jane treated Dominic with a heartrending coldness I would not have believed her capable of. "If you ask him here I shall run away," she said.

Dominic spent his time bicycling from Valley Cottage to us; each time he put a letter in our mail box. Jane tore them into bits without reading them.

"Jane couldn't you be a little bit kinder?"

"No, I can't," Jane snorted through her nostrils like an indignant little horse. "He's revolting. I hate him."

Poor Dominic! He was certainly not attractive in his long and gangling stage with his tense white face and unkempt red hair. Does one redhead instinctively dislike another? I thought. Then why his passion for Jane?

Dominic eventually went to Australia where he became an astronomer of eminence. He has probably forgotten there was a Jane.

It was the bees finally that finished White House Farm for me. "Please have Christmas Rose," Jane had gone on pleading. "I'll do the milking." "I'll look after my pony. I promise," Paula urged. "You're both at boarding school," I pointed out, "I can't deal with cows and ponies," but I had thought I would like having bees. "They're wise," I told James. "Besides they make a garden, fertilising it. You have to tell them everything that happens in the house." I could see myself going to the hives to tell them of, say, Jane's first baby—some years off I hoped; Paula's winning a prize at school—unlikely; an old aunt's death—the Goddens, Fa's sisters, were dying one by one—the advent of a new pekingese. "And we'll have our own honey!" It was the honey in reality not the bees that finished me.

We had established our hives with great excitement in our last autumn at the farm; in the June of the next year there came a night when we took off the honey—I called it Honey Flow and wrote a short story about it afterwards.

Oliver Andrews, our friend and my bee mentor, came from the village to help and teach us. We had five hives standing like towers at the end of the orchard; one hive had been given three supers, three hives, two each and the fifth—added for a June swarm— only one. The new extractor was ready on the kitchen table, a new pail below it; there was a tall jug holding the two de-capping knives and, on the draining board, stood tiers and tiers of glass honey jars, each with its glittering metal cover, each freshly washed. At dusk, a late dusk, we all went to the orchard.

It was a hot night, James and I stifled in our veils and gloves. Oliver Andrews had only his old panama on his head and worked with bare hands, puffing smoke into each hive, working the smoker along the hive door and closing it with a narrow slat of wood. Then we lifted off the roofs, next the top two tiers of the outer walls.

When the white walls were gone, the supers showed built up, again like wooden towers; for all their quietness we knew they were humming with life. Slowly we peeled off the calico quilts that lay on the hive tops; only a bee or two were left there on the combs. Oliver Andrews smoked them, tenderly moving surplus bees out of the way with his bee brush, then he lifted the supers off and set them on a sheet on the grass. Bees were swarming in the brood chamber below the closed trap door as he swiftly put back the quilts, the walls and the roofs, making sure the hives were shut.

The supers, each with eight frames of comb, were almost too heavy for me to lift—I had once dropped one and been badly stung. The edges were sticky with propolis, what Oliver Andrews called 'bee cement', the resinous wax the bees use to fill cracks and strengthen their combs; the actual honey was not sticky, it was sealed in the combs. "And try not to bust them as you carry the supers down," Oliver Andrews warned us, "or you will have a nice mess. Spill the least drop and the bees will trace it and you."

When the nine supers stood on clean paper on the kitchen floor, all windows and doors tightly shut, I poured boiling water into a tall jug to heat the knives. "Keep the kettle on the boil all the time," Oliver Andrews told me. "The knives must be hot. *Hot!*"

He lifted a frame from the super. "The extractor holds three frames," he said. "You want to choose three with the same weight of comb. This," he said, "is a perfect comb, see, filled to the edges, sealed all over."

The comb exactly fitted the wooden frame; under the white wax the cells were filled with honey that shone gold through it. The wax was like pearl.

Oliver Andrews stood the comb upright on the table, holding it with one hand; with the other, he took a knife, steaming hot and, in one movement sheared off the waxen caps in a thin slice, then turned the frame and sheared the other side. "You have to find the air space, see? There's a thin little space of air between the wax and the honey. That's what you cut—if you can find it. It needs knack!" said Oliver Andrews.

"Give me a frame," said James.

Miraculously he sheared it, not as thin as Oliver Andrews but thin, then another and another. It seemed he had the knack. "Ar!" Oliver Andrews was a shade put out and, "I'll leave you to it", he said. "Goodnight."

When I had seen the first trickle of liquid dark gold coming from the extractor, three opened frames clamped into it, I had an overwhelming sense of harvest; harvest, the product of labour, the infinitesimal, ceaseless labour of the bees—and my labour, I thought. I had fed the bees last autumn with sugar syrup and wintered them, quilting the hives warmly, while James weighed down their roofs with stones, tying them with ropes against wind storms so that the great bee clusters would be snug in their stored frames. I had opened the hive doors again in spring and, slowly through the summer months, added the supers one by one, heavy, wooden, each holding the light comb frames.

But the harvest went on and on.

James whirred the extractor, loose honey and comb flew off the frames leaving them clear; the comb was churned round and round and the honey drained through the tap to the jars I held below. Jar after jar. At midnight there were still five full supers on the floor; we had not done half.

Sometimes the knife slipped or James made slashes so that jagged pieces of comb fell off onto the floor; honey oozed in great blobs and we both grew sticky. The handle of the extractor was sticky and I had honey between my fingers and in my shoes. The closed kitchen was almost unbearably hot. "Some people have a proper bee room with screened windows," I said. "Not people with only five hives," said James.

At a quarter past two there were two supers left.

"Let's pitch them in the pond," said James. "No-one could want so much honey."

"It's our harvest." I knew we had to honour it.

It was half past three when the last honey from the last frame ran into the last bottle.

"We're finished!" I said, "Finished!"

"Finished my foot!" said James. "Oliver Andrews said we have to put those supers back."

"Back?" I asked in dismay. *"Now?"*

"Of course," said James. "Don't be an idiot. Where else could we keep them? *And* we must lift the extractor into the cloakroom to let it drain—we should be able to get another pail of honey."

"I don't want another pail of honey." As other needs dawned on me I could have wailed. "We must wash the outside of all these bottles *and* put them away; not a trace of honey must be left, *and* wash the stove and the sink and the table."

"And the floor," said James.

"And now," he said when we had finished the honey and at last I was straightening my aching back, "you will please cook me some bacon and eggs."

We still had to put the supers back. They were light now; even I could carry two at a time. The dawn was pale in the garden, the orchard grass was wet with dew as, shaking with cold and tired-ness, we lifted the hive roofs and quilts and fitted the supers back into position carefully unlocking the little trap doors in the divid-ing boards. "The bees will clean them," Oliver Andrews had told us. "You'll see. They'll take every scrap of honey down into the brood chamber; then you lift the clean supers off and put them away for the winter and then you start feeding the bees again."

"I don't think I will," I said. I gave the bees and their hives to Oliver Andrews.

"You are feeble," said his look. I was. My vicissitudes had left me without much physical strength but all the same I was—and am—fascinated by bees, could have devoted myself to them, been a small echo of Brother Adam of Buckfast Abbey in Devon but they were not compatible with writing. Nor was farming. In the years at White House Farm I wrote one book, a novel I prefer to forget.

'Never write a novel that comes to you from anyone else,' I wrote to Jon about the book—James had suggested it.

> A biography, a study, yes but not any imaginative work. That has to come from within you, a response to something you see, read, remember—once for me it was a picture. But never never from anyone else.

And about the farm:

> We are losing so much money that it is frightening and with James away all day I get hardly a moment's peace; and there are so many other things.

I was still the only daughter of our family living in England. Jon and Nancy came and went from Calcutta. Rose had resigned from the Red Cross, spent a while in South Africa, came back to take a secretarial course, and went to work in a travel agency in India so that I seemed the only settled one and soon Fa and Mam followed me to Buckinghamshire.

'I'm afraid Mam has come to dread being left alone with Fa,' I wrote to Jon. Now he could no longer shoot, fish or sail, all joy had gone from Fa's life, and he sat all day in his armchair filled with gloom, a difficult sad old man. I found them a house in the next village to ours.

> To Jon
>
> Mam looks a different woman now about ten years younger and says she feels it. It is a good house for them, if only Fa liked it, but it hasn't a proper dining room, only an alcove off the kitchen. "I did not think I should end by eating in the *kitchen*," he says over and over again; a pity, as the house is so easy, warm, sunny and looks sweeter every day.

I had had the small garden landscaped for Mam but she had planned it and planted it, and revelled in it. The house was called Grace Cottage, Lacey Green which suited it but Fa called it Disgrace Cottage, Lousy Green and, "He'll have Mam out of there," I said in despair.

"Well, she had him out of Windmill House," said James.

Were James and I going to be like that?

I had found that I hated farming. "It's all petrol and killing," I wrote in that same letter to Jon. For James, too, the dream was fading; far from being axed he had been promoted and worked longer hours, spending most of his time in London. On the farm we had too much produce for the family, gluts of fruit, vegetables, eggs, yet not enough to sell regularly or take to market. The crux came when we spent a whole week up ladders picking cherries— no-one who has not picked pounds of cherries on the stalk can know what painful work that is—fingers get sore and blistered. Then, when James took them to market, the wholesale price had fallen to fourpence a pound.

There was something else far deeper; from the moment we came to live there I had felt there was a feeling of repellance about White House Farm. I had only yielded over the buying of it because James had set his heart on a farm but, though I never spoke of it, the repellance grew. White House Farm was the only house I have lived in where I was afraid to be alone. A curious dejection would come over me, an unreasonable depression, especially at dusk. I would find myself staring out of the windows at nothing, could not settle to anything. Then we discovered a man had hanged himself at the gate.

Everything was sold: house, henhouses, sties, the doughty dwarf tractor, Mrs. Pig, piglets, hens. We would have liked to have taken the geese with us—Chinese geese are good in a garden, they keep the grass down and do not damage flowers—but four days before we left they met their end when Clamour bravely, but vainly, tried to defend his three wives against a fox. The Farm seemed empty already with their cackling gone.

"Another move," everyone was to say. Well, as Keats said to Fanny Browne, 'It is better to be an imprudent moveable than to be a prudent fixture.'

Pollards was in Whiteleaf, another Buckinghamshire village on the side of a wooded hill; we had lost so much money that we had to retrench and the house was small and plain white, with pollarded willows to screen it from the road. Opposite was a row of Elizabethan cottages we called Rabbit Row as they were continually being rented by young married couples who, it seemed, almost at once produced a baby.

To Jon.

It is almost cosy! We shall feel being, as it were, shut in, after the Farm but house and garden will, thank God, be easy. James has been kind about it. I think he likes it. Jane already loves it, Paula not yet; she too, misses the space but she can get away as, ironically, now we have left the Farm, she has her pony.

At long last we had given in and told her she could have a pony, "When you have saved half the cost, say sixty pounds," thinking that would take her two or three years; she saved it in six months, scrimping on everything else with her allowance, asking for money instead of presents on her birthday and at Christmas, working in the holidays, for anyone who would employ her, cleaning shoes, cars, weeding gardens so that we had to honour it. Nancy helped her choose a good looking sturdy Welsh mountain pony of a roan colour flecked with white. His name, unoriginally, was Taffy. The first thing we had to do at Pollards was to build a stable for him. "Here we go," said James but did not say a word about Paula being spoiled. He had, too, recovered his sense of humour. We had tried having an au pair girl to help in the holidays, the French Chantal. Chantal was longing to go to London, to see what all foreign girls seem to want most to see, Buckingham Palace, Harrod's and the crown jewels in the Tower. We were able to arrange for Chantal to do this with a friend; also, as they were set on going to the theatre, arranged that they should stay in James's bachelor flat in Dolphin Square. I was a little anxious about this; we were responsible for Chantal who was young, and so made her promise she would telephone James at the office in the morning to confirm that all was well.

When she telephoned, James was in a meeting. His extremely proper secretary—the same who had tried to squash me over Mrs. Pig—answered, and asked, "Would you like to leave a message?"

"Yes," said Chantal, "will you tell Mr. Haynes-Dixon that the French girl who spent the night in his flat enjoyed herself very much."

The secretary was even more shocked when James laughed.

James did not say a word either of his disappointment over the farm. "I would have done it for you if I could," I longed to tell him but he did not want to talk about it. As if in reward, a new kind of peace settled on us; we had become partners in the truest sense of the word. Quietly but firmly, James took over from me all the businesses of writing, the contracts, the demands, becoming a buffer and a shield. I let him and was at once aware of the boon of having more time, even peace. We grew closer and closer yet I was free as I had seldom been before.

To Jon.

I had an elegant day in London wearing my new grey coat and a green scarf to match my precious umbrella.

Jon had bought it for me when we were in Rome.

It makes me feel elegant all through.

Jon and Roland had taken me to Rome and Florence but it was with James that I learned what it was to travel and really know the countries. With him, agents and bookings were not needed; he seemed to know all the places, hotels from luxurious ones to special small inns, and was usually met with embraces. Poor James though; everytime we embarked on a holiday it seemed to turn into a writing adventure. For a long time he had wanted to take me to the Italian lakes, Como, Maggiore, Garda and Locarno—I was soon to know them well. We went there, for the first time, in our first spring at Pollards; on our way home we drove over the Grand St. Bernard Pass, highest in Europe, and stopped at the Hospice and Monastery.

Tourists were crowded round the kennels where the famous St. Bernard dogs are kept but we went into the Hospice itself. We saw the refectory with its long marble topped tables, given by Napoleon, where even now genuine pilgrims and poor travellers are fed.* We saw the chapel which, after the plain white-washed

---

*Tourists have now to go to an hotel but there was a time when agencies exploited the Rule laid down by St. Bernard himself that no payment was to be asked for food. The tourists, who were innocent, used to leave a few francs or lire as a tip—so that as there were often something like two thousand lunches a day, the monks were in danger of being literally eaten out of their monastery and the Rule was allowed to be changed.

walls and stone flagged floors of the rest of the Hospice was a surprise in its richness. As I was to write:

> It has the Italian beauty of proportion balancing height and length; the walls of the nave are painted in green and gold, the ceiling frescoed and arched, and in the centre hangs a silver lamp that bears the cross of Savoy and the lilies of France. By the entrance is the monument put up by Napoleon to General Desaix who was killed at the Battle of Marengo—Napoleon stayed here at the Hospice; his bedroom is still kept as it was when he slept in it, as is Queen Victoria's at the twin Hospice on the Simplon Pass.
>
> High up in the sanctuary is a window inset with one stained glass pane of a Madonna and Child that is like a little Memling; its blue, even on a dull day, shines to match the jewels of the altar vessels; the monks have nothing of their own but the Order possesses valuable treasures given to it by pilgrims, royal or otherwise.

As we looked through the clear glass to the mountain peaks beyond, in April still in deep snow, I felt a familiar stirring and, "James, I want to write about this," I said.

James was brave enough not to groan.

At the foot of the Pass on the French-Swiss side was the little town of Martigny. We went to see the Abbot or Prévot, head of the Order. He received us in the parlour, a toweringly tall, bearded and handsome man; with a weary smile he handed me a booklet about the St. Bernard dogs, "This will tell you all you need to know."

I gave it back to him. "Monseigneur, I don't want to write about the dogs. I want to write about you, the monks and the Order, its purpose, its history, its present day." It was the beginning of a long rich friendship.

St. Bernard has become the patron saint of all who travel or work or live on mountains anywhere in the world, from the famed mountaineers and Sherpas who climbed Everest far across the seas, as much as of the Swiss girl herding the big-belled cows on the monastery pastures; his monks and their dogs are known worldwide. The Grand St. Bernard Hospice is the Mother House of the Congregation; she must be one of the sternest mothers in the world. On the third storey of the Hospice is a red line to mark where the snow can reach in bad weather; then the monks are completely cut off from the valleys and live in the harshest rigour and sometimes peril. Who would guess that the young almoner in a black soutane and beret showing the way to the Kennels, selling postcards of the puppies in the souvenir shop, politely answering tourists' questions as he looks at them through his spectacles, would, if they were in mountain trouble, unquestioningly risk death to help them. During the war the Pass was the escape route from Italy; the Hospice hid many prisoners, helping them to escape.

The monks have to be fit, not only in the physical sense but in the deepest, ready to endure loneliness, hunger, danger, even martyrdom. As late as nineteen forty-seven, one of them, Maurice Tornay, was murdered in Tibet where the Congregation had a mission until the Communists expelled it.

Every day, until the beginning of this century, a monk from the monastery would go out, with a dog, and make a detour on the two sides of the Pass to look for travellers but the coming of the telephone altered this routine; in winter or bad weather, when any party, however small, has to cross the Pass, the Hospice is telephoned from the villages below; the monks reply and give warning of the weather. "La montagne est chargée," comes the warning. "La montagne est mauvaise." In times like these the mountain becomes a personality, one with wicked moods.

When a call for help comes, the Prior chooses the most suitable. "Will you go?" he asks, which means, "You will go." The monks change into outdoor clothes (they used to have to ski in their soutanes, turning up the skirts, but now they wear ordinary sports clothes, though usually in black), put on their skis and disappear down the piste. If no-one comes back a new party is sent. In avalanche or fog, the skis are left behind and the dogs are taken. "Without them we could not find the path at all," the monks say. "They smell out where the travellers are even if snow has buried them."

Of course I did write about the dogs.* The St. Bernard dog is a cross between a bulldog and a Pyrenean sheepdog; he has the

---

*The long article I wrote—what is known as 'a feature'—was published first in the American magazine, *Holiday*, later worldwide in the *Reader's Digest*. It brought the Order a small windfall of money.

courage and tenacity of the first, the intelligence and protective instinct of the second, and he has been bred, true to type, at the Hospice for hundreds of years. He is smaller than the lumbering silken-coated St. Bernards we know in England and America; "You keep the kind we kill," says the Claviendier who looks after them. "Yours would be too slow and heavy for us and the snow would cling and ball on their long hair."

The true St. Bernard is compact and sturdy enough to carry a man; his coat is short, a tawny brown, and white, his head broad, his expression extraordinarily sagacious and sweet. Close outside the chapel, with his snout almost inside it, stands a St. Bernard dog, stuffed, the only one kept. Usually their hides are used as floor rugs in the guest bedrooms, "They serve also in death," says the Guest Master but this dog is Barry, who rescued forty-one people and was shot by the forty-first, a Swiss guide who was half buried by an avalanche. Barry was sent out alone to find him and, when the guide saw the big shape looming out of the blizzard, he thought it was a wolf and shot him. Barry brought him in but died.

When the article was written we still went to the Grand St. Bernard Hospice or to the Simplon almost every time we went to Europe.

One of the monks, Canon Giroux—they were all Canons—was sent to London to learn English as he was destined for Vietnam and spent his weekends with us. Simon, when he was eighteen and waiting to go to Cambridge, stayed three months with the monks learning to climb and speak French more fluently; in return he taught English in the boys' school they ran. When we took Jane and Paula, each with a friend, on a continental 'grand tour' we spent the night in the Simplon Hospice. I had Queen Victoria's bedroom; her bed had white curtains draped from a mahogany rail, a red plush sofa and chairs, and a washstand with a blue-and-white basin and ewer with the customary dog-hide rugs on the floor.

The girls were next door in white curtained cubicles that had been for the ladies-in-waiting. Like the ladies, in the morning, they had to break the ice in the ewers before they could wash.

The night before, after supper, we had sat round a great open fire, drinking wine with the monks and listening to their stories until after midnight. "You have to say writing sometimes is rewarding," I told James.

*   *   *

The American poet, Phyllis McGinley of 'light verse'* fame wrote a poem with the refrain: 'Where in the world did the children vanish?' It ends:

> Prince, I warn you under the rose,
> Time is a thief you cannot banish.
> These are my daughters, I suppose
> But where in the world did the children vanish?

I seemed only to catch glimpses of Jane, while Paula was disappearing into her own world of horses.

My diary: 1953

A milestone! We opened her own bank account for Jane. No more allowances.

To Jon.   April.

Jane has been here getting ready for Paris.

She had left school with honours and was to do a year's course at the Sorbonne.

We have been up to London for clothes and currency, passport renewed etc. She is a good child and so very sensible over clothes; she had a budget and wouldn't budge—surely the correct word— off it. What a contrast to us at that age!

May.

I have to learn that, when the girls come in, I must not ask questions. I remember Laurence's mother, Florence and her questions as soon as I came in at the door. For some reason it was like sticking pins into me and all the experiences melted away. Yet, when you see their brows thick with what happened, how hard it

---

*For centuries poets of calibre have written light verse. Phyllis wrote of herself, 'In the seventeenth century, poetry was witty, light almost like an intellectual play; it was not until the nineteenth century that the gulf between what is considered light verse and serious poetry grew up.' Phyllis bridged that gulf with firm skill. She won the Pulitzer Prize for Literature: W. H. Auden wrote the preface to her Collected Poems *Times Three*.

is to stay outside. Even if they told me, though, I would never really know.

Paula no longer writes home. She has hired a secretary for her letters! The secretary, I must say, writes and spells a good deal better than Paula.

Why was it so difficult at Pollards to settle down to writing? Real writing? The Grand St. Bernard article had been a by-line, I am a novelist but I see now that, for some reason, Buckingham-shire was not good for my work, though I wrote two novels there, *Kingfishers Catch Fire* and *Episode of Sparrows,* I did not feel 'in them' or they in me.

> The girls are away, James, of course in London. I have been alone all day which should have been ideal for work but no. In the end I corrected proofs which made my eyes ache, while all the time I was trying to think of that one small song for Impunity Jane.

I seemed able to write quite reputable children's books and the song eventually came, word by word.

I have always been fascinated by the miniature which is perhaps why, in that long ago first winter in London, I had sold my fur coat, my only warm coat to buy a doll's house and my books for small children are about small things, doll's house size dolls, pocket dolls, mice and, long ago in Cornwall, I had begun to wonder whether a really strong plot could work in the compass of a doll's house. "You do go out of the way to make things difficult for yourself, don't you?" was Spencer's comment. It was in a way a murder plot, but only one small boy out of the, by now, thousands of children who had read *The Doll's House,* or had it read to them, has realised that. 'How could you,' he wrote—he was eight years old—'How could you let Birdie be *murdered?*'

Birdie, one of the dolls who lived in the house, was a celluloid doll who had come out of a cracker. It was not murder; she gave her life to save the little boy doll, Apple who, egged on by the villainess Marchpane, climbed onto the table where a tiny lamp lit by a birthday cake candle was burning. Apple's fringe caught on fire. Birdie threw herself between Apple and the lamp; being cel-luloid she went up in flames.

> There was a flash, a bright light, a white flame, and where Birdie had been there was no more Birdie, no sign of Birdie at all, only,

sinking gradually down on the carpet beside Apple, floated Birdie's clothes, burning, slowly turning brown, and going into holes; last of all, the fire ran up the pink embroidery cotton of her apron strings and they waved up in the air, as they used to wave on Birdie, and then were burnt right up. 'Tinkle. Tinkle. Tinkle,' said the musical box. Marchpane smiled.

In the eighties, *The Doll's House* was a television series called *Tottie* done by Oliver Postgate. It made television history because it was not acted by cartoons or puppets but by dolls who moved by electronic control. Humans, grown ups and children, were shown by 'stills', the narrator's voice sounding over them; the moment the doll's house door was shut the dolls came to life moving and speaking.

Over Birdie there were parents' protests. 'My little daughter sobbed herself to sleep . . .' and so on. Kay Webb of Puffin who produced *Tottie* remained calm and wise, "Children often have to learn about death and if you had told your little daughter to stop sobbing and listen to what Tottie said afterwards, she would have gone to bed comforted and wiser."

Since it appeared, *Tottie* has, so far, been repeated three times.

It was John Betjeman who first noticed *The Doll's House*. He called it 'a little masterpiece', a real tribute from someone who really was a master and as truly humble as he was sincere. I cannot judge my own books but know I have not touched this standard since except perhaps in *The Mousewife*, again one of those rare books like *The River* that are vouchsafed—I wrote it in fifty-five minutes and did not have to change a word. That happens once in a lifetime if the author is lucky enough but, since *The Doll's House*, between each novel or biography I have tried to write a children's book.

Though I seemed able to do only a smattering of my own work I could attend to Jon's; the proofs I was correcting were hers; she had been writing steadily and was now in the midst of her most ambitious novel, *The City and the Wave* but she had not been happy with her first American publishers, Reinhardt. I did not tell her in this letter that Blanche Knopf had asked me about her, and, on my 'elegant day' in London I had been to see Alfred and Blanche Knopf. Blanche was a thread of a woman—I seldom saw her eat more than a few olives or nibble at melba toast while she regaled her authors with lavish luncheons and dinners but her brain was acute, as big her heart. She and Alfred were the only people in the writing world with whom Jon felt at home which was strange because the Knopfs were far out of our ken, oozing with riches— Alfred, on his visits to England always brought his chauffeur and his white Rolls-Royce. There was none of Ben's simplicity but while I grew fond of Blanche, Jon loved her.

We brought Jane back from Paris for the Coronation of Queen Elizabeth. Quite apart from the occasion, I had been chosen by an American radio network, the redoubtable Mary Margaret Mc-Bride's, to broadcast live to America on the eve. Mary Margaret McBride herself was to be in Westminster Abbey next day.

The others on the programme were the Marquis of Bath, who was to describe his coach, his robes, all the splendour, and the American General, Omar Bradley, telling of his feelings as an exalted guest from overseas, while Mrs. Bradley described her dress and hat. My part was to speak of the ordinary people, the crowds who had been outside the Palace and on the procession route not only overnight but some for three or four days, and try to evoke a feeling of their loyalty and love.

It was a daunting experience; the responsibility was great but I was able to tell those unseen multitudes what I had seen on my way to Broadcasting House and how we, as a family, would have to get up at four o'clock in the morning to get to our seats in time for the procession.

As we picked our way through the crowd next morning, sometimes having to step over a whole family sleeping on the pavement, I had to try and reconstruct it for Mary Margaret to use in her own broadcast that night.

"What's she doing now?" asks a persistent small boy in the crowd as he strains his eyes through the morning mists towards the palace.

"I 'spect they're calling her with a nice cup of tea," says his mother. She would like one herself as she has spent all night on the pavement.

"What's she doing now?" asks the tired small boy trailing homeward with his aching legs.

"Sitting in a n'easy chair in her own room I hopes," says his mother "having a nice talkover with the Duke, and a little bit of peace."

It was a wonderfully good-humoured crowd. I remember, on our way, James throwing an apple to a young policeman who was obviously glad of it. People made room for us to pass, not at all grudging us our seats. "Hope you get a nice view, love."

We were lucky enough to be able to go to the Savage Club in Carlton Terrace—the Club had built a stand on the terrace itself overlooking the Mall and only a few hundred yards from the Palace. When the procession had passed in all its pageantry we were able to go inside and watch the arrival at the Abbey and the ceremony, have a champagne lunch, come out on the terrace to see the great cavalcade, then on its way back.

The 'royal' who, next to the Queen and the Queen Mother, had the most cheers of all was the stupendous and regal Queen of Tonga, who sat in an open carriage in the drenching rain so that everyone could see her. The British liked and honoured that.

It was not only Coronation Day. As we had walked through St. James's Park that dawn—there was no other way but walking, no car or taxi could have got through—the newspaper vendors were already calling, "Everest climbed." "Everest conquered." "Hillary and Tensing reach the summit." "Everest conquered." I think I was one of the few people who were sorry.

To me, great mountains should be mystical. Now even the one of all the Himalayas I love best, Kanchenjunga with its twin peaks, always held to be impregnable, has been climbed. If only I could see them again, a longing I cannot speak of, only feel.

When during the war we had stayed on a tea-garden below Darjeeling, I used to walk up to a ridge above the house from which I could see, on clear days or evenings, the whole panorama of the Himalayas.

I leave my work and the children and go up to the viewpoint to see if the sunset will turn the snows red. The road leads between two worlds, the ridge of the viewpoint, and Chinglam. Chinglam was the name I gave to the tea garden.*

Chinglam is a world of valleys, mountain folds and ridges, floating with clouds, and with its river embedded at its foot. It is all enclosed by mountains. The viewpoint is open, open to the great snows, to the Kanchenjunga range and the Sikkim snows that are

*i.e., the name in the small book *Rungli-Rungliot* I wrote about the tea garden. Its actual name was Jinglam.

not snowed at all now but faint pellucid blue, with snow streaks on them.

The top boundary here is the sky and the other side of the ridge, above Chinglam is a sheer precipice. Walking along the ridge you look on one side down at Chinglam and its river and clouds, and on the other across, and far far up to the snows.

I am quite alone on the hill. The pekingese whine to go home, but I stay. The snows do go red: first yellow—then gold not yellow—then pink, then red, I leave them red and run all the way home.

I was to go back to India twice more but I did not see the snows again.

You never get to the end of surprises in people. At Pollards we had a neighbour, an elderly Colonel, who seemed to prefer not to know us, especially not our young or our animals. He had a most beautiful garden; every spring it was awash with thousands of bulbs in flower. One spring morning he came to see me which was astounding. "Mrs. . . . er," he seemed not to know my name. "I have to go to . . . a . . . friend's funeral, passed away and all that you know."

"I'm sorry."

"Yes . . . er. I suppose I should take some flowers", and with a rush, "Will you let me pick some of your daffodils because I don't want to pick my own?"

One of the penalties of being an author is getting letters asking for autographs, often not simply autographs but a photograph as well. I have learned that, if the asker does not send postage, the request should be dropped in the wastepaper basket but in those days I dutifully sent back an autograph—not a photograph, that was really too expensive. I had a letter from America with the usual request, sent an autograph and a little later had a second letter; 'Thank you for your autograph. We have had your hand-writing analysed. You are mean, petty, selfish and greedy.'

The only person now who was not pleased with James's new role in my life was Spencer Curtis Brown. Spencer was always possessive of his women authors, preferring them to be unmarried, widowed, divorced or at least detached and, if James as much as looked at a contract, Spencer would go into a fury. He would seldom answer the most reasonable query or letter if it came from James; if I wrote a covering letter, his answers were caustic.

One evening the three of us met for dinner at the Ritz Grill, for what reason I cannot remember. At first it was friendly, almost genial, and I was beginning to relax with relief when Spencer had one of his swift turnabouts, was suddenly angry, became offensive, and shouted which was embarrassing. James signalled to me that we must leave before we were asked to go, which we did, but Spencer followed us outside, still shouting. Then he hit James. No-one hit James with impunity and there, on the pavement under the Ritz portico, it became fisticuffs. I saw the commissionaires hastening towards them, one blowing a whistle. I hailed a taxi and went home alone.

Next day Spencer drove down to Pollards to apologise.

I would not ask him into the house—to give Spencer his due, I do not think he would have come in. We drove to our local inn and had a drink, both of us miserable. It was perhaps two years before I saw him again but he wrote,

> I have a suggestion to make which I believe you may welcome. The trouble about you and me is that I have watched your books from the day when I first found an English publisher for you, and have felt *too* devoted and perhaps too proprietary an interest in your affairs and in yourself as an author.
>
> Because of my devotion to you and to your work I am wondering if it might not be better if in future your work was handled in this firm by one of the other directors, Graham Watson. Graham is four or five years younger than I, and would therefore view you with the proper respect which is so lacking in myself. Whereas I would always try to tell you what I believed you ought to do, Graham would efficiently and impersonally carry out your instructions. You need have no worry at all about his skill in so doing, for he was himself a publisher for some years before the war and his knowledge of contracts and of the market requirements is as good, if not far better, than mine.
>
> I make this suggestion on one condition, namely that you should have lunch or dinner or a drink with me on every single occasion, or nearly every occasion, when you are in London.

How ironic it was that for some little time I held off from Graham, he who was to become like my brother; his wife Dorothy of the creamy skin and dimples, with her loyalty and forthrightness, another sister. All sisters censor but Dorothy never hurt and my life now would not be conceivable without them; how glad I am that, at last, I brought myself to write an initial letter to Graham suggesting that we might meet to make some 'arrangement'—if he had time.

His answer came by return.

> It was nice of you to write so warmly and I very much look forward to meeting you.

He proposed lunch at what was to become our favourite restaurant, the Aperitif in Jermyn Street—now closed which is sad. Graham added,

> I am quite sure that we can work out some arrangement such as the one you suggest in your letter, and I do assure you that the one thing I don't lack is time!

That is the astonishing thing about Graham; he must have acted for more authors than any other agent, eminent authors and many of lesser attainment, yet far from being impersonal he always made you feel when you met him, and in his letters, that you were the only one that mattered. Nor did he only 'carry out instructions'— a Spencer dig; Graham advised, restrained, encouraged, sometimes had to criticise firmly but gently.

Graham too had been bruised by Spencer and knew how it felt.

To our lasting distress, Silk died when we were not there. She had become old, frail and had caught a chill. As we had a business meeting with Ben in London, I had had to leave her with my new, completely trustworthy secretary.

Mrs. Lacey telephoned me at Athenaeum Court. "She didn't suffer. She ... she just died." Mrs. Lacey was overcome. "I'm so so sorry."

"At least she died in her own time in her own way," I tried to comfort Mrs. Lacey though I could hardly speak myself. Ben was amazed at our grief, particularly James's—silent though it was. I do not think Ben had ever known, perhaps hardly seen a pet animal. Everyone needs a bit of nonsense and my succession of pekingese have been mine, beginning with Piers whom I bought on my sixteenth birthday with a deposit of five pounds given to me for buying a Persian kitten—I paid the balance with a pledge from my allowance of half-a-crown a week for a year; Piers, Sol, Wing, Moon, Candytuft, Silk, Gossamer, Cumquat—the miniature apricot-coloured, named after the Chinese plum—Tuck, Picotee, Jade Button, Chin Chin. Silk II is my thirty-third pekingese.

Pekingese too, have ways, unknown in other dogs—if they can be rated as dogs. Their puppies play with flowers for instance, picking daisies and tossing them in the air, yet do no damage to flower beds. When you lift them up, they give a polite little spring as if to help you bear their enormous weight. If they want anything the big eyes open, shut, open, shut, in a pleading more eloquent than words. Nor do they bark to ask you to play or take them for a walk; instead an insistent feathered paw will come out to touch your feet and remind you of their presence. Mine are of no interest to anyone but myself, but that carnival of joy when you return, no matter how long you have left them, the trust, innocence, warmth and gaiety have made all the difference to me in the inevitable loneliness of being a writer.

Time, in those years, seemed to spin itself away in little happenings.

To Jon.   April

I went to Paris to see Jane. She is really plunged deep into French life. It was all very fast and giddy. We went to a French bridge party, a ball—both complete agony for me—and the theatre where we saw *Lucrece* with Madeleine Reynaud, Jean-Louis Barrault and Edwige Feuillière; she was completely wonderful as I had always thought. Jane took me round and I had to pretend I had never seen Sainte Chapelle, the Louvre, the Jeu de Paume and Les Deux Magots before. She was a little dashed though when, taking me, as an extremely sophisticated surprise, to the little night club, Club l'Abbaye in Saint Germain des Près, she found I knew its owner, the negro film director and actor, Gordon Heath who, with his partner Lee Payant, had made the Club famous for the wit and delight of its French and Negro songs.

The beechwoods at Whiteleaf were beautiful. Sometimes in the evenings we walked through them up to the Cross; on the crest of Whiteleaf hill a cross had been cut, looking far over the Chilterns. We watched the sunset gilding one roof after another far below.

My diary.

On Sunday morning we have breakfast, the only real breakfast of the week. Coffee, hot rolls and always for James, hot sausages. The pekingese—who do not attend breakfast any other day of the week—sit round, their eyes opening, shutting, beseeching.

One year we gave a dance, turning the terrace into a vine-covered arbour. Our small cottage served ninety-six suppers that night. All the cottages in Rabbit Row let us use their spare rooms or nurseries—babies being hustled into their parents' room to make space for those guests who came from London. For music, we had records and a wandering musician who doubled saxophone and concertina. I still have vivid pictures of boys and girls—no, young men and women—dancing the Gay Gordons on the lawn. It was moonlight.

My diary, 1955

I love my hut room when Celia, our daily woman,* has cleaned it. It has the quiet feeling of a well-kept church, freshly washed wood with the smell of damp and polish, or is it because of Celia's goodness? I don't know.

Celia is lovely in her bigness with her plait of grey hair round her head, her fierce dark Welsh eyes. No-one works harder, or gossips with more full-bloodedness or is warmer. When any of us are in trouble, the fierce words melt away and though Celia scolds, she rescues us.

She is the leader of the Baptist church choir and sings hymns in her deep Welsh voice as she works. One day she tells me her 'trouble'; it is that she has never been baptised. She could not face the Baptists' total deep immersion. "I never told," she says triumphantly, "I'll never tell either!"

Late Autumn.

When I went to give Taffy his hay, late in the afternoon, I found him at the bottom of the slope because, higher up, they were burning the leaves. In the almost dusk the white smoke and mist, the flames, the colours still in the trees, and leaves, the heaps of brown leaves on the ground, the red of the garden boy's jersey, and Taffy's roan and silver coat seemed to glow with their own fire, even the

*Freda was now too far away to come to us.

dark of the twigs gleamed, polished and, all over the grass, in a pale shine was the dew, not wet as in the morning but held there because it is so chill.

Pollards was the happiest house we have had.

PART THREE

Towers, Domes,
Theatres and Temples

We left Pollards with extreme suddenness.

When it becomes clear to me that something has to be done I do not believe in putting it off, perhaps hoping the need will go away. I like to do it quickly even if it is a wrench but not usually as quickly as with Pollards.

More and more I was becoming involved with London. James, too, was working longer hours often having to stay away the night which he did not like. Pollards had always been too small, also it was not truly country, verging on the commuter belt, though the drive into London was tedious. These were valid reasons but what brought them to a head was Jane.

From the time she had been a little girl Jane had wanted to be a nurse—Laurence's family had, on both sides, been doctors and nurses and before going to Paris she had been accepted for training by The Middlesex Hospital in London. The Board told me that when they asked Jane why she wanted to be a nurse she answered, "Because I like making people comfortable," which they said was one of the best answers ever given. She was though, too young. "Let her do something absolutely different for a year," Miss Marriott, The Middlesex's redoubtable Matron had told me; which was why Jane had gone to the Sorbonne. When the students came down that December she had taken a Christmas holiday temporary post at D. H. Evans, one of the London Oxford Street shops, and James had allowed her, with a friend to have his flat in Dolphin Square, where it seemed they had been caught up with a happy-go-lucky, extremely silly set. Part of the silliness came from the naiveté of some of the girls. I remember a party one of them gave when she had had the, to her, brilliant idea of borrowing a large copper or cauldron. It was a bottle party and as each guest arrived their bottle, no matter what it contained, was emptied into the cauldron. The result was a minor orgy and they were all quite horridly ill next day.

All this was comparatively harmless—had I not been giddy and silly myself? But now, though Jane had begun her training at The Middlesex Hospital and so had to live in the Nurses' Home, the parties at Dolphin Square went on. James had not told me but the management had complained. "And they seem to frequent pubs around the Charing Cross Road," said James. "Places where I'm sure you would not want your young daughter to go." Jane, too, began staying out after hours, cleverly slipping in through casualty. "You could jeopardise your whole career," we told her. "Miss Marriott wouldn't overlook this if she heard."

"It's just fun," Jane protested but, as James had predicted, it became far more than fun. "Some of the men are older," he told me. "They take advantage of the girls." It culminated in one of the mothers telephoning me, distracted with worry, to ask if, by any chance I knew where her daughter was.

"You *must*, must talk to Jane," said James.

"Talking's no good," I said. "We must move to London."

He knew what was in my mind. Living in Nurses' Homes, the girls could only go out with people, not ask them in. "If they saw Jane had a background . . ."

James nodded again. Then, "If we're going to move," he said, endorsing my view, "it had better be at once."

We did not have to go to house agents; next morning I saw an advertisement in the personal column of the *Times* and took the next train to London. I was just in time. "You must make up your mind in half-an-hour," said the landlord. "I have promised to let some other people know this afternoon. Though I should prefer you and your husband . . ." I telephoned James. "Use your own judgement," said James. By four o'clock I had taken a ten year lease of part of the Old Hall in Highgate Village, London.

If we left Pollards quickly it was sold even more quickly.

For the lease of the Old Hall I had to give references and rang Jay Simon, in his office, to ask if I could give his name. "Does this mean you are selling Pollards?" he asked. "If so, Jimmie and I would like to buy it." He instructed his solicitor, I ours; the deal was made that afternoon.

Standing at the top of Highgate Hill, facing the Grove and its line of gracious houses, just behind the famous Flask Inn, the Old Hall in its acre and a half of garden must be one of the most beautiful houses in London.

There had been several houses on its site but its date, as it stands now, is given as sixteen ninety-one. Parts of the earlier rooms have been kept though the drawing room on the ground floor, with its splendid panelling, wide oak boarded floor and plaster work ceiling came from a house in Yarmouth: the carving over its fireplace has the date fifteen ninety-five.

This room is known as the Cromwell room because Oliver Cromwell often visited here—for a short while the Old Hall belonged to his grandfather, Sir Henry Cromwell—and it is said that it was in this room that the death of King Charles the First was decided.

The house had, too, literary associations. Francis Bacon had died there having been overcome by cold when making an experiment with a chicken on Highgate Hill as he tells in a letter written on his death bed to the then owner of the Old Hall, Lord Arundel,

> My very good Lord, I was likely to have had the fortune of Caius Plinius the elder, who lost his life by trying an experiment about the burning of Mount Vesuvius; for I was also desirous to try an experiment or two, touching the conversion and induration of bodies.

He had been 'taking the air' with a doctor friend in his coach.

> Snow lay upon the ground, and it came into my thoughts why flesh might not be preserved in snow as in salt. I was resolved we would try the experiment; we alighted out of the coach and went into a poor woman's house in Swine's Lane (now Swaines Lane) and bought a hen, and made the woman excenterate it, and then stuffed the bodie with snow.
>
> As for the experiment itself, it succeeded excellently well but I was taken with such a fit of casting, as I know not whether it were the stone, or some surfeit, or cold, or indeed a touch of them all three. But when I came to your Lordship's House, I was not able

to go back and therefore, was forced to take up my lodgings here, where your housekeeper is very careful and diligent about me.

She put him into a good bed warmed with a pan; but it was a damp bed that had not been lain in for about a year before, which gave him such a cold that in two or three days he died of suffocation.

Dickens used the house in *David Copperfield* as the home of the Steerforths, including Rosa Dartle.

In the nineteen twenties the Old Hall had belonged to Lord Rochdale who was reported killed in the Second World War, whereupon his heir, son or nephew, stripped the staircase out of the Old Hall, the drawing room panelling and its exquisite ceiling and sold them to America, as well as the Peacock Fireplace from the first floor and, I believe, the fine scrolled iron entrance gates. Lord Rochdale had not been killed; he was a prisoner-of-war and when, freed by the armistice, he arrived back in London, was so outraged by his heir's desecration that he went straight over to America and bought back what he could; the staircase was irretrievably lost but he put back the drawing room panelling as well as the ceiling—we were constantly asked by Antique or Preservation Societies to allow groups to see it. Lord Rochdale also managed to rescue the Peacock Fireplace and the gates but I suppose he was too heartbroken to live there again or not rich enough. The Old Hall was sold to be divided into six flats or apartments—some were double—including the attics on the third floor which, above the tops of the trees, gave wonderful views over London.

We had the main part of the house and its main entrance which opened into a large white panelled hall that we used partly as a dining-room. The magnificent drawing room overlooked the garden as did the White Study which became mine. Below our windows was a wide terrace from which a back staircase led up to the other flats. On our floor there were smaller rooms, bedrooms, kitchen, secretary's room while, as the house was on different levels, in a sort of basement, but open on the garden side was a separate small flat of hall, bedroom and bathroom for the girls. "They'll only be coming and going," I told James.

Beyond the terrace the garden with its wide lawn and a rose garden stretched to a balustrade above the old Highgate cemetery; on clear days we could see as far as the plateau of Blackheath.

In the drawing room, its big windows giving onto the garden, I never stopped rejoicing in the fine plaster work of the ceiling; its bunches of grapes, pears, apples, scrolls and flowers; in, too, the richness of the oak panelling, the wide polished floor boards, the huge curved fireplace. We had log fires, the flames reflected in two big silver knobs of the twin andirons that supported the iron fire basket. I had curtains and covers made in a soft aquamarine silk and found an unusual carpet; for it we were advised to go down to the docks where Oriental carpets, Persian, Indian, Chinese are held in bond—London is the greatest carpet dealing port in the world. The carpet was again one of my treasured Persian Kermans but this time a Kerman version of a French Aubusson, its date about eighteen seventy with cream and blue flowers on a deep rose ground—the rose being distilled from madder. The carpet glowed on the oak floor and against the panelling.

We had flowers. Every Thursday morning we would get up at five and James would take me to Covent Garden Market's Floral Hall, arriving at the time when the wholesalers, having done their main business, 'broke the boxes' and would sell bunches instead of boxfulls. This brought a queue of barrow boys and nuns as well as us. The nuns waited till last when they would go round the stalls and be given single flowers; they were, too, welcome to any they could pick up off the floor and would garner large bunches for their altars and shrines. At Christmas Jane and her fellow nurses would do the same for their wards but they bullied the stallholders, or charmed them, into giving far more.

James did the bargaining, he knew the stallholders—any of them would take his cheque—we would fill the boot of the car with flowers, go to the Strand Palace Hotel or the Waldorf for an excellent breakfast. I would drop James at the Central Office of Information—then in Baker Street—and with our spoils, drive home. I remember I had lilies all the year round; there was a special stall for them in Covent Garden.

An old friend had told me in a letter,

Flowers in a room often send you a reminder of their presence, a waft of sweetness, a scent.

This is true. Books, she told me do the same.

From their shelves, a line, a poem, a thought suddenly speaks.

Jane was in and out of the Old Hall, coming every time she could get away and bringing new made friends; the old ones had mercifully disappeared out of sight. We had breakfasts when she and the other apprentice nurses came up after night duty. They were an extraordinarily good looking set, "Too good looking," Miss Marriott said; almost three quarters of them married before they finished their training. They all ate ravenously—with their hours turned upside down, our breakfast was really their dinner— they stayed to sleep far into the afternoon. Jane often came as well to dress for parties, brought friends to supper before dances. "Deo gratias," I said to James.

I was ready for London now; the Old Hall seemed to give impetus to the writing as my literary life unfolded and quietly blossomed.

I have never been a sensationally popular author but the net seemed to be stretching further than Europe. America had always been there—at one time I thought of myself as an American author—but now it was Canada, Australia, Africa and particularly, Japan. The Old Hall was a good place to work. James was at office all day—we had cleaning ladies Alice and Kitty and an evening cook, but they went about their work without disturbing me in the White Study.

I worked all morning, broke for a rest, worked again from four o'clock but always took the pekingese out for a walk, for my own sake as well as theirs. We had another bitch, Gossamer, black and silver grey and a delicious apricot miniature, as small as Candytuft but plumper, Cumquat. I would take them on the Heath or to Highgate ponds.

January 1957

This wintry day, when the dogs and I were alone except for one forlorn small boy fishing, the ponds grey white in the mist, I saw what I have not seen before, swans taking off from the water and coming down. It was surprisingly loud; they beat the water with their feet as they rose; the wings, moving so close to me, made a chuff chuff sound like an engine. As they came over they lowered their feet, held them stiffly and their wings wide until, at first touch of the water, the feet began to beat, again sending spray high in the air as the big bodies slowed. Then they folded their wings and sailed majestically away. One day I am going to do an anthology of swans.

A rest in the afternoon is for me essential; being brought up to the siesta, I have never been able to abide the afternoon which is exactly the time most British and Americans are energetic and busy. In Rome, shops, many firms, even banks close from one o'clock until four when they re-open until eight which I call civilised. At four o'clock I, too, started work again but tried to be ready and changed when James came home. Often we went out and, if it were to a theatre, film, ballet or recital, would come home for a late supper which we had at a small table in the drawing room, in winter by the fire—with a bottle of good wine. James's abominable stepfather had been a vintner of the City of London and had taught James more than a little about wine.

Margaret Rutherford, that delight of an actress, lived in the flat above us with her husband Stringer Davis—their drawing room had the Peacock Fireplace. We would hear them come in from the theatre, our door to the garden opened on their stairs, and often they would come in and have a glass with us.

That August I had a novel nearly ready, *The Greengage Summer*.

Long, long ago—when Jon was seventeen, I fifteen—Mam had taken the four of us to see the battlefields of France; she had hoped in her simplicity that it would make us more thoughtful and less selfish in which I am afraid, she failed. Added to this, on the way to Château-Thierry she was taken ill in the train with what proved to be septicaemia, as with Paula long ago, dangerous, in the days before penicillin. She was so ill that instead of the planned week at Château-Thierry we had to stay two months. For Jon and me nothing was to be the same again.

It is difficult, with the novel and the film that followed it, to disentangle what actually happened, what was transposed in the novel, and what has been overlaid by the film; each seems to shimmer through the others. I still do not know if we really had to walk from the station, Jon and I one on each side of Mam, holding her up, a boy pushing our luggage in a handcart, Nancy and Rose trailing behind as, "Hotel des Violettes," we said over and over again.

August 1959

I can still smell the 'Violettes' smell of warm dust and cool plaster, of jessamine and of box hedges in the sun, of dew on the long grass—the smell fills the garden—and, in the house, it is of Gaston, the chef's cooking: of furniture polish, damp linen and always a little of drains. There are sounds that seem to belong only to des Violettes: the patter of the poplar tree leaves along the courtyard walk, a tap running in the kitchen with a clatter of pans and china, mixed with the sound of high French voices, especially of the chambermaids as they call to one another out of the bedroom windows; the thump of someone washing clothes in the river sounds close and barges puff up-stream; a faint noise comes from the town and near, the plop of fish; a greengage falls.

When the book's first draft was written, James and I went to Château-Thierry to check on details. The town had been badly bombed in the war—the Second World War—and was partly in ruins. The hotel was rubble; I only recognised it by a shred of the blue satin wallpaper on part of a wall left standing in what had been the dining-room. There was a sad stillness as I stood there looking at it but the sounds of the river came from beyond the door in the garden wall and, in the orchard, the greengages were ripe.

With research it is always difficult to break into what you need but James, with his knack of solving difficulties, had the brilliant idea of consulting the town clerk. I had visions of an elderly man with a white beard, solidly bourgeois. Pierre Latour was young, tall, dark, handsome as a fortune teller's prediction and enterprising; he opened the town for us, even to my being allowed to see the police records of the time, where I found, to my astonishment, that the owner of the hotel, Madame Chenal's* lover, a Canadian, was in actuality a spy. I had come close to that when, for the book, I merged him with an Englishman, a Mr. Martin, also staying at the hotel and made them one. Mr. Martin was discovered to be an international thief; while we were at des Violettes he carried out a large robbery in a Paris bank, absconding in the night. He was never caught.

In the next two years we went back several times to this beautiful green and gold part of France, the 'champagne country.' A good deal of the film was made there. We went to watch, taking Paula and Simon and always staying at the old-fashioned Croix d'Or in Soissons which we cherished for its superb food—its sole cooked in champagne had to be tasted to be believed.

*A fictitious name.

People often say the French are avaricious and will exploit you. The morning we left after seeing the film and paid our bill the patrons, Monsieur and Madame, were away; there was only a young Mademoiselle at the desk. We paid for a fortnight's stay which included the four of us. Perhaps ten years later I, on my way back from America, arranged to meet James in Paris; he drove there from London and thought, for old times' sake, he would stay the night at the Croix d'Or. As soon as he arrived and went to the reception desk, Monsieur who was there, said, "Ah! Monsieur Dixon!" turned to a pigeon hole and took out an envelope. "We have been hoping you would come back. Last time you stayed with Madame and the young Monsieur and Mademoiselle, you overpaid. You should have been charged, not by the day but the week and *en famille* which is less. We tried to find a way to send you the money by post but it was too difficult so we kept it for you."

After ten years!

Renoir had wanted me to stay with him after *The River*, to work with him on scripts, an almost unbelievable compliment from so great a man. Now and again I wish I had; we might have arrived at a partnership like that of James Ivory, and the gifted Ruth Prawer Jhabvala, but I am a novelist not a screen writer.

Even with my own books I seldom want to do its film. A book bought for a film is old, it may be four or five years old and there is nothing as dead to a writer than a book when it is written—it is like a cat with kittens; she is full of care and concern when they are dependent, yet has no interest in them when they are grown-up. To make a film means spending months, perhaps a year, working over old material when you might be working on new, but the making of the film of *The Greengage Summer* was, for me, near perfect. I was consultant—this time a real consultant. Victor Saville and his Director Lewis Gilbert could not have been more cooperative over the script, the casting and design. I was welcome to come and go as I liked.

One of the flaws was that I could not imagine Danielle Darreaux who took the part of Madame Chenal, falling in love with Kenneth More, the best actor available to play the chief part of Eliot my charming thief. I had wanted Peter Finch who would have been exactly right. Kenneth was too British, ordinarily British, to appeal to Danielle, also too nice to be a cheat. The rest of the cast were

impeccable, especially Susannah York as Joss—in real life Jon—
and Jane Asher as Cecil—me. It is interesting that every one of
the films made from my books has led to the discovery of a star;
Jean Simmons in *Black Narcissus*, Adrienne Corri in *The River*, Susannah York in *The Greengage Summer*—she had had a part in
Tunes of Glory but this was her first major part. In *The Battle of the
Villa Fiorita* it was Olivia Hussey, for *In This House of Brede*, Judy
Bowker; and it was impressive in *The Greengage Summer* to witness
how thirteen year old Jane Asher, in the scene where the girls get
drunk, stole it completely from Susannah.

It was a time of actors. As I have said, Margaret Rutherford and
Stringer lived above us. Margaret, in real life was exactly as on the
stage, cloaks and scarves flying, the scattiness and the inimitable
face with the mouth that could purse, pout, smile as no other
could, the eyebrows that could suggest by a fraction of a lift or a
lowering. Behind the genius, there was nobleness, a quality that
would have surprised Margaret to know she had—she was innately humble—and so generous that at one time she reduced herself and Stringer to a poverty that finally drove the tax authorities
to arraign her. She was not allowed to sign cheques, have any help
in the flat—nor any drink—they were put on the smallest household allowance. She was not even allowed a car to bring her back
from the theatre; a taxi driver who owned his own taxi heard of
that and arrived at the theatre every night to drive her up to Highgate. He would not take a penny which did not surprise me; in all
the years I knew Margaret I never knew a taxi driver to take a fare
from her.

I was witness to how she fought her way out of that plight,
playing in films she detested and, for the first time since they were
married, agreed to be in a play in which there was no part for
Stringer, something she had always insisted on though Stringer,
charming and handsome as he was, could not remember his lines.
I used to see her every morning at seven passing below my window on her way to the studios at Pinewood—the Company did
send a car to fetch her; on matinée days it took her straight to the
theatre; if there were no matinée it brought her back to the Old
Hall by five o'clock so that she had perhaps an hour's rest before
leaving for the West End and the theatre. That play ran for over
a year and every night, wet or fine, snow or summer, at eleven
o'clock Stringer, often with a vast umbrella, would go out to wait

for her and bring her in. We always tried to waylay them for a drink; often Margaret needed a stiff whisky.

At first we had been careful to keep out of her way—Margaret was often mobbed and was beset with hangers-on—but one afternoon from my White Study I saw her below on the terrace; she was walking up and down in true Rutherford fashion wringing her hands and I saw she was crying. At last I went out to her. "Miss Rutherford, is there anything the matter?"

She clutched my arm. "Dear, you come from India, don't you? Then you must know about monkeys. *Please* help me. I've got a monkey coming to tea."

"To *tea?*"

"A chimpanzee dear, and I'm terrified. Terrified."

Before I could ask further the side garden door of the Old Hall opened, a woman came through, and beside her, a small chimpanzee, dressed in red rompers, a red bow in its hair—evidently a female—walked or ambled, holding the woman's hand, peering at the garden, then looking up confidently at the woman.

Light broke. I had heard Margaret was in a Norman Wisdom comedy film, as an eccentric old lady who kept large animals in her house, including a giraffe, a bad role for Margaret who had a fear of all animals, not least of chimpanzees. "I'm supposed to bathe it," she gasped. "It's come to make friends. Stay with me. Please, please stay."

"It will want to shake hands." I said it sternly to help her control. "Its hand, I mean paw, will be cold—all monkeys have cold hands—so don't jump. It's a girl chimpanzee; she'll be perfectly amiable or they wouldn't have brought her."

"But you'll stay," Margaret still clung.

The chimpanzee behaved very well—except that in the middle of tea she would suddenly turn a somersault, once unfortunately holding her cup; she poured another cup over her head and Margaret was eventually, not won over, but able to accept. She even laughed.

At the Old Hall, for the first time since my dancing days and the herb farm, I managed outside activities first of all in poetry, doing two series of poetry for children at the BBC, two winters of lunchtime readings in Foyles art gallery to promote young poets; John Betjeman opened one season, Christopher Fry another.

The charge was a shilling with coffee provided; people brought their own sandwiches. There were never enough chairs so some brought camp stools—we built up quite a regular audience—or they sat on the radiators or mats on the floor.

> From my Diary
> at Foyles.

Today's poet was Elizabeth Jennings, shy, young but already an acknowledged poet—her third book, *Song for a Birth and a Death* had been published that year. Jill Balcon, most gifted of readers was with her but, for some reason, the atmosphere was tense. With Elizabeth beside her, Jill Balcon began.

As she read the opening lines:

> "The bells renew the town, discover it
> And give it back itself again ..."

from outside, in the city, the sound of a bell broke in. Our readings began at twelve o'clock and this was the Angelus, coming in with exact coincidence. The beautiful voice went on with, in perfect accompaniment, the full toll of bells. The audience stirred and murmured, everyone relaxed with smiles, even Elizabeth.

James and I were responsible for fifteen Sunday evening readings at Kenwood House in Hampstead; they were held in the Orangery. Our readers included Dame Sybil Thorndike with her husband, Lewis Casson; Flora Robson with Christopher Hassall; Michael Hordern with Margaretta Scott; Ralph Richardson, Marius Goring, both solo; Barbara Jefford with John Neville and many others, it was a time of actors.

Paula was drawn in too. Feeling she needed a little time abroad after the end of school we had sent her to Switzerland to a School of Languages in Vevey, ostensibly to study French and Italian. It was a mistake, she would not speak a word of either; she was too miserable. At a loss to know what to do next, she agreed to take a course of cooking for a year and went to Tante Marie at Woking which she enjoyed, becoming a superb cook and qualified caterer.

I knew all the time she had yearned for horses—Taffy had to be given away when we left Pollards—but, "Horses are a luxury," we told her, honestly believing it. "You have to be able to earn a living," so, perhaps from being plunged among actors, Paula decided to apply for a place at the Central School of Speech and

Drama for their course in stage management at which she had shone at school. We went for the interview held at the Albert Hall which impressed us.

There were eight places; Paula came ninth which, out of some sixty applicants, made us proud of her. As a reward we gave her a fortnight in Devon where the Dartmoor farm of Sherberton offered pony trekking. While she was away, the secretary of the Central School telephoned to say one of the eight candidates had withdrawn; Paula had the place. I sent a telegram of congratulations to Sherberton and had a telegram back.

'Refuse place. Am staying here. Have been offered a job.'

Soon she, with another girl, was in charge of the ponies and trekking, quite handsomely paid and utterly happy. How crass it is of us parents not to let our children follow their instincts.

To Jon.

I have been commissioned to arrange a poetry reading for the Arts Council, a far more exalted affair than I have done so far.

The poets, R. S. Thomas and William Plomer could not have been more different, the first a Welsh Clergyman who preferred to live almost withdrawn from the outer world and seemed to find any publicity an agony, the other urbane, witty, much travelled, but both were men with a passionate inner fire; for Plomer it was his anger over Africa where he was born and his abomination of apartheid; for Thomas the struggle and bitter toil of the Welsh farmers and labourers of his parish.

It is not easy to arrange over an hour of poetry, especially with two such well-known poets, persuading them to include, not simply the poems they like and think their best but those that will give a balance to the whole. Fortunately both poets recognised the necessity of balance and were endlessly patient.

With William Plomer the reading led to a small something that gave me great delight; we discovered we shared the same birthday. Plomer rhymes with Rumer and every birthday for years he sent me a witty little quatrain of poetry; I sent him four lines of doggerel.

Then the Arts Council asked me to go on what was then called their Poetry Panel. I am no good on committees; to my disgrace,

I had resigned after one meeting of the PEN* but managed to survive two years at the Arts Council and was asked to stay the discretionary third, although, at first, the gathered poets had looked askance at a novelist daring to come among them. Why is it that a poet can write a novel and be acclaimed for it, but a novelist must not write a poem?

I particularly liked the Greek poet, Trypanis with his courtesy and sense—and went to see him at Oxford but my chief bonus from the Arts Council was Stevie Smith. I arrived for a meeting one afternoon to see, sitting at the far end of the paper-strewn table—it held twenty-six—a small figure, obviously a witch; she had a little black pointed hat, badly cut black hair, white face, eyes that darted looks along the table and grew more and more bright with amusement—something that did not normally lighten our proceedings; except once when one of the universities wanting a grant for furnishing a poetry room had asked the august body for a rhyming dictionary.

That afternoon we all had to give, turn by turn, our view on the allotting of a bursary of seven hundred and fifty pounds to a young poet, 'so that he can afford to live while he writes his poems.'

I, who believe in struggle, even garrets, said I felt the bursary should be given to an older poet who had already proved himself and needed a sabbatical to write some theme special to him.

The question came to Stevie Smith. She spoke, not quite in the chant in which she sang her poems—it always took the audience aback then completely won them—"Suppose," said Stevie, "you give seven hundred and fifty pounds to a young man. He has never had as much money before; fearful, he consults a friend. The friend is a stockbroker who invests the money so that it will earn a little more, invests it so well that it doubles. The poet now has fifteen hundred pounds. Delighted he invests it again, maybe again. What has happened? You have gained a stockbroker and lost a poet."

The motion was not passed.

When Stevie Smith was three she had gone to live with her Aunt in Palmers Green, the 'lion aunt' of the play *Stevie* Hugh Whitmore was to write and which became a film. Stevie stayed in Palmers Green for the rest of her life but worked in London for the publishers Sir George Newnes and Sir Neville Pearson. She remained their secretary though her poems were quickly recog-

*PEN—Poets, Essayists, Novelists.

nised as unique, the most famous, 'Not Waving but Drowning' ends,

> He was far too far out all his life
> Not waving but drowning.

When Stevie died of a brain tumor, a memorial was planned for her—a most unusual memorial—by her trusted friend and guide, the publisher James MacGibbon; she made him her literary executor. In her days of working for George Newnes, Stevie in a lifetime of lunch hour wanderings, had come to know most of the ladies' rooms in the West End from Piccadilly to Bloomsbury; of them all she always said the Ritz was the best. Her favorite meal had been tea and we were bidden to an afternoon tea at the Ritz, held in the privacy of the Marie Antoinette room—it could not very well be held in the ladies' room.

It was more evocative and moving than any service I have been to, especially when, as a valediction, the poet Patric Dickinson read the poem Stevie had written a few days before she died:

> I feel ill. What can the matter be?
> I'd ask God to have pity on me,
> But I turn to the one I know, and say;
> Come, Death, and carry me away.
>
> Ah me, sweet Death, you are the only god
> Who comes as a servant when he is called, you know,
> Listen then to this sound I make, it is sharp,
> Come, Death. Do not be slow.

It is the tea parties I remember best at the Old Hall which is strange because I am not, normally, a giver of teas, nor do I willingly go to them but one day, "You are having," said James, "some Japanese to tea."

Working in the Central Office of Information, James had often to entertain people from overseas—especially from the Commonwealth—white, brown, black, yellow, mixed but we had not had Japanese before, nor were these usual Japanese visitors; it was the first time Japanese women had come in their own right to Britain, not as appendages to men. They were women Trade Unionists, guests of the Foreign Office and the Ministry of Labour, Miss Sai Hamazaksu of the Railway Workers' Union, Miss Masako Hashi-

moto of the Silk Workers' Union and Miss Kyoko Miyashita of
the Postal Workers' Union.

They had been taken on tour, notably to Tolpuddle where the
first tentative trade unionists, the Tolpuddle Martyrs, were exe-
cuted; to Nottingham to see how Nottingham lace, linen and cotton were made, and had been shown facets of British trade and the
British way of life. For this last they were invited to high tea in a
Council house and now, "We want to show them a traditional
afternoon tea," James's Director had told him—he used the dreadful word 'classy'.

"You mean an embroidered cloth, silver tea things, cucumber
sandwiches, cakes and little cakes?" said James.

"Yes. Your wife's drawing room is perfect for it."

In the party were the three delegates, an interpreter, a lady
'bear-leader' from the Ministry of Labour, a diplomat from the
Foreign Office as well as James and his aide, and other possible
guests, a dozen at least.

"I haven't enough matching cups for as many as that," I told
the Director when, after James had agreed, he rang me. "Not a big
enough tea-set."

"Buy one," the Director said at once.

"You may as well buy a good one," said James, "We'll pay
half." It was gold and white Worcester and has been called The
Ambassador's tea-set ever since. It is now in Jane's house.

The party was to come at four o'clock. Everything was ready. I
had no silver tea things but the white and gold was elegant as
were my fine organza embroidered cloths on little tables. I had no
idea what Japanese liked to eat except fish—there were fish paté
sandwiches as well as cucumber, plenty of little sugar cakes; Indian
tea, China tea, lemon tea, cream. Alice, our cleaning lady, who had
a sense of occasion, appeared in a black dress with a muslin apron.
There were flowers—knowing my clumsiness with flowers I had
persuaded our extremely good flower shop owner to come in and
arrange them which she did; even Japanese, I felt must approve
them. There was another tea spread in the kitchen for the chauffeurs.

Four o'clock came, quarter past, half past. James telephoned the
Foreign Office. They were on their way. Five o'clock. It was not
until a quarter past five that the motorcade appeared, the bear-
leader lady flushed and flustered.

So far, through the tour, the Japanese had worn Western

clothes, the almost regulation navy suits, white blouses, berets, stockings and shoes but, in honour of this, they had been told, different occasion, they felt they must wear full Japanese dress, as for the tea ceremony—kimono, obi, white one-toe socks, thonged sandals, their hair piled up with flowers and stick pins studded with gold and silver and ornamental butterflies. They looked gorgeous but it seemed when Masako Hashimoto of the Silk Weavers, who was of peasant origin, saw the kimonos of the others, she had refused to come. The long delay had gone in argument; the other two had finally retired to change into lesser kimonos. "You see, I am entitled to wear five crests on my kimono," Sai Hamazaksu told me when we met afterwards. They were printed, one on the back, two on the breast, two on the sleeves of her kimonos.

When I came out to the hall to meet them, all three bent low and extended their fans to me; it would have been desecration to shake hands.

We found it difficult to make them feel at home. They sat in a row on the sofa; every time anything was offered to them they gave a little hiss which was disconcerting until I realised it was in appreciation but they ate hardly anything; the interpreted conversation was stilted until I thought to show them photographs of the children which apparently was after their hearts. They plied me with questions. Success came again when I showed them the kitchen which, the interpreter told me, they much wanted to see but were too polite to ask.

When we met them again at the civic reception given for them as a farewell, they hailed us as old friends. Sai Hamazaksu and I wrote to one another for years.

There was another tea, not as pleasant—it left a sour taste.

For some two years a woman—I will call her Rachel—had been writing to me from Massachusetts; not only writing, she sent me the *Hornbook*, America's prestigious magazine for children's literature which comes out quarterly; there is no equivalent in Britain so that I was grateful for it and when she told me she was coming to England and could she come to tea? I said 'yes'; though I do not often invite readers home. Rachel said she had one or two friends with her, could she bring them?

At the Old Hall I was lucky enough to have, as part-time secretary, Celia Dale, who should not have been a secretary as she was an exceedingly clever, spine-chilling novelist and a discerning critic; for years she wrote the Book Page of *Home and Garden*. At lunch time on the day of Rachel's visit, Celia came to me perturbed. "You said this Rachel told you she had one or two friends. I've rung the hotel to check the time. The desk said Rachel was out with her tour. She has twenty-three friends," said Celia.

"Celia!" I looked at her blankly. "We must cancel at once."

"We can't. They're out for the day—until they come here," said Celia.

I had provided tea for three, at most four. It was already one o'clock and in Highgate it was early closing day so that no shops would be open. I rang up Tante Marie; they nobly—and I must say at cost—sent up from Woking every available cake, scone, biscuit, they had. Somehow, with the help of the Ambassador's tea-set we mustered enough cups. Alice stayed to help.

At four o'clock a coach arrived. Two dozen middle-aged or elderly ladies got out, beaming, giving vent to their happiness in enthusiastically loud American voices. Alice told me afterwards that the driver staggered into the kitchen, clutching his head, "Give me a cup of tea, quick. Blimey! I've never heard such a noise! I've had it all bleeding day."

Alice went round removing the ashtrays and teaspoons. She need not have bothered. The ladies were librarians, delightful, interested and completely innocent of any intrusion, which Rachel was not.

It turned out that she ran an annual tour, "Meet the Famous in Their Own Homes" for which the price was quite high. Working on each tour for months, in my case two years, she insinuated herself by letters, cleverly baited as she had baited me with the *Hornbook*. This particular tour had been to Stratford—an actor; to St. David's—a bishop; the House of Lords—a Viscount. I suppose she hoped, that faced with the ladies—they were true ladies—none of us would have the heart to turn them away. At least they enjoyed themselves; Celia and I enjoyed them. Rachel would not meet our eyes. Nor did I hear from her again.

It is indicative of my sense of fulfilment at the Old Hall that I was able to write the complicated novel *China Court*, a companion to the novel *Fugue in Time* based, like that, on Dunn's theory of time, that still fascinated me but using five generations not three.

Fugue in Time was set in a London house, *China Court* in the country, Cornwall, the Court itself being partly derived from Darrynane, partly a house in Blisland I had come to know and love.

To Jon—in exasperation.

I am so *slow*! The work grows infinitesimally!

At work I could be called the portrait of a tortoise. Indeed a new friend, Elizabeth, had given me a little silver tortoise with a winkle shell to put on my desk. Now she sent a silver hare which perhaps was right. It had taken me eight years to write *Fugue in Time*; I was to write *China Court* in eighteen months. I had, of course found the key.*

I suppose the more you have to do, the more you learn to organise and concentrate—or else get fragmented into bits. I have learned to use my 'ten minutes'. I once thought it was not worth sitting down for a time as short as that; now I know differently and, if I have ten minutes, I use them, even if they bring only two lines, and it keeps the book alive.

There was an odd offshoot of this time.

I had come to know the nuns of the Cenacle Convent, then in London, occasionally driving for them and helping in their work for old people. Talking one day to the Superior, Mother Thornton while she was sorting out a cupboard full of books, we came across some little pamphlets, childishly illustrated called *Prières dans l'Arche*, short poems in French. "Give them to your grandchildren," said Mother. On my way home in the bus I read them and realised at once these prayers of animals were not for children but everyone.

> Lord
> I am the cat.
> It is not, exactly, that I have something to ask of You!
> No—
> I ask nothing of anyone—
> but . . .

*See page 33.

The prayer of the donkey:

> O God, who made me
> to trudge along the road
> always
> to carry heavy loads
> always
> to be beaten
> always . . .

The cock:

> Do not forget, Lord
> I make the sun rise . . .

It so happened that Harold K. Guinzburg, co-president with Ben Huebsch of the Viking Press, was in England and was having dinner with us that night. I showed him the poems. "Do you think I should try and translate them?"

"You must," said Harold. "These are rare and must reach a far wider audience. It is so seldom that anyone has an original thought."

The first problem was to find the poet. She was a woman, Carmen Bernos de Gasztold. I tried the Institute of Poets in Paris, tried bookshops; no-one had heard of her until, turning the pamphlets over, a friend I was with—the same quick-witted friend who had given me the silver tortoise and the hare—said, "I wonder if she is a nun," and pointed out what was in small print, so minuscule that it had escaped my reading, the words *Editions du Cloître*. Next time I was in Paris I tried Pagés, a Catholic religious bookshop and there, on the counter was a display of the pamphlets *Prières dans l'Arche*.

"Ah, oui," said the proprietor, "*Les Editions du Cloître* are from the Abbaye Saint Louis du Temple, a Benedictine House at Limon," which was not far from Paris. "The nuns used to be the famous Benedictines of the Rue Monsieur until they were driven out by the war. You will find your poet there."

Carmen Bernos de Gasztold is not a nun. She was born in Arcachon where her father was Professor of Spanish. He was subject to fits of insanity so that they were extremely poor—Carmen remembers the shame when she and her brother had to take charity vouchers to the butcher. The father died and during the Second

Ben Huebsch in his garden in Sweden

Jon

R.G. with the Japanese delegates

Jane and Anthony on their wedding day

R.G. with James and L. Quincy
Mumford, Librarian of Congress

Dame Felicitas Corrigan with a
young nun

Paula with Titania

Simon

Jon and R.G. with Harold Macmillan at the Yorkshire Evening Post *luncheon*

Lamb House Garden in Rye

R.G. with James, left, and Orville Prescott on the steps of Lamb House

Miniature Jade Button of Alderbourne; his size can be seen by comparison to the sprig of holly

Mark, Elizabeth, Emma, and Charlotte at Lamb House

Paula on her wedding day

A witch of a child

World War she and her mother made their way to Paris where, in the occupation, she was conscripted by the Germans to work in a factory. At the same time, to help her widowed mother, a sister whose Polish husband had deserted leaving her with three small children in a tiny flat, Carmen worked as well in a kindergarten. It was no wonder that she had a nervous breakdown so bad that she was put in a public asylum.

One of the nuns at Limon, Mère Anne Geneviève, happened to be Carmen's godmother. Hearing what had befallen Carmen, Mère Anne Geneviève persuaded her Abbess, as it was wartime, to allow Carmen to come into the enclosure and sallied out to rescue her —which none of Carmen's own family had tried to do. It would take more than Germans or strict enclosure to thwart Mère Anne Geneviève when she had made up her mind. She brought Carmen to the Abbaye, put her on its farm and nursed her back to health. Eventually the colombière, the Abbaye's big dove house, was turned into a guest house and home for her and she has been attached to the nuns ever since, but is now at Joques in the South of France where a second abbey has been built, again by the nuns themselves with the help of des clochards—drunks or dropouts whom nobody else would employ.

It was in that time of overwork in Paris, and in that tiny flat, in acute suffering that Carmen wrote the *Prayers*. No-one knows what else, besides conscription the Germans did to her; she had been, they told me, a beautiful girl and had still a look of the young Napoleon in the painting by David *Crossing the Alps*, the face fierce yet vulnerable, but it was obvious that most humans had become terrible to Carmen which is why she turned to the animal kingdom; the observations of her animals are not flattering to the human race.

It was, I am sure, through that acute suffering she was able to find, in each of these workaday often infinitesimal or unfavoured creatures, its intrinsic being which is, in itself, a prayer if only we had ears to hear them, sensibility enough to sense them. Yet she writes of them in the most matter of fact and tenderly ironic way as in the *Prayer of the Ducks*:

> Dear God,
> Give us a flood of water,
> Let it rain tomorrow and always.

or in the joyous flea—

> I jump. I bite.
> I jump. I bite.
> How it amuses me
> Lord!

She is the reverse of sentimental—Carmen has no use for pets; to her a pig is to be eaten. 'Lord, why did you make me so tender?'; a dog to be kept on a chain as a guard. The Old Horse on its stiffened legs is 'an unprofitable servant' and how many of us have not, at some time felt, like the ox:

> Dear God, give me time.
> Men are always so driven!
> Give me time to eat.
> Give me time to plod.
> Give me time to sleep.
> Give me time to think.
> Amen.

All the poems end with Amen—so be it.

Even when I had found Carmen, gained her permission to translate, there were still endless difficulties; Mère Anne Geneviève is a little hornet of a nun, fiercely protective of Carmen and, at first was sure I, an English novelist, would exploit her. "Using her work to make your name. Jamais!" I offered to do the poems anonymously but the publishers would not accept that. "You are set," accused Mère Anne Geneviève "set to make money from the prayers."

"Of course," I answered, "but my share will be ten per cent for my expenses. Carmen's will be ninety."

"Vraiment?" she said incredulously.

"Vraiment, ma Mère."

None of the nuns spoke English—Carmen not even a word— so that when I showed a first draft of the translations to them they consulted a dictionary. Naturally the poems would not conform. "You don't translate poetry word by word," I told them and asked for an arbitrator, only stipulating that he or she must be bilingual, "*and* a poet," I said. They did not know anyone who spoke English, nor any poet but their own. At last they accepted a Stanbrook Abbey nun, Dame Marcella, who had translated Rilke and

Rousseau. Even then we ran into trouble; Dame Marcella had used 'a column of water' in a poem about a fountain. "But the dictionary says a column is of *stone*," said the puzzled Mère Anne Geneviève. I myself think 'plume' would have been better but Mère Anne Geneviève would have said "A plume is a feather."

There are, of course, insoluble difficulties in translating poems, especially from French to English; think of the contrast between our heavy 'the', 'these', 'those', with the lightness of the French 'le', 'la', 'les'. Also these poems were so short—it was their shortness, their very simplicity that made them such a problem as well as the subtle play on the double meaning of some of the words and an integral rhythm almost impossible to catch; there is in each some phrase or word that is utterly elusive.

How, for instance, in *The Lark*, can you render in English the opening,

> Me voici, o mon Dieu,
> Me voici, me voici!

with the insistent, shrilling sound of that French i-i-i? Or find a word in *The Little Bird*, for intarissable—'cette intarissable musique' that repeats the sound and meaning? All our corresponding words seem to be weighted with "sh". Or in *The Old Horse* replace that word encense in

> Ma pauvre tête encense
> toute la solitude de mon coeur!

which gives, in two syllables, the double picture of the old horse's swinging head and a censer swinging to offer up in the Catholic sense all that he has left, his loneliness? The dictionary translation of encenser, which, when used of a horse, means "to toss", which is too young and lively.

I had done all I could and there came a day when I travelled to the Abbaye and met Carmen.

To James.

I am up in the colombière which is like a tower in the room next to hers—a warm room—it was January, snow outside—comfortably furnished with wide window sills but only a flicker of light, obviously they economise on electric bulbs. There is hot water—though limited.

I did not have a bath all the time I was there.

The loo is smelly as usual.

We dined in a parlour of the Abbaye: soup, cold duck, followed French fashion, by buttered endives. Cheese, plum tarts, wine, much talk. At first Carmen was too shy to speak; clearly for her my coming was a terrifying ordeal but she warmed, especially as we walked over to the tower by starlight.

Worked all the next morning with her and Mère Anne Geneviève, both prickly and uncertain but feel I am slowly, gently getting nearer the poems.

After déjeuner Carmen went for her daily treatment: without it she cannot exist. It seems she must have been searingly ill and still has relapses. While she was gone I had a long interview with the nuns, they behind a grille, sheets of poems passing through the drawers. Once I opened one on my side to find a Siamese cat. It reminded me of the Franciscan Rule, 'You shall have no animal but one cat'.

I knew I was on weak ground. I am no French scholar; I cannot really speak French, only read and understand it. Who could help doing that after two years with Renoir? It was only a feeling for language and poetry that made me try but those days at the Abbaye were as exhilarating as they were fruitful. I came to have a real rapport with Carmen which has lasted ever since.

To James

My last day, Ash Wednesday, Carmen and I worked away in her tower room which is sunnier than mine. Déjeuner not at all Ash Wednesday—celery mayonnaise, omelettes, salad, cheese, patisserie, wine. I have been so stuffed that last night I could not eat the excellent fish and, "Pas de succés" the young nun who served us said reproachfully. Then another long session with Mère Anne Geneviève and another nun, Mère Christine. All seemed amicable and Carmen has lost her anguish and worry.

At the end I dared to ask, "Can I take it then that you accept the translations?"

They answered, "*Acceptons! Nous les applaudissons.*"

*   *   *

There was a blessed ending to all this and it has not ended yet.

In America the first printing of *Prayers from the Ark* was sold out in four days; it was almost as successful in Britain. There were sales to magazines and the *Reader's Digest*; the prayers have been set to music by, among others, Ivor Davis, Edmund Rubbra, Marian Prideaux for Peter Pears and Osian Ellis and Dr. Paul Nordoff in his work for children; every month we seem to have to say 'no' to other composers. There are translations now in some dozen other languages.

When I found Carmen she was penniless, paying for her keep at the Abbaye by working in the library and garden and as a fitter for the stained glass windows for which it is renowned. Then came this, what Mère Anne Geneviève calls 'La Pluie d'Or'.

In gratitude I too, say "Amen".

And every New Year's Eve at the Old Hall I kept the ritual which has become a tradition: it is that I have to write the New Year in, best of all begin work on something new.

James would call me after midnight struck. We would walk down through the garden, once or twice in snow to the balustrade and look far over the lights of London where the bells were ringing.

> Ships, towers, domes, theatres, and temples lie
> Open unto the fields, and to the sky;*

The fields were gone but the sky reflected the lights in golden domes over the city; each year we stood spellbound.

Then we would go in to a leaping fire, its flames reflected in the silver knobs of the fireplace's andirons—I called those knobs Gog and Magog. James would open a bottle of champagne.

---

*From Wordsworth's sonnet "Composed upon Westminister Bridge."

Three Hundred and
Sixty-five Roses

"I want something different" said Jane.

She had always wanted that, to be different; perhaps it was the mark of a child with a mother slightly in the public eye though I had tried not to cast a shadow. It was why, at school, she had wanted to play the harp. While it lasted that was appealing; the sound of a harp stirs a house to life as does the soft whirr of a spinning wheel. A harp, though has its disadvantages; it must never be left strung tightly ready for use. The first small harp we bought for Jane had, before we could take delivery of it, been left strung in a bow window facing the road; a heavy lorry passed and the harp split from top to bottom. When we bought another, every time it travelled it had to be re-insured. In the end, Jane found she was not musical enough to go on with it, but she had had her harp. Now it had come to her twenty-first birthday dance.

She was in her second year of training at The Middlesex Hospital, doing well now; more and more we liked her set of girls; most of them seemed to be having twenty-first birthdays which was, in those days, a real family celebration and they too wanted 'something different'. One had her dance in a Bank, another on a steamer in the Thames. I felt helpless but James produced the answer as it were out of his pocket; "You will have your dance," he told Jane, "at the Zoo."

James was a Fellow of the London Zoo and had persuaded the Committee, also the Members, to allow us to hold a dance in the

Fellows' Restaurant—something that had not been remotely thought of before.

It was ideal. The Fellows' Restaurant has a glassed-in terrace or foyer where Members could sit for drinks before luncheon—I do not think the restaurant usually served dinner. The terrace was perfect for a reception to which our older relatives and friends came; Jane was the eldest grandchild on both sides so that for the family it was a notable occasion.

The restaurant's large dining room became a ballroom, though dinner for some sixty guests was served before the dance. Soon after dancing began, the keepers brought in some of the smaller animals, a lemur, koala bears, baby chimpanzees, a small python which brought shrieks from some of the girls, little crocodiles. We ended with a three A.M. breakfast of bacon and eggs and kedgeree.

It was not long afterwards that Jane said to me, "You don't know how wonderful it is to go out with a man instead of boys."

The 'man' was a subaltern of the Royal Artillery serving in the Parachute Brigade whose officers were nicknamed 'Red Berets' which enhanced Anthony in Jane's eyes. She had met him when, making up a foursome, he, though unknown to her, was her host. She wrote next day to thank him. "The only girl," Anthony told me later, "who has ever done that," which was the beginning of the real attraction. The first time she brought him to the Old Hall he was in full dress before a ball. With his fair curly hair—and a certain plumpness—he looked like a cherub in uniform, an ebullient and irresistible cherub.

As if there were not already too many things I had to do, I found myself committed even further. "Why not?" said Spencer. "It will do you no harm to come down into the marketplace."

Though I certainly had not lunched or dined with Spencer every time I came to London—as he had laid down—he still surfaced now and then and still seemed to have his old power. I could have said that, particularly since we came to live in London, I was already in the marketplace but he meant an especial book market, the Book Society which in those days had a considerable influence, its choice, perhaps, more particularly, its 'recommendations' bringing handsome sales. I had been asked to go on its Panel. "Say yes,"* Spencer urged me.

*Graham Watson would have said, "Say no."

There were five of us. The work was punitive, a choice having to be made each month with some six to ten recommendations; one month, one hundred fifty-three books were submitted which sounds impossible but we had a system; the books were divided equally among us; if we found any book of note, the other members were alerted and we all read it, cover to cover. Also a technique soon came, taught to me by Daniel George, one of the last —and finest—of our full-time literary critics who had been longest with the Book Society. "Read the opening," he told me, "dip two or three times into the middle, read the end"—I called it 'sniffing'—"then either lay it aside, which is what you will usually do, or read it through." It was a good guide though I am sure we missed several good books; I know now why, unless there is one special reviewer chosen for one especial book, reviewers seldom give a fair review—with so many to read it is not possible.

We met once a month, generally with fierce argument—I once found myself in opposition to everyone—then, after a long discussion, voted for the choice; as we were five, one of us ultimately had the casting vote. One of us again had to review the 'choice' which meant a long review; this was decided by the Society's full-time secretary and administrator, Colin de la Mare, son of Walter de la Mare the poet. After this had been allotted the 'recommendations' were parcelled among us; a book would come out with its jacket carrying a banner *Recommended by the Book Society*. Each recommendation had to be reviewed.

"Pamela,"—Pamela Frankau—"you're good at funny novels. You do so and so."

"Maurice,"—Maurice Cranston—"you for travel."

"Rumer's much better."

"Oh no!" I said. "This book's about Africa. I've hardly been there. Richard has"—Richard Church.

But no matter how we dodged, it was usually three reviews apiece.

Feelings were soothed by a delectable lunch which always began with smoked salmon. It was not until we were home with our load of books that we realised what we had undertaken. I did though make two 'finds'—from the Book Society's point of view. They would have, of course, soon have 'found' these themselves but I remember the excitement when I opened a book in a curiously dark jacket, saw with relief that it was short and did not have to go further than a few pages before I was on the telephone to

Daniel George. "A new voice . . . totally original talent. This novel must *must* be a choice." The panel decided the book was 'too morbid' for a choice though it was highly recommended; it was Muriel Spark's *Memento Mori*.

The other was of a different calibre, not a 'literary' find; a novel called *The Shadow of the Moon* by Molly M. Kaye came to me. "I think you should take note of this," I told the Panel. "Here is a born story-teller." The style was not to our liking but the power of Molly's story-telling overrode everything and I was not surprised when, more than ten years later, encouraged by Paul Scott of *The Jewel in the Crown*, Molly Kaye published *The Far Pavilions* which brought her instant and worldwide fame, a film, tours of India, appearances everywhere and a fortune. "It would happen to me," Molly wrote to me, "when I have one bedsock in the grave." That was typical of the delightful and modest person she is. In actuality, not many people know North West India and the Frontier, scene of her novels, as Molly does. Her husband General Hamilton was one of the few army Generals who spoke Pushtu and was taken as blood brother of the tribesmen.

Sometimes at the Old Hall when I felt I had written my eyes out I used, in the early evening, to go through the door at the end of the garden to walk in the vast old cemetery that spread down the hill.

Dogs were not allowed there. The pekingese had to stay behind wistfully looking out of the study window, but a Siamese cat had been added to our family, the first cat I had owned—or been owned by—and Simba used to come with me. He loved to leap from cross to cross, monument to monument as they rose from the mass of mare's tail weed that half engulfed them. Half way down, the cemetery had a labyrinth of eerie catacombs, crumbling into ruin, some of the coffins had burst, showing a skeleton which was macabre but some of the monuments were endearing. I particularly liked a huge marble lion, lying couchant on the tomb of an Arthur Wombwell who had kept a circus and menagerie; also one with crossed tennis racquet and tennis balls in memory of Mr. Spalding. There were writers—Arthur Waley, Mrs. Henry Wood, Radclyffe Hall, John Galsworthy, and, in the lower, better kept cemetery was the huge monument of Karl Marx which brought endless Russian pilgrims or comrades.

Sometimes, surreptitiously, I did take the pekingese—if we

heard anyone coming, by tacit agreement they went into hiding among the graves. At the bottom gates we walked across the road into the beauty of little Waterlow Park with its lake and its ducks, its statue of kind Mr. Waterlow who had given the Park to us, and the house Charles the Second had built for Nell Gwyn. There is a story that when their son was born there, the King could not make up his mind to give him a fitting title. This outraged Nell so much that the next time she saw King Charles riding up the drive she went out on the balcony over the portico with the baby and called to the King, "As you won't acknowledge your son I shall drop him."

"Madam! Madam! Don't drop the Duke of . . . ."
and that is how the baby got his title.

One of the rewarding results of living in London was being close to agents and publishers. In Curtis Brown there was Graham, a steady relief after Spencer, my counsellor and friend in difficulty as well as joy. Graham and Dorothy; you could scarcely think of them apart. "Fearfully dull," Dorothy would say of herself, even of Graham, knowing quite well they were never for a moment dull, always travelling—as I write they have one daughter they visit in Moscow, a second in Australia; we have been to Paris together and to Italy. They are always doing interesting things, perpetually entertaining or being entertained. Dorothy is a superb cook and both are equally sympathetic as guests or hosts. I re-member telephoning Dorothy one evening; a gurgle of laughter came down the line. "I am sitting on my bed," said Dorothy "with nothing on but stockings and a diamond necklace." She must have looked exceptionally pretty. They were going to a banquet at the Guildhall and, as in the de Maupassant story, she had been lent a diamond necklace.

When Harold Macmillan resigned as Prime Minister so that he could devote himself to writing, also to the firm, and came back into the firm, within days Rache Lovat Dickson was out of it; I still do not know why. Rache went back to Canada and Harold Macmillan told me I would have a new editor, Alan Maclean.

Editor/author is a curious relationship. You give away so much of yourself in your books, even when they are totally invented, that they cannot be other than intimate, so much so that you often shrink from the encounter; for a time I avoided Alan, my memory of him being of someone tall, thin and inconspicuous which is what Alan and his wife Robin, prefer to be, but it was not long before I felt his quiet power; and recognition of his quality quickly came. There has not been, or will there be another editor like Alan—or such a friend. We have been through vicissitudes together—at least mine were vicissitudes, Alan's were tragedies— yet still quiet joys remain, joys we have shared. All my books written since I met him are in reality dedicated to him.

The Americans of my writing world came to London: from Curtis Brown, Edith and her hats arrived on what was her last literary visit. Edith was not a good traveller; on her first two days she was so jarred and exhausted that she was unable to eat.

I took her to Prunier's knowing I could rely on their tact and delicate cooking. Their Monsieur Pierre was solicitous—he was captivated by Edith's porcelain prettiness, the tilt, even in her distress, of her little velvet hat. We coaxed her to try Prunier's famous turbot soufflé, "and a little glass of dry champagne," coaxed M. Pierre which was clever of him because Edith drank nothing but champagne. "I couldn't possibly."

"Try," I coaxed.

"Just a mouthful," crooned Monsieur Pierre.

Under our eyes she revived, ate the soufflé. We had more champagne.

Alan Collins came. All thoughts of his playboy reputation had vanished as soon as we had stayed with him and his wife Catherine at their home in Hopewell, New Jersey. Catherine was born a Pomeroy and this had been the Pomeroy estate; it had its own graveyard with, at the foot of its hill, another graveyard for the one-time slaves; when Alan and Catherine married, they gave the graveyard to Hopewell's black community. We went to see it; though it was immaculately kept, that day it was littered with broken whisky bottles and the debris of tall silver paper tridents from a recent funeral. "They hold a wake by the grave," Alan explained to us. The tridents were for flowers carried high in the procession, the bottles were smashed on the headstones all around to bring good fellowship for the soul that is gone. "And they sing of course," said Alan.

> Swing low, sweet chariot
> Coming for to carry me home . . .
> Coming for to carry me home.

and,

> My father died a shouting
> Singing Glory Hallelujah!

We heard that splendid singing. Beside the cemetery, Alan and Catherine had built the community a church. "Would you like to go to their service?" Alan asked that Sunday.

He drove us down the hill to it, deliberately not to seem like patronage, taking the oldest car on the estate to find, in the church car park, a glittering array of Cadillacs, Buicks, imported Mercedes and Jaguars.

We were the only whites and watched as the congregation thronged in; men in best suits, women in gaudy floral dresses and magnificent confections of hats and turbans; little girls prinked out, boys looking like miniature men in trousered suits and bow ties. All the children had tambourines or castanets; there were two electric organs and, in the well of the church, a skiffle band with drums. When the revered Elder gave his sermon—he had a full rich voice—he began in ordinary speech; it turned to a chant with pauses when, "Hallelujah. Hallelujah," the congregation joined in. Drums began to beat, at first softly, tambourines tinkled as castanets clicked, all in rhythm. The band, lastly the organs followed until the sermon became a paean, loud, louder until the whole church shook.

Next there was, "Sister Betty, would you like to give witness," and Sister Betty described a happy event that came to her in the past week. "Brother Paul ..." "Sister Gloria ..." "Sister ..." "Brother ..." Then the Elder turned to Alan. "Our friend, Mr. Collins," and our playboy stood up. "I should like to give thanks," said Alan—Catherine had been through a serious operation—and he made one of the most simple, sincere, moving prayers I have heard. Soon, softly, the people joined him. They and he prayed together. It was obvious how much he and Catherine were loved.

We had to witness too: "Our English brother", "Our English sister".

At one o'clock Alan whispered that it was time for us to leave. "They go on till two o'clock or more." We tried to be quiet but, outside, the ancient car would not start. Alan tried and tried, no sound, no stir. The whole congregation came trooping out; finally the magnificent Elder of the sermon drove us back to the house in his Cadillac.

And every year brought Ben.

I have booked on the Queen Elizabeth, he wrote, due in on Friday night. After London I make for the Continent . . .

where he would go from capital to capital seeing authors. He would end up in Sweden with Alfhilde and her sisters where he could assess his finds in peace.

He always had a plethora of people to see in London but we tried to spend his first evening together. It was a joy to find him waiting for us at Athenaeum Court in his accustomed sitting room and looking exactly the same; Ben was always so fresh, his skin like a child's, his grey-white hair like spun silk, his extraordinary bushy eyebrows over eyes that, looking at you, looked deep. The fineness of his tweed suit was always immaculate, his shoes hand-made. The talk was seldom personal; he talked of music—we went to the opera together—of painting, and books, books, books, but the personal link was strong.

From Ben on his travels:

> Savoy Hotel
> Baur en Ville
> Zurich.

Let's write to each other when we feel like it and not regard a communication as a debt that has to be paid at a particular time. I have two reasons for writing now, and neither requires comment from you at present, much as I value anything you send.

It has been one of my griefs, and disappointments that Jon never had the friendships that have come to me through my writing; she seemed deliberately to block them. Though she enjoyed a good luncheon or dinner with her publishers or agents—Jon was an inveterate gourmet—and enjoyed the few occasions when we were on radio together, also when we spoke together as at a Yorkshire Post luncheon, she rejected almost all overtures. What was saddest of all was that she seemed arrogant; certainly she was proud but the arrogance was a shield to hide what was her greatest handicap, her deep distrust of herself. This led to a timidity which was an anomaly because she was such a force in the family; I think she had been so hurt by people that she shrank from any contact with them—except a very few.

There are no letters from Jon at this time because she was here in England with us. After nearly thirty years of marriage she had left Roland at his own request, sudden and completely unforeseen.

Roland's deception is still difficult to believe, so much so that I still think he meant what happened only as a passing affair but the young woman was determined to marry him—never mind her own husband and her children. In her Australian eyes, Roland was the acme of an English gentleman and she wanted him. Roland was weak, Jon proud, and refused any thought of reconciliation. It was a bitter divorce; she at once went back to her first husband's name—Nigel who had died tragically—was again Mrs. Baughan, but alone.

She had no idea, poor Jon, how hard that was to be. For all those years of her marriage Roland had pampered and protected her until she was spoiled in every sense. Everything had been done for her; she had not as much as sewn on a button, or washed out a handkerchief, or packed a suitcase. She had lived in complete luxury, never travelling except first class or de luxe, being taken, met and guided. For years she had not been on a bus or gone by underground, seldom taxis, usually it was a car and chauffeur. She had not dealt with money, only spent it.

Spent far too much; if it had not been for James she would not have had any, except the little Nigel had left her. Fa was too stunned by Roland's defection to cope on her behalf but James faced Roland, and made him settle capital on Jon, not a great deal but some. It was as well; Roland married his young Australian and died within a year; Jon's alimony died with him.

Two things were fortunate. Fa had long ago had Mam out of Grace Cottage; the next house was a disastrous interim and I was then given what seemed an impossible assignment: I was to find them a house, small enough to be easily run but large enough to take the family portraits. It had to be near enough to a village to have domestic help available but not to be in sight of anyone else's roof, and was not to cost more than four thousand pounds, inadequate even then. I managed to fill all these conditions except the last, though I had to admit that in winter when the trees were leafless, you could catch a glimpse of a roof.

Because the builders were still there, when Fa and Mam first saw Lydd House it looked so bare and stark that they were dismayed, giving me traumas that I had made a terrible mistake on their behalf—it has proved a haven. Originally a cottage, a long sitting room was built on to it with big windows which looked far over the weald, giving vistas east, south and west so that all day and far into the evening the house was filled with sun.

It has seven acres of land and another smaller cottage which James and I bought thinking to come down from London at weekends to bolster Fa and Mam. We scarcely had it long enough to use it.

Jon at first tried to live with Fa and Mam; that did not, could not, work, she had so far outdistanced them that James and I ceded the cottage to her. It was an ideal arrangement; she was only two hundred yards from them yet was independent. She loved the little house and it was in Lydd Cottage that she wrote two of her best novels, *Told in Winter*, the story of an Alsatian bitch's jealous love for her master and in particular, almost my favourite of her books, *Mrs. Panopoulis*.

It had lain dormant, in the way books do, from the time when she had visited the Isle of Spices, Madagascar. As the blurb described,

> From the moment that the ship drops anchor off the coast of Portuguese East Africa, Mrs. Panopoulis senses an immediate affinity for the coral island that lies ahead, with its ancient fort and chapel and cemetery, its burning colours and bone-dry winds. And before the day is over she is to find out what the island has to tell her.

A complete change from Jon's macabre writing, it was a little gem of wisdom and beauty.

My diary
29 January.

St. Francis de Sales* day. Made a pilgrimage to the little church in Warwick Street to find him.

Warwick Street, narrow, small, runs parallel to Regent Street and holds the Portuguese Embassy Church which is so small it is

*St. Francis de Sales is the patron saint of writers.

scarcely to be noticed except for those who know its peace. It has the only statue I know of St. Francis de Sales, first shown to me by the writer G. B. Stern.

> Jon came too and lit a candle. She knelt beside me—she is so different now, grateful in a new spring way, a spring of appreciation it seemed she had lost with Roland. I pray the book is a success. She deserves it.

My diary: June 1960

In the afternoon, Ann* brought the Japanese doll's house garden.

I had written a children's book about two doll's house size Japanese dolls, Miss Happiness and Miss Flower who were sent in a parcel to England; it was also about the loneliness of being a stranger in an alien place. The children in the story wanting to make the dolls feel at home, made them a Japanese doll's house. As plans for this were included I, too, had to make one to be sure the plans worked: the sliding paper screen walls, floor matting, firebox, a niche for a scroll, everything and, as with most Japanese houses in Japan, the garden is almost more important than the house, there had to be a miniature and living garden as well. Ann had planted mine with a willow tree, seven inches high, a pine, real irises and peonies, a half hoop bridge, a stone lantern that could be lit.

> An exquisite perfection in miniature; one has only to kneel in front of it and watch the shadows under the tiny trees—as in the evening at sunset—to set the whole imagination free.

Jean Primrose who illustrated the book—she is the sister of William Primrose, the viola player—when she came to sketch the garden and saw the cascade of miniature stones that made the stream, whispered, "It sounds."

*Ann was Miss Ann Ashberry of Miniature Gardens where she propagates and grows her plants and makes her gardens. She does many for disabled children so that they can tend living plants raised on stands. She made a rose garden for the Queen that could go on a dining-room table with live and scented climbing, standard and bush roses.

*   *   *

Children's book editors must surely be among the nicest of people; true, some of them get a power complex but that is because they believe passionately in the importance of what they are doing; I have never met a cynical children's editor.

The first of real stature I had was Viking's formidable May Massee, pioneer in getting books for children to be treated as literature, serious literature. She was more than influential in the, then, innovation of the especial and superb children's libraries, which flourish now in the United States and Canada. May's office at Viking's was panelled in oak with niches in which were toys sent to her from all over the world. When the Viking Press moved, her office was moved too and re-installed, panelling, niches and toys. That was the way publishers used to treat their valued editors.

To May, her authors were her children; like children she expected us to obey. I once had to oppose her over an illustrator; she was amazed at my temerity—as was I—but she cherished us. The last time I saw her in New York when she had, at last, retired—in her mid-eighties—she insisted on seeing me safely across the road. My last glimpse was of her standing on the opposite kerb waving, her white hair blowing in the wind.

May had two disciples—they were far more than assistants; one, Annis Duff took over from her at Viking—it was years before May really allowed her to act; the other, Marni Hodgkin, eventually came to Macmillan in London so that, by providence, I had two outstanding—and pedigree—editors.

Marni swiftly made Macmillan's list one of the best in London, perhaps in the world. As with Alan Maclean, she became my touchstone; though we had our battles, every book I did with her was a delight.

For one book, *A Kindle of Kittens*, published almost at the end of Marni's and my time together, when James and I had come to live in the 'ancient town' of Rye, Marni found an extremely gifted 'cat artist', Lynn Byrne. Lynn was still at art school in Birmingham—only allowed by her carpenter father to go there on condition she lived in a convent. What he would have said to her current young man, a Greek, Costas, I do not know but the nuns were sympathetic; they could not ask Costas into the convent, but they used to serve dinner for him and Lynn in the greenhouse.

A Kindle of Kittens was Lynn's first commissioned book; and we arranged for her to come down with Marni to see the cobbled town, its walls and its houses. Late the night before, Lynn telephoned to ask if she might bring Costas, if so they would come on their own.

Marni arrived, ready to spend the whole day. "What shall I give them to eat?" I had asked her knowing Lynn's unsophisticated background, "Posh or plain?"

"Posh," said Marni without hesitation.

We were to start work at ten o'clock, so Marni had taken an early train. The book concerned Rye's Town Cryer and I had asked him to come in his full ceremonial dress; thrilled to be in a book he was punctual. Half-past ten came, eleven, no sign of Lynn. "Would you like to go and come back?" I asked him.

"It takes half-an-hour to put on this gear," he said. "I'll wait."

Unfortunately his breeches were so tight he could not sit down but had to rest himself on the arm of the sofa; I could only ply him with coffee and sherry—it was altogether an uncomfortable morning—Lynn and Costas did not arrive until nearly twelve; however she was so disarming, we could not be cross. With her advance from Macmillan, she explained, the first money she had ever earned, she had bought Costas a car, "For one hundred pounds," she said in awe. "For us to drive here in and give you a surprise." The car, of course, had broken down; they had had to leave it, get to the nearest railway station, "We ran all the way *and* had to change trains."

The book was worth it; the cat drawings are ravishing; I cherish one of the originals which Lynn gave me. Luncheon fulfilled everything Marni had advised; the butcher had made us a crown of lamb; Lynn's eyes lit up with wonder when she saw the white paper frills on the end of the cutlets. We had rosé wine—I had thought she would revel in its pinkness.

"Costas, you behave," she told him. "Don't tie your serviette round your neck," she twitched the napkin away from him. "Take your elbows off the table," and, echoing Marni, "This is posh!" She was utterly contented.

Marni was Lady Hodgkin. Married to the scientist, Alan Hodgkin —her father, husband Alan and Alan's cousin, Dorothy Hodgkin had all won the Nobel prize for science; how Marni escaped into being a novelist and children's book editor, I do not know; fortunately Alan loved music, paintings, books—I had not imagined that a scientist of his eminence would have read my novels; Alan had read them even before I met him.

Much as I liked him, for me, Alan represented a danger. While he was President of The Royal Society life was easier for Marni; the President has a flat in the Society's Carlton Terrace headquarters so that she was only a few minutes walk from Macmillan's—for years, from their home in Cambridge she had bicycled to and from the station, catching the early train to London. She had always managed until, in his meteoric career, Alan was appointed Master of Trinity College, Cambridge. Then what I had dreaded, happened; Marni had to retire. A Master needs a Mistress as I found out; once when I rang up, Nightingale, the butler answered—the Hodgkins had inherited him but had found their own housekeeper, Ruby. "Ruby and Nightingale," Marni used to say, "It's like a pantomime." "Nightingale," I asked, "please can I speak to Lady Hodgkin?" Nightingale's voice came back, "The Master's Mistress is not available."

Staying with them at the Lodge in all its gracious beauty was a privilege. To how many students, I wonder, has Trinity's Master's Lodge been a revelation? With its great staircase, the panelled double drawing room, its floor polished to set off the colours of Persian rugs, the paintings—and flowers. As the drawing room is on the first floor, from the deep window seats looking down on the Great Court, you could sit and watch comings and goings of students, faculty and tourists and feel the quiet purpose and dignity of this great university. The private garden of the Lodge gave onto the River Cam, where punts passed, going under the arch of the bridge to St. John's.

Marni ran it all with her own mixture of simplicity and capability, everything exactly right for each occasion as she, in the dresses she made herself, always looked exactly right whether she was going to dinner at Buckingham Palace with the Queen or, if it could have come to pass, with Lynn and Costas in the convent greenhouse.

June.

Margaret Rutherford came in dressed to go to the Women of the Year luncheon at the Savoy. She was wearing a gorgeous draped confection in brilliant shaded colours and a hat with osprey feathers that only she could have worn. I was washing up in a butcher's apron. "My dear," she said, disregarding the discrepancy. "I hope I didn't make too much noise this morning. I was in a tantrum with inanimate objects."

There were often crises in the flat upstairs. "The whole of brute creation is against me!" Margaret would cry, her wonderfully carrying voice penetrating every flat. Only two mornings before I had been working in the White Study when I heard 'drip, drip, drip,' turning into 'splash, splash.'

In the hall water was coming through the ceiling. Alice had, at that moment, finished cleaning the silver and had pushed a trolley load of it into the hall; it was awash as more and more water fell, added to which the water was hot, near boiling. Dashing upstairs, I knocked frantically at the Rutherford door.

Margaret answered it. She seemed perfectly calm and unflustered.

"Margaret. There's water ..." but, "How nice to see you," cooed Margaret, "come in and have a sherry."

"*Margaret!* Have you left a tap on? There's water."

"Water? My God!" said Margaret.

She was having friends to lunch and was giving them red wine; she had been told that red wine should be served warm—there was seldom anyone as ingenious as Margaret and she had stood the bottles in the sink, plugged it, turned the hot tap on and forgotten it.

Margaret I loved and honoured yet, of that time there was no actress friend to compare for me with Sybil Thorndike. Though, of course, I had seen her act, notably in Shaw's *Saint Joan*, I only came to know her in her later life. She had the gift of making you feel you were the one person she was most delighted to see; at Swan Court she always came with you to the lift as if she could not bear to part with you, but it was towards the end, when she was so crippled with arthritis it was torture for her to move that she meant most. In that suffering I can never forget her face—it seemed almost transfigured with light and love. One day she said to me, "I am glad to have this pain. All those years when I was so well and strong, I never understood compassion; being able to share. Now I can."

Why, why do we have pet animals? They are so vulnerable it only leads to heartbreak.

From my diary.

This morning the postman rang; he had a package that would not go through the letter box. The little bitch Cumquat ran to greet him and stood wagging; she is so small he did not see her and pulled the heavy front door to, caught her in the crack and crushed her.

It was three hours before our vet could come. In the days afterwards, Gossamer pined so woefully I had to send her down to Jon. A house without pekingese is, to me, empty.

Some of our best times were when we joined Jean and Dido Renoir in Paris. Once Jean had to go to Le Havre on the Brittany coast for a gathering of Les Anciens Combatants, Veterans of the First World War, at which his most famous film, the wartime *La Grande Illusion* was to be shown. He asked us to go with him. James drove us down and, as James was himself an Ancien Combatant he was invited with Jean and was required to speak, Jean interpreting. Dido and I, left behind, explored the restaurants of Le Havre—she was a connoisseur of restaurants. The Combatants returned much later and the worse for wear. Dido berated Jean in French, English and Portuguese; he only laughed, but we did not start back for Paris until mid-morning of next day and by lunch time had only got as far as Rouen.

Food was enormously important to Jean and Dido; during the filming of *The River*, as we drove out to Barrackpore, they spent the time in nostalgic talking about the food they especially loved and missed, particularly tête de veau—in all its ghoulish detail. Now Jean—or was it Dido?—remembered a restaurant in Rouen of which tête de veau was a speciality. The restaurant was in the Place; remembering Mam and *The Greengage Summer*, I at last saw where Joan of Arc was burnt.

In the restaurant the patron who was also the chef kept coming in to look at us, standing against the wall, his arms folded and, we thought, frowning. "We are making too much noise," said Dido. The frown became so marked that Jean apologised.

"The brouhaha is too much?" he asked.

"Pas de tout," the patron came over to us. "The fact is that I cannot help thinking how like you are to the film director, Jean Renoir."

"Je suis Jean Renoir!" bellowed Jean.

There was embracing, almost tears. Cognac was produced. We did not leave for Paris until six o'clock.

On one memorable Paris evening we joined them after dinner when they had been dining with Young Cézanne as Jean called him though he must have been in his forties. He was the grandson of the painter and ran an antiquarian bookshop on the Left Bank, tucked away in a courtyard, a tall narrow house above it. When we arrived they were all upstairs, still at table, but room was at once made for us with a warm welcome.

The room had bare boards; there were not enough chairs, some of the family sat on packing cases. The children, who had grave delightful manners and entertained us with hula hoops and singing, were shabby, bare legged, wearing cheap plimsolls, faded shirts, frayed skirts and trousers; Young Cézanne's jeans were patched. I heard a whispered colloquy between him and Jean who unostentatiously produced notes and the eldest boy went out for more wine. "They can hardly exist," Dido told me afterwards, yet all round the room, some only pinned to the walls, were pictures, finished paintings, studies, pencil sketches. "Si, Si," nodded Madame as I looked, "All, all, Cézanne."

"There is a fortune in paintings in that house," Jean confirmed as we drove home but, "Of course," said Dido, "they would not think of selling any."

One of my most endearing memories of Jean—I do not think anyone knew about it except him and me—was when he came on his own to stay with us and, one evening, took me aside. "Rumer," he said, "I have heard that"—only he said "I 'ave 'eard zat"—"here in England people often have what is called 'morning tea', a tray of tea while they are still in bed," clearly to Jean incredible. "Is that true?"

"Quite true, Jean."

"C'est épatent! And after they eat an English breakfast?"

"Yes, some."

"Formidable!" said Jean. "Rumer," he whispered. "Don't tell anybody but I should like to have this experience. Will you call me in the morning with this morning tea?"

"At half past seven? Jean are you sure?"

"Yes. Yes. I shall like it very much."

*   *   *

Knock. "Jean. It's half past seven." Knock, and I went in. "Jean."

A form like a whale rose up out of the bedclothes. "Nom d'un nom . . ."

"You asked for morning tea. Here's your tray."

Comprehension dawned, but the small eyes blinked up at me bleared with sleep. "Put him down."

I put the tray on the bedside table.

At nine o'clock I tiptoed back. Morning tea was on the floor, untouched.

June 25th, 1958.

Jane and Anthony were married at St. James's, Spanish Place.

To Her Highness
the Princess Birabongse,
Punta Campagnola
Malcesine-sur-Garda
VERONA   19 February 1962

This is a letter from a complete stranger. My only excuse is that Helena Wright, my doctor and a mutual friend, suggested that you might be able to advise me. I understand from her you have a villa on Lake Garda just beside Malcesine where we have often stayed and that you know the Lake from end to end.

I have a belief—it will sound topsy-turvy to many writers but it is a firm and proved belief—that, when writing a novel or any imaginative work it is better to write the story first, go to the place and do the research afterwards even when the book is set in a place, or in circumstances unknown to you, otherwise you will probably have a documentary novel, almost always lifeless which is why when I had finished the first draft of yet another novel, I wrote to the Princess.

I am a writer, seeking a villa—large or small—where we (my husband and I) could come and be in seclusion, from just after Easter —about the 24th April—until the end of May. An hotel wouldn't do as we want to be quite alone, nor would we wish to be paying guests in a family. Do you know of anyone willing to let such a villa—on or near the lake—about this time? We would be careful and quiet, would need a cook and maid, or a cook-maid. We would, of course, pay whatever is reasonable for the villa and staff.

Prince Birabongse and his brother Prince Chula were the pair of ace, and royal, motor racing drivers from what was then Siam, now Thailand. Both married English women, Prince Chula and his wife settling in Cornwall not far from Darrynane, but Ceryl Birabongse had tired of the pace of the racing driver circuit and had retreated to her small villa on Lake Garda.

The book in question was *The Battle of the Villa Fiorita*, written because I had grown tired of the innumerable novels—they came to me on the Book Society—about child victims of divorce. 'Let's have a book where the children will not be victims but fight back,' I thought and, in the book, the children, a school age boy and girl, instead of going miserably back to school, run away to Italy where their mother had absconded with a film director, determined to fetch her back. No book of mine has been more unpopular, especially in America.

When it was filmed—it made a good film—actress after actress refused to play the part of the mother because it was too near the bone. With Ingrid Bergman I came near real trouble as, by an unfortunate coincidence, I had been in Beverly Hills when she left her first husband Peter Lindstrom for Rossellini, also a film director. In Italy as in France, film people are usually called by their surnames and I had no idea Rossellini's first name was Roberto, the name I gave to the film director in the book. Worse, by Peter Lindstrom, Ingrid had a daughter. I had always heard the child called Jenny—they were friends of the Renoirs—now it appeared her name was Pia. I had called my Roberto's daughter, Pia. Finally Maureen O'Hara took the part and gave the best performance of her career.

Ceryl Birabongse found us the Villa Fiorita—not its real name —next door to her own, two of the rare villas on the lake side of the busy road; both were built close above the rippling or often troubled lake.

Lake Garda, in all its grandeur is a cruel lake—a storm can sweep down over the mountains turning the water into an inferno of waves and there are currents deep down.

"On Garda many, many peoples drown," said Celestina with gusto.

Celestina was our cook and the cook in the novel.

And she went on in her mixture of broken English, German, and Italian with tale after tale. "Five fishermen," said Celestina. "Village fishermen, drown fifty metres from the villa. Here in the villa we hear their cries for help, 'Aiuto! Aiuto!' and we can do nothing. Nothing! It grow dark, the cries go fainter, then only the women, praying in the garden, sobbing. "All drown," said Celestina gleefully.

Often no bodies were found. "In lake middle, deep, deep," said Celestina plunging downwards with her hand. "Three hundred metres down, caves, big big caves. Water strong; sweep them like that. . . . Never find," said Celestina. She came closer. "Lastest year, three doctor, three in motorboat. Gone. Kaput. A little girl, Papa see her kneel to look big feesh. Never find."

As in my book, the two elder children, his and hers, go sailing into such a storm I had to find a way in which they did not 'go down' but survived. Ceryl had a friend, Bruno of great Italian charm who was also a yachting fanatic and had sailed on Lake Garda all his life.

The four of us spent evening after evening in Ceryl's villa or ours, looking at maps, planning or plotting or driving along the shore, every now and then scrambling down to find a place where, after the boat had capsized, clinging to the floor boards, the boy and girl could have been swept to the shore and lived. Ceryl said, "These children have become so alive they inhabit my house."

Our Villa belonged to an Austrian Contessa who died soon after we left. The book was finished in London but as I worked I seemed to be still in the villa. "Let's go back," I said to James but Ceryl told us it had been sold, with everything in it: its inlaid furniture, Persian rugs though they had grown so thin they lifted when the wind came under the doors, as it often did, its pretty small chandeliers; the bed painted with roses in which I had slept, the silver, fine china, old Venetian glass and, "I wonder what happened to my angels?" I said.

I called them mine because I had grown fond of them, a pair, fifteenth century, standing perhaps three feet high, carved of wood, gilded and painted. They had stood, holding garlands one each side on the huge overmantel above the open fire, their gold glimmering against the grey stone. "I wonder what happened to them?"

"They are in the garage," said James.

He had written to the Contessa's daughter, bought them privately and driven out to Italy to fetch them—I thought he had had to go on business to Milan—and kept them until I, as he had hoped I would, asked about them.

The book had already taken us to Milan because I needed to see the Opera House of La Scala where, by the kindness and influence of the British Council, we were allowed to attend a rehearsal, sitting mute and still in the Royal box. They gave us tickets for the current opera that night; afterwards we went round to the stage door to see behind the scenes—it is the only stage I know that is guarded by soldiers.

The opera was *Rigoletto*. By luck it was a gala night so that the vast proscenium, the whole first tier of the circle and its boxes, were banked with carnations. Tito Gobbi and Renata Scotto were singing; it was she we went round to see.

The principals' dressing rooms opened off a panelled lobby that had, suitably, a red carpet and heavily impressive mahogany doors, bearing that night those famous names.

Renata Scotto came to her door herself. She was wearing a short quilted nylon dressing gown that might have belonged to Jane or Paula. With her was, it seemed, her entire family; we were introduced to father, mother, grandfather, grandmother, aunts, all eating cold sausage. The only exception was a small boy sitting on the floor in a corner; he was eating the carnations Renata had been pelted with.

Italy was the country James loved best, next to his own and we went back there on every or any excuse.

One night in Venice—it was years after *The Battle of the Villa Fiorita*—we were sitting after dinner outside Florian's Café in the Piazza San Marco. Being Sunday, the tables were full while the great passeggiati—evening walk—was in spate, passing and repassing, whole families down to small children, girls, arms interlaced, young men who gave soft wolf whistles after them, soft because of the music. There is another café opposite Florian's and, when Florian's orchestra had a rest, the other café took over, the crowd surging over to it across the Piazza.

It was a warm summer night with a full moon, fit for music and the light hubbub of voices.

Florian's orchestra began to play arias from *La Traviata*. As they began, 'Ah, fors'e lui che anima' from somewhere among the tables a voice rose, soprano, full, beautiful, matching or outmatching the night.

In England, or for that matter in France, no-one would have taken much notice but the Italian crowd at once came to a standstill, hushed—even the carabinieri stood fixed, their long swords still as 'sol-in-ga ne' tu-mul-ti, sol-in-ga ne' tu-mul-ti . . .' the voice sang.

When it came to an end, a ripple, a vast contented sigh passed far over the Piazza until the applause came. "Brava! Brava!" She sang again. Then it was over. "She might have been Callas," whispered James. We never knew. We did not know either that it was the end of our times together in Italy.

James was finding his work at the Central Office of Information increasingly frustrating; it culminated in a face-losing—for the Directors—case of leaking secrets. Twice James had warned them; they ignored him until the scandal broke, all the more poignant for us because I had been at school with the lady concerned. To be proved right is not always to be liked and, "I don't care for the climate," said James. "I would rather go and work as a gardener,"—we had learned that, in America, a gardener was paid more than a senior Civil Servant in Britain.

At the end of nineteen sixty-two James retired and was given the usual farewell party and presentation but it was not all usual; his personal staff in the department had come to him and told him that, approve or not, they were giving him a present, so, "What would you like?" they asked. James guessed they had visions of a silver salver or cigarette box and said hastily—he knew they had not much money—"Please just give me some roses for my wife."

They gave him a book about roses and a garden token for three hundred sixty-five roses, one for every day of the year.

Speaking, not Writing

"Light the lamp
And lift the latch
And look at the lovely lady!"

"*Look* at the *lovely lady* ..." "Light. Keep it light. Light," called Mona.

"A wrathful rhinoceros rushed with a crash
Through the forest; he wrecked all he saw:
He rooted up rocks, rent branches and trees,
And his tusks and his terrible jaw
Struck terror ..."

"R. R. Rrrrrrrrr. Sound your R's."

"To Acton and back
On their narrow track
The trams clang
And rattle and bang;
And with angry crackles ..."

"Did you see the dappled deer, half-hidden in the shade,
As they drank from the pond in the woodland glade,
And the timid, delicate does go to the woods?"

"D's are *so* difficult! especially at the end of the word," I moaned.

I am in Mona Swann's* sitting room, standing away at its far end, learning how to throw my voice—even a whisper should be audible at a distance; learning about diction, differences of tone, summoning power, difficult as I have an extremely soft voice but, "If you are going to speak at all," said James, "you must do it properly."

That was long long ago but it was the beginning.

Few authors can speak or read adequately in public; we are not meant to, it is not our voice but it seems to have become part of an author's life. I had already had quite a fierce baptism; two years before this, I had been brought over to the United States by my publishers for the Annual American Library Association Conference at Cleveland and found myself faced with an audience of six thousand.[†] I had to speak immediately after the Mayor who had opened the Conference; as he stepped off the rostrum to make way for me he had whispered, "Beware of that mike. It suddenly switches off." I had never used a microphone before and it was a full hour's talk! By luck the mike did not switch off and I survived but swore to myself, "Next time I shall come prepared so . . .

> "Light the lamp
> And lift the latch
> And look at the lovely lady."

If Italy and the Continent were James's territory, I had been over to the United States so often that it was becoming mine until, one day at the Old Hall he said, "Wouldn't it be fun if we went to America and really saw something of it? Coast to coast," said James. "A lecture tour."

"Fun?" I was dubious.

"We could make it fun," he said, which came true.

He and I did two long talking tours in America[‡]—I refused to

---

*As well as teaching me the techniques of writing, naturally only the techniques —no-one can teach anyone else to write—Mona had long taught speech and drama, notably for Michael St. Denys: the theatrical producer.

†As a matter of fact it is easier to talk to an audience as large as this—if you know how to project your voice—than it is to an audience of sixty of whom you are more conscious. With a large number you simply pick out one or two faces and talk to them.

‡I did more on my own.

call them lectures—I could not lecture anyone—but we talked our way across and up and down the North American continent.

These talks were arranged by an agent, Colston Leigh. I would not have dreamed of demanding such fees for myself but before he would act for us, I had to have an interview with him. "Mr. Leigh is *extremely* particular whom he sends out," his Personal Assistant told us. She, his secretary, my literary agent—not Edith Haggard now but her successor, the tall dark-haired, elegant Marilyn Marlow, James and I were gathered in Mr. Leigh's New York office on Fifth Avenue perhaps on the tenth floor, where he, in his bulk, was seated at his desk in a swivel chair which he swivelled or tilted back while he talked not to me, at me, as I sat opposite.

It was a peroration with all the old clichés: I was not to be afraid, "I'm sure you're confident—you look very confident." Not to worry about the subject of my lectures—he insisted they were lectures. "It's how you put it over that counts. You can put it over, I know . . ." No need to change the talks, "I have an actor, a very fine actor, who has been going round the States giving the same lecture for five years, and he hasn't finished yet." I wanted to ask, "Hasn't it finished him?" but had no chance against the volume of that flow.

I could see James was getting restless; then more restless. Suddenly he stood up which stopped the flow. "Mr. Leigh," he said, "I think you are making a mistake. I am Rumer Godden. You are talking to my secretary."

For a moment I thought Colston Leigh and his chair were going backwards through the window, down all ten floors. Then he began to laugh.

I have never fathomed why the British look down on American lecture audiences, especially Women's Clubs. There have been accounts by writers who have toured there, such as Victoria Sackville-West who returned angry and exhausted—she had obviously not been a success. Osbert and Edith Sitwell wrote wittily about their experience but underneath the wit was a decided sneering. I wonder if any of them gave a serious thought to their audiences; how many British women, old or young would be interested enough in things outside their own small orbits, to join perhaps a Women's Forum which has a speaker every fortnight, speakers on politics, science, economics, medicine, education besides the arts. Young women with children take it in turns to come, the 'stay behinds' looking after the children; some of the women had driven over a hundred miles. Few of them have a chance to meet the speaker, only the committee members do that because the numbers are too great, which does away with another myth; that the audience only comes to lionise. Who coined that objectionable phrase, 'culture vultures'? We met genuine interest, responsiveness to every least nuance or phrase; I took two versions of each talk to America, an easy one and one more difficult; I never gave the easy one. Above all, we met enthusiasm, something the British seem to distrust, yet how refreshing it is; in Seattle for example, we had to do the talk twice, the first evening for three thousand, a repeat next morning for an overflow of eighteen hundred.

Sometimes we met this curious despising in Americans themselves. At a large university in Texas—which had better be anonymous,

From my diary

We were appalled at the Dean. She met us at the airport, drove us round the campus and took us into a faculty common room, littered and untidy, offering us coffee in paper cups from a machine. "It won't matter what you talk about," she said when I asked her about the students. "They won't listen. They never do," and, "You must forgive their manners."—What about hers?—"They're very low grade, you know. You mustn't be upset if they walk out. They frequently do."

She did not offer to take us to the auditorium. "You can find your own way, I expect."

We were met at the entrance of the auditorium by two students, a white boy and a black girl; they had brought flowers, a buttonhole for James, a small corsage for me. "I'm Melody," said the girl. She was beautiful enough to have that name.

"I'm Sam."

I asked them which talk I should give; without hesitation they chose the difficult one. A few did walk out but came back at the end to explain they had had conflicting classes; most stayed for over an hour afterwards, asking questions.

I say 'we' because James was always with me, we made a team. To help conserve my voice, the talks were broken with excerpts; sometimes we did these together, sometimes solo; his triumph was reading from Benvenuto Cellini's description of how he cast his statue of Perseus—now in the Palazzo Vecchio in Florence—and how, when the metal ran out, in his dedication to his art, Cellini threw into the furnace all the household pots, pans and vessels to the despair of his wife. There was an actor hidden in James.

So much, to me, is memorable of those tours; endless scenes come back, some of them irresistibly funny. After those days in Seattle we had to leave by an early flight to New York and boarded the plane at half-past seven in the morning; it sat on the ground, sat and sat until at perhaps nine o'clock, a voice announced on the tannoy that we were to transfer to another plane which would take us to Chicago where we would be put on yet another flight to New York. "We apologise for the inconvenience." That was followed by, "Would passengers please remain in their seats until certain passengers are taken off." The next moment an airport official and a stewardess came to me and James where we were sitting. The official said, "Please, Sir and Madam, will you come with us?"

We thought we were going to be arrested except, "Don't bother about your hand luggage," said the smiling stewardess. "We'll bring it." They brought our coats and, before the eyes of the other passengers, we were ushered out, carefully piloted to another aircraft, and given front seats. "We do hope you are comfortable, Sir and Madam."

During the flight, when breakfast was served, ours was brought to us on china, the tray beautifully laid. James had only to move and the stewardess came up.

At Chicago once again the passengers were asked to wait while we were taken off, escorted through the crowds to a private room. "Refreshments will be coming," said the stewardess taking our coats—she was obviously not a stewardess but a hostess. "Please ask for anything you want. When your flight is ready we will come and fetch you."

Though completely mystified we enjoyed the sandwiches and drinks; then, again, were escorted back to the plane—this time the other passengers were held back by a cord and there was a red carpet. Once on board, front seats again, newspapers were offered. Then the hostess took her leave. "I do hope you have been comfortable"—we thought we heard—"your Excellency". Comprehension began to dawn and was soon confirmed; as we took off, a passenger across the aisle bent forward and touched James on the sleeve. "Excuse me," she said, "what country do you represent?"

"England," said James in a gruff voice and buried himself in his newspaper.

It was soon explained. While we had been waiting at Seattle the morning papers had come out; one of them carried a report of my talks with the flattering headline, 'The Best Ambassadors Britain Has Sent Us'. I suppose no-one had bothered to read the print below. Americans, too, seldom recognise double-barrelled names; James's Haynes-Dixon became simply Dixon and the British Ambassador in Washington at that time was Sir Piers Dixon. Seattle is a long way from Washington.

As we realised our mistake, the airline realised it too; nothing was done, nothing said but we were ordinary passengers again.

It was wonderful while it lasted.

And we did see at least some of America including 'pockets' to which most English people do not go. "Don't let's keep to the big spots," James had said. "Some of the smaller will be more interesting, even if the fees are less." At first Colston Leigh did not believe us, and objected, "You are here to make money," then he said, "Maybe it's a good way to build up a reputation," and he splashed out on embarrassingly enthusiastic leaflets.

"When we get home," said James, "you will do nothing but cook, scrub and darn my socks for three months."

I have loved New England from the first time I saw it, its mixture of the prim, trim small towns with their puritanical names: Concord, Providence, Bethel, Canaan; other names came from the Pilgrim Fathers' homesickness: Portland, Dorset, Cambridge, New London mingling with the Red Indian forests, hills, lakes such as Lake Waramaug; near Boston are Cohasset, Assinippi, Ponkapoag, in Rhode Island Quonochontaug, Pawtucket and Woonsocket.

I like the white clapboard houses, often round a green, where square-dancing goes on in summer evenings, everyone dancing from grandmothers to three year olds, while others watch from the peacefully rocking rocking-chairs on the wide porches. I like the churches, white clapboard too, the farming, especially in autumn when ripe pumpkins were set in gateposts, maize on the cob hung up under the eaves. It was, too, a surprise to find the plumbing old-fashioned.

We learned to prize Oregon, far on the West Coast with its almost Canadian mountains, fir forests, rivers, and autumn colours, just as we liked Maine where we stayed with friends who had a house on the beach itself. In the evening, Naomi, the wife, would put a deep pan of salt water on the cooker; then she and I would go out of sight and hearing while her husband Ned pulled the wicker lobster pots out of the sea; we would each have a fresh lobster for supper, delectable!

We travelled the great stretching tracks of the grain fields of the middle West and golden California, and came to know San Francisco where we always stayed, not at the St. Francis, but at the Mark Hopkins Hotel on Nob Hill with its roof restaurant's view far across the city. From our bedroom we could watch trams clanking up and down the Hill—from that height they seemed like tiny beetles—or look far over the Bay and the Golden Gate. We went to the redwood forests and saw those unbelievably enormous trees—the cars drive through an arch in the base of one of them. I always went to San Francisco's Chinatown, to me the best of any, even more fascinating than Calcutta's. Some of my friends had an enamelled bowl especially made for me there, in turquoise and bronze, by the famous Jade Snow Wong; it has her signature on the bottom.

We had so much to learn; our first time in Chicago I was scheduled to speak at what was called The Women's Athletic Club. We had pictured an audience of gusty young women wearing perhaps polo necked sweaters and jeans—it was eleven o'clock in the morning but, as we came to the entrance, a car drew up, a dark green Rolls-Royce. A footman in livery to match got out, let down some steps and carefully helped out an old lady; she was, I have to say, 'gowned' not dressed, wearing a hat with a veil, furs and gloves.

Ushered in, we were taken straight up in the lift to a small reception room where the Committee was waiting, all women who matched the old lady in elegance. We were offered hot bouillon with sherry.

The auditorium was the Club's ballroom, filled with gilt chairs. Always, before I start to speak, once the introduction has been given, I say a small prayer; the pause is good, it rivets the audience's attention—perhaps they think you will fail to speak at all;

a Hail Mary is exactly the right length if I make myself say it slowly; never have I prayed as I did on that occasion.

The applause was so polite I could not tell if we had failed or not but afterwards the Committee Members were gracious. The talk was followed by a luncheon, equally elegant, with orchids on the table. James was the only man in the building except the janitor who, when James wanted to go to the lavatory, had to be fetched.

I believe that one of the secrets of speaking is a sense of responsibility; after all the audience has paid handsomely to hear you. Also if you think about them and about the meaning of your subject, you forget yourself and cease to be self-conscious.

Of course, sometimes you are brought abruptly up against yourself. One particular day began, for me, with being called for at half-past five in the morning to appear on the popular television show *The Today Show* which started at half-past seven. It was fascinating; we, who were being interviewed were, each with our particular interviewer, in a small set, furnished as a sitting room or study, the front open, all on the perimeter of a circle, in the centre of which was a turntable for the camera, sound, lights and crew. That morning I was with Hillary, the mountain climber and the Duke and Duchess of Bedford. As the programme went on the air, a little man crawled along the floor up to the set whose turn had come, and as a warning, held up three fingers for three minutes, then two, then one and we began. When the end was near the fingers appeared again; three, two, one, cut. It was difficult to avoid looking at him.

That same evening I had been engaged to talk at a notable school for girls, Miss Porter's School at Farmington. Driving up from New York we arrived in Farmington in the late afternoon and drove straight to the auditorium, in reality a beautifully equipped small theatre and were 'received'—not merely met—by the Head of the English Department. I always ask to see the auditorium, test the microphone, and especially the lectern as I am so small, five foot two, that I tend to be hidden. Once, at a small country club something had to be found for me to stand on; no-one could find anything. I suggested telephone directories—they only had a local one. It was a dilemma until resourceful James went out to the kitchen and found three baking tins in graduated sizes which he balanced a little precariously. "Be careful how you move or they'll come down," he whispered to me, "and don't move your heels; they'll sound like a drum."

As I tested at Farmington—where everything was perfect—I saw the majestic English mistress continually looking at me, obviously perturbed; something was wrong but I could not think what it was until we were taken to the Alumnae House where we were staying and, in the bedroom, I saw myself in the looking glass. Miss Porter's school is renowned for plain living, high thinking and I was still wearing the make-up from the *Today* programme. In those days television make-up was heavy; I had garishly rouged cheeks, scarlet lips, bright green around the eyes. In the limousine with me on that long drive had been Marilyn, James and the chauffeur; not one of them had noticed!

We were fascinated by Arizona and the desert, by the vast spaces, interrupted by sudden mesas or hills, the arroyos or gullies where the streams had run dry and the sand had built up high walls and curves; by the strange shapes of giant cacti and twisted juniper trees but most of all I remember the great scape of cloudland. When the clouds are dark with rain the whole desert seems filled with foreboding—but that day they were puffs of white that cast patterns of colours and light. We saw too, the gentleness of sunrise and sunset when as I had seen in my first flight across America, the desert turns bright red.

Years ago, Jean and Dido Renoir had taken me to see the old adobe mission churches in New Mexico. Now I found them again, with their intrinsically rich colours and the gaudy plaster statues that are so deeply loved; the Indian women may have the shabbiest of clothes but they delight in dressing and redressing their Virgin Mary and Holy Child in an array of robes, crowns and jewels; their church is the beauty and meaning of their lives.

I had an introduction to a writer, Ann Nolan Clark who had been born in New Mexico and had lived and worked with Mexicans and Indians all her life.

Ann was a gifted writer yet had come upon that gift almost accidentally; for years she had been in the Service for Indian Children, and finding there was a great need in the schools for books written from the Indian point of view—there seemed to be none —she wrote them herself. They appeared in double form, English/Spanish; English/Navajo, English/Sioux and so on; they have Indian illustrations. No-one knew more about Indians than Ann who exactly caught the rhythm, design and pattern of Indian speech especially in the well-known picture book for children, *In My*

Mother's House which is set down in short lines with breaks in the sentences, the way thoughts come:

> The pueblo,
> The people,
> And fire,
> And fields,
> And water,
> And land,
> And animals—
> I string them together
> like beads.
>
> They make a chain,
> A strong chain,
> To hold me close
> To home,
> Where I live
> In my mother's house.

When we met her, Ann had retired and was living alone far outside Tucson where I had been speaking at the University. Her small adobe house was surrounded by two twelve foot fine meshed wire fences, one close to the house, the other thirty feet away as 'protection against coyotes and rattlesnakes'. "Are you ever afraid?" said James. "Of what," asked Ann. At seventy-six she was a little boney woman with wispy white hair and scintillating blue eyes that could, though, easily fill with tears as we found, because Ann had made a sad mistake.

No-one knew more about the desert, its moods, creatures, flowers, birds than Ann; by letter we had agreed she would take us for a day into the desert which should have been perfect. I do not know what Ann had heard about this unknown couple of English visitors, but she had thought she would be inadequate—she, Ann Nolan Clark!—and so had asked a friend to come and support her. I suppose Esmé meant well but she was mercilessly voluble and bossy, especially with Ann. Everything Ann had arranged was wrong—from the horses to the picnic. It was the picnic that caused the tears. Ann unpacked it from a basket in the shade of a small arbour thatched with juniper, spreading a clean cloth with sandwiches, cookies she had made herself, cool home-made lemonade, hot coffee, but, "Call that a lunch for *guests*," said Esmé and stalked off to the horses. Ann wept. "I thought she would entertain you."

"Dear Ann, we don't need to be entertained." We only wanted
to be alone with Ann, to be allowed to look, listen, feel the desert.

Cast by an ancient river;
Salted with iron rich cinders;
Covered by the sands of time.

Raised by forces from under;
Worn away by wind and water;
Reddened badlands before my eyes*

The evening made up for it.

When we got back to Ann's house I could see she was exhausted. Thankfully Esmé had a date elsewhere but, "Mind Ann,"
she said as she left, "You must take them into town for a good
dinner. They only had those sandwiches for lunch. I've booked
you a table at . . ." the restaurant sounded like 'Les Altos', "There's
a band there"—we shuddered—"I've booked it."

As soon as she had gone, "Let's unbook," said James. "Ann,
please let us stay here quietly with you, and you tell us about the
desert and the people."

"But you must eat," she looked distraught again.

"First I'm going to give you a scotch and ice . . ."—we had
brought her whisky—"and you'll put your feet up." He pulled up
a long chair and brought a cushion.

In the end she let me make scrambled eggs which we had with
fruit on her verandah or porch. Then she talked and, as the desert,
its people, strange flowers and life, unfolded, her eyes grew bluer
and bluer with happiness.

We were leaving, it was past midnight, when Ann suddenly
said, "Wait," got up and trotted into her bedroom. She came back
with a Madonna, carved in wood, with a fish at her feet, rays all
round her, carved into calm dignity with a beautiful face. "She was
made by the Indians for my mother," said Ann. "Rumer, I want
you to have her. *Please*," she said before I could speak. "She must
be taken care of. You will do that I know," and, "James you must
have something." She gave him one of the Mexican gaudy crosses
sold on Mexican feast days made of wicker work and bright pink
wool, tipped with tinsel and hung with bells.

*Haiku translated by John J. Wagoner who wrote *This Is Painted Desert*.

I still have the Madonna, she stands by my bed. James asked for the cross to be buried with him.

We always came back to New England.

Emily Dickinson, the American New England poet, in one of her famed brief poems had written:

> One Sister have I in our house
> And one, a hedge away. . . .

The second sister was her sister-in-law Sue, wife of her brother Austin; it was in their house that I had a curious experience—I still wonder if I dreamed it.

From the moment I had come upon Emily Dickinson with, I am glad to say instant recognition, I had wanted to go to Amherst where she had lived all her seemingly uneventful life, and when I was asked by The Bodley Head publishers to edit a book of her poems for younger readers, as we were in America at the time, it seemed destined. James and I were driven up by our friends, Lilias and Orville Prescott, Orville the leading book critic of *The New York Times* and a staunch ally of mine.

Amherst is a small and pleasant town in Massachusetts among rolling hills and valleys. It has a College—Emily's grandfather was one of the founders; white frame houses and small shops are set around a green with an old inn, the Lord Jeffery at which we stayed. Main Street where the Dickinsons lived is lined with trees and large houses in gardens of lilacs and snowball bushes. The Mansion, as the Dickinson house was called though it is no bigger than the others, is of brick with turrets of yellow and white and stands in an enclave with the Evergreens, a frame house built for Austin Dickinson almost in the same garden.

For me it was a pilgrimage. Over our centuries of poetry, among poets who can be ranked as major there are only a handful of women—in fact they can be counted on one hand*—Emily Dickinson is one and James, equally with the Prescotts, understood when I asked them if, please, they would let me go into her room alone.

---

*I would rank Sappho from what we know of her, Christina Rossetti, Emily Brontë, possibly Edith Sitwell or Marianne Moore—both have greatness. Some would include Elizabeth Barrett Browning.

It had been kept exactly as it had been in her day, a frugal New England room, a rag rug, probably made at home, on bare boards, plain furniture; white dresses, incredibly small hanging in the wardrobe—after what she called her 'white election', Emily Dickinson always wore white. They seemed to bring her presence close.

I felt I must not touch anything only look, especially at the cherry wood bureau where, after Emily's death, her sister, Lavinia Dickinson, alone now in the big house, went into the room—again one guesses it still seemed to be inhabited—and, in the bottom drawer of the bureau, found a box full of packets of poems. Each packet was made of small sheets of writing paper, threaded together to make small 'volumes' as Vinnie called them; these alone held eight hundred and seventy-nine poems; as time went on, more and more poems were discovered; altogether over seventeen hundred.

When they were deciphered it was clear there had been none like them before. They were not only original, they seemed too original and it was only through Vinnie's persistence that they were published at all. 'Who could have imagined,' one of Amherst's summer visitors, a Professor, was to write, 'Who could have imagined that, all unknown to the thousands that passed her house, there was a mind and imagination that could tell them more of nature and the mysteries of life than the combined wisdom of the College. They should have sensed,' he said, 'the presence of one who was reading the inner life of bee, grass and sky; the secret lives of men and women.' No-one imagined. Poetry then was written in 'poetical' style, exact in metre, thorough and logical in phrase, with exact rhymes; it was lofty, 'beautiful' in thought. Then came this style like glancing light, the paradox of an odd flippancy about serious matters like death and God, with an immense awareness of their insoluble mystery. There was an unpretentious camaraderie:

> I'm Nobody! Who are you?
> Are you—Nobody—Too?

Nobody! Her first small book bound in white and, stamped in silver on the front, in a design of Indian pipes, those seemingly fragile resilient flowers that might be a symbol of Emily, is now a collector's rare piece, and it was only the beginning: two other books of poems followed—then a selection of letters—then selection after selection, collection after collection. Emily Dickinson's biography has been written and re-written; there have been neighbours' books about her, memoirs, more letters, and several scholarly analyses of the poems; probably no poet living within the last century has such a bibliography. She has her own room now, in the Houghton Library at Harvard University, where her square piano, the minute desk at which she wrote those hundreds of poems, her amethyst seal, her watch with a key to wind it, are reverently kept. Amherst College houses most of her manuscripts in a priceless collection.

It seems a great fuss to make over such little poems, but are they little? They are, rather distillations and like all distillations, they are potent; though they are short, it is not wise to read more than one or two of her poems at a time. No-one else has ever written like her and it is safe to predict no-one will because she has a quicksilver quality, impossible to capture.

> This is my letter to the World
> That never wrote to Me—
> The simple News that Nature told—
> With tender Majesty
>
> Her Message is committed
> To Hands I cannot see—
> For love of Her—Sweet—countrymen—
> Judge tenderly—of Me

I went down the stairs saying those words, out into the garden and walked along a path, and found almost hidden in the trees another house, but frame not brick.

This was November, the evening was closing in, so that it was difficult to see but I seem to remember the house was yellow—or was it that white clapboard was stained for lack of painting? The roof was dark—of shingles? I do not know. The windows, too, were dark, no light showed; I was to learn there was no lighting, gas or electric but I could see shapes of furniture—a clutter of untidiness. There was a strong sense that the house was inhabited.

Treading carefully to make no noise, I walked round it on a path overgrown with bushes and came out on a strip of front garden made more private by overgrown hedges. The gate was askew as were the wooden steps that led up to a wide porch behind dilapidated railings. Here was a rocking chair beside a table piled with books; was it my fancy that the empty chair was still rocking? As I stood there, a harsh voice sounded from inside. "Who are you? What do you want? Go away."

Instead of going I went nearer. In this big front room a lamp was lit, though its light hardly reached into the shadows; I had an impression of book shelves all round the room, more books and papers piled on tables, but it shone clearly on a head of white rough cut hair, a face so seamed and brown it seemed almost Red Indian, a haughty face with angry black eyes looking accusingly at me, two knotted hands still holding a book. Man or woman? I was not sure until I saw that, as she hunched in the chair, she was wearing a long skirt, a brown shawl over her shoulders. "What do you want? Trippers are not allowed over here. Go away."

I did not apologise. "Excuse me," I said—I must have been still with Emily Dickinson—"but this must surely be the house a hedge away."

Abrupt change. She put the book down. "You *know* the poem!" Amazement was in her voice.

She got up, asked me in, asked me to sit down. Later she made tea, strong and black as any in Britain; I had to drink it and found it exactly what I needed—I suppose I had had a shock. Then, carrying the lamp which cast only a small pool of light as we went, she took me over the house. "Nothing has been changed," she said with satisfaction, "nor will it be while I have breath."

In the kitchen a heavy old mangle stood in a corner with a copper and wash tub; the sink had a pump; there were slated shelves for pots and pans, all heavy too; a dresser. In the drawing room the upholstery—was it silk?—on sofa and chairs was frayed, the stuffing coming out. Knick-knacks on the table were covered in dust but the square piano was open. The fine staircase was wooden, some of the balusters were missing; upstairs beds, chests, wardrobes, chairs were standing where they had always stood. Outside the windows, trees soughed in the wind; branches tapped the panes as if they had a message. In a way it was eerie, in a way not, evocation followed our every step.

Austin and Sue had three children, Edward, Martha and Gilbert who to Emily's sorrow died when he was eight. Their home must have been as full of bustle and life as Emily and Lavinia's was quiet. Austin's house had many gatherings, small routs but now:

This quiet Dust was Gentlemen and Ladies
And Lads and Girls—
Was Laughter and Ability and Sighing
And Frocks and Curls.

That invisible dust stirred as we sat talking, though the visible lay thick on everything. Nothing I had imagined or read about— I did not know which—had changed except that there were all these extra books and papers. At last, "You are doing something on Emily Dickinson?" I asked.

"*For* Emily Dickinson," she corrected me sharply; there seemed to be a fanatical gleam in her eyes as she looked at me, daring me not to believe her. It was then that I asked, "Who are you?"

"A relic," she said and pulled a wry face. "That's what they call a widow, isn't it?"

"Whose widow?"

"I am Mrs. Hampson."

"Mrs. Alfred Leete Hampson?"

"You know of him?"

"Of course. He edited the poems." He had been their second editor, with Emily's niece Martha Dickinson who had become Martha Dickinson Bianchi.

"He was mistreated."

I did not argue. It would have been embarrassing. Emily Dickinson's first editor, Colonel Higginson, had made the poems conform; Alfred Hampson and Martha Bianchi had gone the other way, exaggerating the irregularities to make them 'quaint' which, in the thirties, was fashionable. Added to which it seemed Martha often failed to read her aunt's handwriting and there were words misread but, "We are bringing out a new edition of all the poems, Martha Bianchi and I."

"Mrs. Hampson, Martha is dead." I did not say it. Mrs. Hampson had not said Alfred and Martha—the 'presences' seemed only in the Dickinson's house—so, "According to Alfred?" I said. It was perhaps a slip but she did not take offence. "According to Alfred,"* she said with satisfaction.

I had guessed now how Mrs. Hampson came to be here in Austin's house; Martha had made Alfred Leete Hampson her heir.

---

*In any case it would not have been allowed. The authorities at Harvard have laid down that, in no circumstances, can any word, lettering, least mark of punctuation in Emily Dickinson's poems be changed.

We talked quietly on until it grew so late that James and Orville came to look for me. As soon as their footsteps sounded by the gate the hostility came back. "Go. Go at once. Understand. I do *not* allow people."

I went out as quietly as I had come and put a finger to my lips to hush James and Orville. As I passed the rocking chair I set it gently rocking.

How stupid it is that in the rush of life, we do not follow the avenues that open from experience. I was too tired that night, or perhaps too full of emotion, to talk about what I had seen and been through. I must though have told about the house because I remember Orville saying, "They are debating what to do with it when the old lady goes, restore it as a museum or pull it down to make a car park."

A car park! That inimitable house.

We left next morning without trying to find out anything more.

I was not alone in feeling a 'presence' or 'presences' in those houses. When my book was published, knowing he shared my passion for Emily Dickinson, I sent a copy to the poet James Kirkup whom I had come to know by letters—I had never met him—when he was Professor of English at Japanese Women's University in Tokyo. He had since been posted to Amherst by, I guessed, his own desire. He wrote that in a limited space I had managed to suggest 'the quintessence of a quintessential being.'

> There is a mysterious white shadow in one of the snaps I took in her garden, but I expect it's only my lack of skill. I secretly prefer to think otherwise.
>
> I shall cherish this little book, and take it with me to show her on my visits to her grave. The little posies I take to her are always missing next time I go. At first I thought it was naughty children taking them, but last time, I saw Emily. She was carrying one of them—a sheaf of honesty the colour of her gown and her face.*

There was so much to see, do and learn on those American tours that we always came home tired, exhilarated, filled with richness but tired.

*James Kirkup sent me a poem, *Emily in Winter*, which has not I think been published. Four of his poems appear in the Appendix to this book.

I remember one December when we flew, not back home but to Lisbon because we were going to Jane, Anthony and their children for Christmas and Anthony was stationed now in Cyprus. We had passages on a boat that would take us from Portugal to Cyprus through the Mediterranean which would give us, we hoped, a day or two's rest.

The Portuguese know how to do things. We stayed at the Ritz, even then a remarkable hotel and not nearly as expensive as it sounds; we arrived at six in the morning and went straight to bed.

I woke to find our big room in dusk and shadow. I stirred, sat up, and looked at the clock. It was still six o'clock. Slowly I realised it was six in the evening; we had slept almost twelve hours. A voice came from the next bed, "Do you know what day it is?"

I had no idea.

"It's your birthday," said James. "Come on. Get up. We'll go and find a restaurant and have a gala dinner."

"James, I couldn't. I couldn't possibly. I'm too tired."

He looked at me. "I think you are. Very well. Go and have a bath. Get into a dressing gown and we'll see."

Our room had an alcove sitting room; when I came, cleansed and fresh, armchairs had been drawn up, little maids in white aprons were running in and out bringing more electric fires to warm us. There were flowers, freesias and carnations in bowls and vases. A small table had been set, lit with candles, the maître domo himself waited on us. "A light, light supper," James had specified. We had sole perfectly cooked, fresh fruit slightly crystallised, cut in pieces which on long forks we dipped into a hot chocolate and brandy sauce—finger bowls were brought sprinkled with rose petals—then we had small rounds of cream goat cheese on toasted wafers, with, not champagne, but our favourite still white wine, blanc de blanc.

"I only want a pekingese to be utterly content," I said.

For once James could not produce one out of his pocket.

The peak of all tours was, of course, to be invited to speak at the Library of Congress in Washington; to speak there is the pinnacle of speaking in America, a privilege and I am proud to say I was invited to speak there twice, the first time, as a double engagement with a reception after it. The stage was white panelled, lit with a chandelier; we came on through double doors at the back, James in a dinner jacket, I in a dress designed for me by Liberty's—plainly cut in deep cyclamen silk. It set off one of the few jewels I had, a pendant, a single aquamarine. When we were planning our visit, James had asked me, "What are you going to wear for Library of Congress?" I told him and said, "I should have liked to wear the aquamarine pendant, it would look beautiful on that dress, but I haven't a ring to go with it." A ring on your hand seems to emphasise any gesture you make but I had no ring with an aquamarine.

"Haven't you?" said James and went upstairs. He came down with a small box which he handed to me; inside was a ring, an aquamarine solitaire as exquisite as the pendant, but set in diamonds.

At the time we married, James had not been able to give me a ring—he had been between posts. He had saved up for this ring and had been carrying it round for six months, "Waiting for the right occasion," said James.

It was the right occasion.

While you are speaking, if you are lucky, there comes a moment when, for a short while—if you are wise you keep it short—you know you have the audience in the palm of your hand and you can do with it anything you wish; that happened in Washington. Standing on that stage I looked at the truly glittering audience—in those days, these were 'dressed' occasions—in that dress, those jewels, heard my voice ring out confidently and, once again I was back twenty-three years ago to a young woman working by the light of an oil lamp, in the bitter cold of a Kashmiri winter, steadily writing.

January 1944

It is too cold in my writing room; the desk has had to go into the sitting room. The children are in bed. I dare not hold my kangri* pressed to me, but can warm my hands on it which helps. It is utterly quiet.

When the Library of Congress talk and reception was over, with, I must own, acclamation, back at our hotel I said to James, "I don't want to do this any more."

For a moment he was stunned—the talks had meant much to him. Then, as James always did, he tried to understand. "You mean, one can't go any higher than this. Is that it?" he asked.

"No," I said. "I mean it isn't writing."

---

*Kangri: a wicker basket holding an earthenware pot filled with live charcoal; one side has a wicker shield—Kashmiris hold it under their pheran or robe, pressing it against their stomachs. It is their only means of heating.

In This House of Brede

"I wish," said Dame* Felicitas "that someone would write a book about nuns as they really are, not as the author wants them to be."

I thought of *Black Narcissus* and blushed.

In an American *Book of the Month Club News* a reviewer had written that, during the past three years, I had produced five books each quite different from the other:

> *Miss Happiness and Miss Flower* in which the lives of dolls and children are interwoven; *Saint Jerome and the Lion*, a humorous narrative poem equally appealing to children and grown-ups; *Prayers from the Ark*, subtle translations from the French; *Little Plum*, another book about children and dolls; still a third children's book, *Home Is the Sailor*, to be published next year.

The reviewer was as encouraging as she was enthusiastic but none of these books were novels and my metier is the novel. It was time I got back to it but I had had a warning.

The Battle of the Villa Fiorita had been a commercial success yet Jon had written:

*Benedictine Nuns of the English Congregation, if they belong to an enclosed or contemplative Order, are called Dame not the usual Sister, while the Monks are called Dom.

I stick to what I said; this is the mixture as before; children, animals, flowers, houses, a little sentimentality and piety, all written and done as you only can do it. But if this is a typical Rumer Godden it is a vintage one.

Jon had warned me before; she was my wisest critic—and my sternest; her letter gave me profoundly to think. What else could I write about? For a while it seemed hopeless and it was not until nineteen sixty-nine that I was able to tell her, 'I have written a novel with, in it, only a mention of an animal—one cat—hardly any flowers and not a single live child.'

Some time before Jon had sent me, from the *Bhagavad-Gita*;

> The god Krishna says: However men approach me,
> even so do I welcome them, for the path men take
> from every side leads to me.

'When the pupil is ready, the teacher will come.' That is a Hindu proverb which for me over and over again has proved true; Mona Swann, Ben Huebsch; now it was Archbishop Roberts, S.J.

I first met him when we were together on the panel of a Brains Trust—an odd place for me to be. As soon as the Archbishop spoke, and by his answers to the questions, it was unmistakable that he was someone as unusual as he was special; I had been told he was a convert to Roman Catholicism, had become a Jesuit monk and, uncommon as it is for a Jesuit to hold a See, been appointed Archbishop of Bombay.

He was small, thin with brown eyes more quick and perceptive than any I have seen. He wore the shabbiest clothes. "Archbishop, you really can *not* wear that suit any longer," James used to say, "it doesn't even fit you."

"No," the Archbishop was unperturbed. "It belonged to Father Barrett," or some other monk who had died. "They were all larger than I, but it's still wearable—just," he had to concede.

When, several years later, he came down to us in Sussex to christen my youngest grand-daughter, Charlotte, we gave him a cheque, "For Mother Teresa," he said with joy.

"For a new suit," said James and, when the Archbishop hesitated, "or else give it back."

A priest is not made an archbishop for nothing but it was only slowly, because he was so modest and not talkative that, we discovered Archbishop Roberts's immense learning, and the width of it. As with Ben, he had an aura—again I almost wrote 'halo' though he would have hated that—an immanence of energy, humility yet fearlessness; he was a thorn in the side of the hierarchy, often stepping beyond their authority. Archbishop Roberts believed passionately, as I do, that India should belong to Indians and that the Archbishop of Bombay ought to be an Indian as, on an obligatory visit to Rome, he told the Pope.

"Where will you find an Indian capable of that responsibility?" asked the Pope.

"I have found him," said the Archbishop. "He has been taking the whole responsibility for the past two years. I have been merely the gardener."

The Indian was Archbishop Gracias who was later made a cardinal.

Archbishop Roberts could be stern yet he had a wonderful understanding, often with a slightly humorous tenderness especially for anyone young. On one of his innumerable sea voyages outward bound for Bombay—this was in the days when most of us travelled by ship—there was a young Scots girl who had been at his table in the dining saloon. She was going out to India to marry a man she had not seen for two years and was naturally full of trepidation. "I tried to comfort her," he told me. As usual with those big liners, on the last night there was a gala dinner, after which everyone at the table signed a menu card for the others as a keepsake. The Archbishop signed hers, Thomas Roberts, S. J. † customary sign of a bishop. Next morning when he met her she said with a pleased blush, "Thanks for the wee kiss."

After that Brains Trust I had driven him back to Farm Street, to the Jesuit Presbytery, next to the Jesuit church. On the way I asked him—it seemed you could ask him anything—why he had become a Catholic. "Evidence," he said. "Evidence."

Evidence? and I remembered what I had long believed yet had not liked to voice because the very thought might disturb those who are happily settled in their religion; it is that the Roman Catholic Church is the only Christian church founded divinely by Christ, not by men.

"thou art Peter and on this rock I will build my church ... and I will give unto thee the keys of the kingdom of heaven: and what-soever thou shalt bind on earth shall be bound in heaven: and what-soever thou shalt loose on earth shall be loosed in heaven."*

There is a version of a psalm that says God has no love for tepid men; I began to see I must declare myself, no matter what it cost. "But I have one stumbling block," I told the Archbishop.

"Only one?" He smiled.

"It's the chief and I think it has troubled many many others besides me. It's where Christ says, 'I am the way, the truth and the life: no man cometh unto the father, but by me,' "† and I burst out with the question that had been troubling me and stopping me, "What about all the holy spiritual people I have known and you, Father, must have known, in India for instance. You must have known many more than I: Hindus, Muslims, Buddhists, Zoroastrians? Are they to be shut out?"

"My child," he said—I was a child in belief though I was older than he—"My child, Christianity is still in its infancy. It is only two thousand years old. We haven't begun yet to know what Christ is."

Like an echo there came into my mind lines I had learned to love,

> For Christ plays in ten thousand places,
> Lovely in limbs, and lovely in eyes not his
>   To the Father through the features of men's
>   faces.‡

Jane was the first of our family to become a Catholic, Paula the last; she held out for five years, from her first dismissing it as hocus-pocus nonsense—we never argued—until her final reception in Cyprus with Anthony as her godfather. Mark, my grandson, now five was allowed to attend; he was impressed when we were given Communion under both kinds, especially the wine from the chalice. "What does it taste like?" he whispered to me.

I whispered back, "Nectar," which it is.

For Jane it came in a practical way—she is a practical rather

*Matthew. Chapter 16, v.18/19.
†John. Chapter 14, v.6.
‡From the sonnet "As Kingfishers Catch Fire, Dragon Flies Draw Flame," by Gerard Manley Hopkins, also a Jesuit.

than a mystical person; it was from her experience as a nurse. "Those Roman Catholic priests seem the only ones who are not afraid of death or embarrassed by it," she had said. Archbishop Roberts baptised and confirmed her.

After the private ceremony at Farm Street Jane and I took him out to lunch. The restaurant was the l'Etoile in Charlotte Street, exclusive but homely, a family concern. When we arrived, the cloakroom girl took the Archbishop's old hat, ancient greatcoat, and deplorable purple knitted muffler, with disdain; eyebrows were raised. Then, as we went to our table, drinking our apéritifs, he let his hand rest on the table.

It was the young waiter who first saw the amethyst ring; to the astonishment of the other clients, he immediately knelt and kissed it, then whispered to Monsieur, the proprietor. One by one, the proprietor, his wife, the staff down to the kitchen boys in their aprons came in, knelt down and kissed the ring; the Archbishop, while continuing to talk to Jane and me, blessed each one.

By one of those unexplained coincidences Anthony, when he met Jane, had been taking instruction to become a Catholic. He made his first communion at his wedding and managed his sword as well.

From the *Times*:

> 1959: MURRAY FLUTTER—On 17th June 1959, at Towyn, N. Wales, to Jane, wife of Captain Anthony Murray Flutter, R.A.—a son (Mark).
>
> 1961: MURRAY FLUTTER—on July 19, at Aberystwyth General Hospital, to Jane (née Foster) and Anthony Murray Flutter, a daughter (Elizabeth Rumer).
>
> 1964: MURRAY FLUTTER—On April 8, in the Buchanan, Hospital, St. Leonards-on-Sea, to Jane (née Foster) wife of Captain A. Murray Flutter, R.A., a daughter (Emma Selina).
>
> 1965: MURRAY FLUTTER—On April 5 1965 at the Buchanan Hospital, St. Leonards-on-Sea, to Jane (née Foster) and Captain A. Murray Flutter, Royal Artillery—a daughter, sister for Mark, Elizabeth and Emma.

That was Charlotte. It was my namesake, Elizabeth Rumer, who brought me to Stanbrook Abbey, before she was born.

*   *   *

It had always been Paula, now strong and wiry, who had been the delicate one, Jane the picture of health until those babies were born. There was a bad miscarriage after Mark and when another baby was on the way the doctors were unanimous that Jane was not strong enough to have it. "Too great a risk," they said but she and Anthony—it was almost worse for him—were firm. "This is our baby. No-one must interfere," but I could not help being deeply worried.

In the months of suspense—we were still at the Old Hall—coming out to take the pekingese for a walk I met a friend, Leonard Clark, the poet. It was on the pavement outside the gates; Leonard too was going for a walk with his small son; we stopped, talked lightly until, "What is worrying you?" asked Leonard—he was always sensitive to other people. When I told him he said, "Write to Stanbrook Abbey and ask the nuns for their prayers."

It was the first I had heard of a place that has become a lifeline for me.

Dame Felicitas, like many of the other Stanbrook nuns, has every day a heavy bag of mail yet it was she who wrote to Jane every week in those months of anxiety, never with off-putting piousness—"We don't talk pi," say the nuns—but simply, steadily, sustaining her. "Don't worry. We have you tucked in our sleeves," those ample sleeves, particularly of the wide black cowls they wear in choir and the chapter house.

My diary—July 19 1961

Elizabeth Rumer born early this morning. I was in London and "a little girl," said the nurse on the telephone. "A perfect baby."
James and I went to Stanbrook to say thank you.

Stanbrook Abbey stands in its great park above a village in Worcester, its bell tower can be seen for miles. It is a Benedictine monastery of enclosed contemplative nuns of the English Congregation which is why they have the letters O.S.B. after their names. 'Monastery' comes from the Latin word *monos*, to be alone, living a community life yet alone with God.

Each moniale has to make her own way; a Stanbrook nun often will have no idea what the nun next to her—or any of the other Sisters—is doing and, in all the years I have been with them, I have never set foot in the Enclosure. Except for the doctor—at one time the dentist—only three categories of people are allowed in; the reigning monarch of the country, cardinals and plumbers, meaning workmen. I pleaded that I was a 'plumber' but, "That's cheating," Lady Abbess said firmly.

There are, though, a row of parlours, small private rooms—one door leads to the Enclosure, the nuns come in by that, the opposite door is for visitors—and through them come people of every sort and kind. Some, of course, are the nuns' relations and friends; some are would-be aspirants but many are in need. There is, as well, a notice-board put up in the cloister close by a statue of Our Lady of Consolation—the votive light kept burning there seems an emblem of hope. On that board are letters, cards, messages, each a cry for help.

Stanbrook makes no claim to miracles; the nuns simply call such happenings as baby Elizabeth 'providence' which it is; Jane had an excellent gynaecologist but I would not be surprised. I have seen extraordinary things done by prayer and Stanbrook is a power house of prayer.

> We do not engage in works outside our monastery
> For we have chosen to live in silence
> > and concentration
> At the hidden springs, the deepest level
> Where the struggle is enacted
> > between the powers of good and evil
> Where our union with Christ bears fruit
> > for all mankind. . . .
>
> We have chosen a stillness
> > more powerful than all activity.
> A detachment more fulfilling than all possession,
> A wisdom exceeding all knowledge
> And a love beyond all.

The nuns wrote that in a small pamphlet saying for me, in a few words, what I had taken a whole book to try and express. The pamphlet was to help me to answer the near avalanche of letters the novel brought; a surprise because, when I wrote it, I thought no-one would want to read it—perhaps an echo of Fa's long ago remark when, with *Black Narcissus*, I had told him I was writing a book about nuns, "Don't," said Fa, "no-one will read it."

*　　*　　*

"Not as the author would like them to be."

In This House of Brede is the story of Dame Philippa Talbot—as I have said I can only write stories—told from the day of her entry into the enclosed life of the monastic Abbey of Brede. In it, no professed* nun comes out, leaps over the wall, though, of course, aspirants, postulants, novices come and go. "Mostly they goes," an old lay Sister said to me. Professed nuns—there are, maybe, a million or more of them in Britain and Europe—abide, keeping their vows. Nor do they fall in love with the chaplain or become lesbians; in fact one critic complained that the only sex in my book was in the word 'Sussex'.

It would have been far easier to write about an active Order; people can see, understand and admire the good they do. "Sister," said a young American soldier when, in India, he watched a nun bandaging the rotting and malodorous finger stumps of an old leper, "Sister, I wouldn't do your work for ten thousand dollars a day."

"Neither would I," said the nun.

All of us, believers or not, can honour the selflessness of that, but to be a contemplative nun, bound to one House for the rest of your life? That seems so incomprehensible, even wrong, that reason after reason is invented for it; they have entered because of a broken heart or are misfits, which leads to the favourite explanation that they cannot cope with the world and so settle for shelter and security; they want to escape. On the contrary; if they have entered for a 'reason', a human reason, it is rare for a contemplative monk or nun to succeed. Often one of them will tell you she, or he, did not 'choose' to come; no words are more true than Christ's, "You have not chosen me, I have chosen you ...". It is as if God put out a finger—if a spirit can have a finger—and said, "You".

It can be too the most unlikely person, breaking a settled life, interrupting a career. "My life was so beautifully arranged," says Dame Philippa in my book. "I was succeeding, becoming a personality; then this came like dynamite and blew it all to bits."

---

*A nun is 'professed' when after perhaps six months or more as a postulant, two or three years as a novice, at least three years in 'simple vows', she takes her solemn profession, usually for life.

†St. John. Chapter 15, v.16.

Among nuns I have known, some had been doctors, lawyers, artists—one had been a beautician at Elizabeth Arden. They may be aristocratic, middle class, working class but all make the same acknowledgement of that 'call'. It is, too, paradoxical; one girl may want it with all her heart; it does not come; she has no 'vocation'. Others who hear it, recoil. Dame Felicitas, herself, as a young novice asked her novice mistress, "Mother, do you think I have a vocation?"

"Yes dear, I do."

"Damn!" said Felicitas.

When they are 'chosen' in this mystical way, what good, people ask, can come of it? "Someone should give those women something to do," said Queen Victoria when, after the Duke of Clarence had visited Stanbrook, he told her of it. Queen Victoria was not a percipient person but can be excused because, except for that row of parlours, that notice-board, the heavy post-bags, the line of tramps that are fed every day, the work of a contemplative nun is not apparent; they themselves can seldom gauge what they achieve—"or don't achieve," says Dame Felicitas.

The Abbey is famed for its printing and has its own Press—the oldest in England and still used; from it come books, spiritual and temporal, many written or illustrated by the nuns. They do translations from Latin, Greek and modern languages. The Abbey is known for its art, the beauty of the vestments made there, for its plainchant, and music; Dame Felicitas is one of the foremost organists in Britain, musicians come from far and near to hear her* but these are offshoots, never allowed to interfere or interrupt the main stem of the Abbey's purpose—prayer.

As I wrote in the novel:

At the sound of the bell, a speaker must stop—"Well, not in mid-sentence," said Dame Clare, "but stop." A writer must stop too even in the middle of a paragraph, the artist must lay down her brush, the cleaner her broom or dust-pan, as though the liturgy of the monastic choir,

each day we lift the world up to God in public prayer and praise.

*Dame Felicitas has also written books including the story of the friendship between her late Abbess, Dame Laurentia and Bernard Shaw, recently re-issued as, *The Nun, the Pagan and the Infidel* which has been produced as a play in the West End. Her *Life of Helen Waddell* won the James Tait Memorial Prize.

To Philippa the chant was the nearest thing to birdsong she had ever heard, now solo, now in chorus, rising, blending, each nun knowing exactly when she had to do her part. On feast days, it took four chantresses to sing the Gradual in the Mass, four more for the Alleluia, rising up and up, until it seemed no human voice could sustain it.

It is not only praise and supplication; underlying all, is the fight against the evil that has always been in the world. Researching *Five for Sorrow, Ten for Joy*, I had to explore prisons, in particular the Maison Centrale at Rennes in France to which only women serving life or long sentences are sent; I came to know and value its balanced—and compassionate—Governor, Jacqueline Mercier. "I don't know if I believe in God," she told me, "but I do believe in the devil. I have met him."

> Our World has lost God
> Each day we search for him
> In our private prayer and reading
>
> Each day we work
> according to our gifts
> for the support of the community
>
> Such is the life of a contemplative nun.

"Give those women something to do!" Lady Abbess allowed me, for one day only, to follow Stanbrook's day according to the Rule, beginning with Lauds at five minutes to four in the morning, ending with Compline at eight. I was exhausted.

Though Stanbrook was its prototype I called my imaginary monastery Brede Abbey because when we left my loved Old Hall and came to live at Little Doucegrove in Northiam, East Sussex, the next village to us was called Brede, its manor house the seat of the Frewens, an old Sussex family. Roger Frewen let me take the name and the site for my book.

Little Doucegrove had belonged to the Sussex born and bred writer, Sheila Kaye Smith whose books, now out of print, included her best seller *Joanna Godden*; it could be called another strange coincidence, my name being Godden except that East Sussex and Kent are full of Goddens. 'Godden' comes from the time when North West France, especially Normandy, belonged to the English

King and the occupying soldiers were recruited from these con-
veniently near counties. The morning greeting then was not,
'Good day to you' but, 'God d'en' so that the French called those
men 'Goddens'.

Little Doucegrove was not little; the house converted from the
original farmhouse and two oast houses was large; it had forty-six
acres of woodland and fields and a row of three cottages. I do not
think I would have liked Sheila Kaye Smith; in Doucegrove house
there were eight lavatories, four bathrooms; the three cottages—
there were thirteen people living in them—had no inside water,
only a cold water tap outside and one outside privy. There was
also a church, built by Sheila and her husband, Penrose Fry; they
were dedicated converts to Rome. I think Penrose, as a widower
quite unable to cope, would have given Doucegrove to us for the
sake of having it in Catholic hands; as it was we paid little for it.

I was not, in fact, an accepted Catholic yet; as James and I were
both divorced I had to wait years before I could be received but
tried to live as a Catholic. I had felt the exclusion acutely, being
perhaps the only one at, say, Easter having to stay in my place
and not go up to the altar, until Father Diamond—he was a real
diamond—our priest in Princes Risborough wrote to me:

> There is such a thing as spiritual communion. When people for
> some reason are unable to receive Holy Communion in the ordi-
> nary way they are recommended, for example at Mass or any other
> time, to make a spiritual communion by a prayer of desire or long-
> ing. Some of the older prayer books used to have suggested words
> but, to me, your own would, I think, be more genuine.

Father Diamond, like Archbishop Roberts, has died, but they
are woven for always into my life.

The small church at Doucegrove, St. Teresa's was open to the
people round; a visiting priest served it, and I found to my dismay
that, as chatelaine of the house I was expected to look after it and
him; lay out his vestments and the vessels for Mass, which at first
I had no idea how to do; worst of all, I was responsible for the
flowers. Altar flowers are even more difficult to arrange than most
as the two sides have to match; I was in despair—as I have told
my hands are clumsy—but we had engaged a young local girl as
a cleaner. Fay was a beauty, a big girl with long fair hair, brown
eyes and a luscious skin with, most important of all for me, a

hidden ambition to be a florist, so that it ended by, on Saturday mornings, I doing the housework while Fay did the flowers.

I do not think Sheila approved. We were haunted by a pure white squirrel—surely unusual? "That is Sheila," we used to say. She was certainly inquisitive, jumping up on window sills to peer in.

Perhaps it was an omen. It had taken us a year to put Little Doucegrove in order, for one thing the staircase was so hideous it had to come out. We had lived in it for only fourteen months—I am glad to think we had started on the cottages, they now had plumbing and hot water—when the house was burned down so completely that only the walls and drains were left. James had just finished planting his rose garden.

It was not until weeks afterwards that I could recall anything of that night, and then it was in a caravan that I had hired to put on site so that, in the aftermath, I could deal with what had to be done.

The abiding memory is of noise and smell; I had not realised fire could be so noisy, a roaring, crashing of timbers as they fell that went on far into the night while the smell clung to everything; of the few things that were saved, most had to be jettisoned. Liberty's carpet representative came down and took the Persians that were left away to clean and repair them; they have hardly a trace of damage.

James and I were out with friends when the fire started; the police came to fetch us and driving home we heard and smelt it a mile off. "That can't be us," I said. The whole night was difficult to believe.

A pan of oil had been forgotten on the cooker—the cook had gone home. Paula, whose sitting room was in the kitchen wing, heard the first strange sound—mercifully she had a friend, Valerie with her—and opened the kitchen door; the cooker was ablaze. The girls could not get near enough to try and smother it, so slammed the door and raced to the telephone but the heat blew out the new picture window we had put in the kitchen; it was a stormy night and the wind swept the flames up to the roof which unbeknownst to us, was lined with tarred felt. The fire ran along the roof and, in a matter of minutes, the house was on fire from end to end.

Doucegrove had a long drive with, at its entrance from the road, an island of grass. The second fire engine—five came—stuck on this, impeding the others. Even with the small lake in front of the house, so that water was available, it was not until the early hours of the morning that the fire was reduced to smouldering. The embers were hot for days.

To me, the greatest astonishment was Paula; I think she grew ten years that night. Though shaken to her depths she stayed cool-headed; she and Valerie had not been able to get back into her sitting room, the passage was too dense with smoke; her dog and the pekingese were inside. The girls ran round outside and smashed the windows with their fists—Valerie was badly cut— got the dogs out and put them safely in the van Paula used for work; she had just opened her own riding school and livery stable at Doucegrove. Then she backed the van up to my study at the end of the house and got my papers out including the finished manuscript of a book; it was *The Battle of the Villa Fiorita*, the manuscript is dramatically stained with smoke and blood. If she had not done that our financial loss would have been far worse—no insurance can cover a book in the making.

When the firemen asked her, before James and I arrived, "What shall we try and save," she said, "The carpets and rugs," and, though those upstairs were burnt I still have the cream of them. Most surprising of all was that she, who had lived for her horses —nothing and no-one else had mattered—thought only of us that night. "Paula, what about the horses?" I said as soon as we arrived. She looked at me aghast. The stables were only some three hundred yards from the house, sparks were flying everywhere. We ran but all we could do was to open the loosebox doors and let horses and ponies out; wild with panic, they stampeded far across the countryside.

I remember kind people leaving their cars on the road and coming in to help—they were extraordinarily brave though the crowd did not help the firemen. Neighbours rallied. I saw James collapse and could not get to him because of the press; a neighbour took him away—he had a nervous breakdown that lasted for months. I remember how the sparks flew high into the sky and showered down so that people were forced to keep away, and how our fantail pigeons refused to leave the roof, their roosting and nesting place, even when hoses were turned on them. Next morning I saw my charred piano lying in the hall, its legs in the air, its lid off its hinges, the men could get it no further. Going through the burnt out kitchen into the china cupboard, full of debris, I saw what seemed intact, a set of antique gold and white Venetian glass we had bought in Italy. I touched a glass; it fell to powder.

Most searing of all was the hideous fight with our insurance company. In my ignorance I had thought if you were insured and had a genuine loss they paid but they queried and squabbled over every least thing, like a porcelain dish broken in half. "It can be riveted, therefore is usable."

"It is *ruined*," I argued. I felt like saying, "Keep your horrible money. We'll go without." In the end we had to have an adjudicator. All the time, in a small hotel that took us in and could not have been kinder, James was helpless, completely unable to cope. He could not sleep; we spent most of the night playing poker for enormous imaginary sums.

I could not grieve as he grieved; for him it was another dream shattered, for me it was, in a way, a relief. I have never liked things, especially houses, adapted from other purposes like lamps made from vases or chianti bottles, and could not come to terms with Doucegrove's round rooms converted from its oast houses. Also it had brought dismay—writers should not have more than they need, overlarge houses let alone estates; all the money I earned seemed to disappear into hedging, ditching, felling of trees, keeping up the drive, garden and cottages.

The fire in a way delivered me but still, after twenty-five years, I go to my bookshelves to find a book I am sure I have—and it is not there; still feel a pang for a few things that cannot be replaced; the portrait of the children that hung over my bed; three little pink cloisonné bowls in graduated sizes—they used to play The Three Bears with them; a Chinese scroll of the Manchu Empress's Imperial Pekingese—the royal red tassels round their necks showed they were imperial—that was hanging on the stairs; it was snatched down but its silk had been scorched so, though I have the painting, it is no longer a scroll—it is mutilated.

That early spring, outside the caravan in what used to be the garden, I found a scylla.

My diary . . . March

I had thought I knew about adversity but this morning I found a bulb, a scylla growing head downwards into the earth, planted by some blind person upside-down and it had flowered. True, its blue was pale but it was perfect.

In Chinese calligraphy the word 'crisis' is made up of two characters: the first means danger, the second a turning point or opportunity, perhaps hope.

Even in the caravan the writing of *In This House of Brede* went on.

It was possible—in part anyway, because I had a new ally, a true right arm.

Author seeks part-time secretary with good typing skills.

They little knew the amount of skill that would be needed unravelling my flymarks.

Shorthand not necessary but an interest in books and poetry essential.

It was the poetry that brought me Peggy Bell.

When we had left London I was faced with a quandary; though I could only employ a secretary part-time she was important to me but where, I thought, in the country, in Sussex, could I find anyone of the calibre of Celia Dale? or even of her successor whom we called The Earwig, she was so thin and small, usually wore tight-fitting black trousers and jerseys; her black hair was cut in a fringe that came down to eyes behind enormous horn rimmed spectacles.

The Earwig had been a phenomenon; a superb typist she could type forty pages a day faultlessly in any unknown language— unless she stopped to think. I once gave her a poem to type based on one of the antiphons for Advent, 'The earth shall bud forth a Saviour'. That stopped her; she had no idea of the subtle interwoven language of Christianity and, 'The earth bud forth ...?' That *can't* be right' she had thought; the poem came back to me with, "The earth shall bud forth a saxicar." "What," I asked, "is a saxicar?"

"Oh! I was so proud of that." The Earwig had been crestfallen. "I found it in the encyclopedia. A saxicar is an outcrop of crystal."

For a writer the feeling between him or her and a secretary is even more intimate than between say, a businessman or woman and their secretary, no matter how much they rely on her; for an author, the relationship is even more nervous than between writer and editor because typing a manuscript, particularly when it is a 'rough' or first draft, is horridly revealing; I always dislike handing one over even into sympathetic hands. I had tried to learn to type, but quite apart from my belief in the bond between pen and writer, long hours at the typewriter jarred my oversensitive back. Also I hated to change; I had been attached to Celia and The Earwig, but, coming to Doucegrove, there was no help for it and the advertisement went into the papers; to my astonishment we had more than thirty answers and interviewed ten women, young and older.

Among them was one with obvious distinction, dark, most attractive, especially her voice. She was quiet and reserved, a little intimidating, having been secretary to Anthony Eden; she reassured me by telling me he had once thrown an inkpot at her—hidden in Peggy is an almost impish sense of humour.

Peggy does not tell anyone her troubles though she has many; as the wife of a vicar she had more demands on her than most women could have coped with but never, to my knowledge, said, "No," to any suppliant yet her work was as faultless as The Earwig's, but enriched with true comprehension. She knows far more about poetry than I; her husband was a scholar and much had rubbed off on her.

Peggy and I went through many things together; she had to leave for two years when Godfrey her husband was extremely ill, but she came back. We were together for sixteen years and all that time her patience was unfailing. I do not know how many times she typed *In This House of Brede*.

It was to take me five years.

"You will want to ask questions," Lady Abbess had said. She was completely my idea of an Abbess, tall, majestic yet in a way in love with simplicity; on her election she had discarded the large gold and amethyst cross—sign of an Abbess—and wore a plain smaller wooden one. Now I saw at once that her long experience of journalists, would-be interviewers, or unabashed outside curiosity had made her wary.

"Reverend Mother, I shall have to ask questions about ritual, observances, tradition but I promise I will not ask any of your nuns a personal question." I did not have to; they told me everything I needed to know and more, stories, happenings, far more strange than anything I could have thought of in fiction. My greatest difficulty was in not betraying to any nun things another nun had told me—what is said in the parlour is as secret as in the confessional, not even the Abbess knows what is said there.

Though I could not 'come in' as they call it or go beyond the 'turn'* I was given a plan of the Enclosure and soon seemed almost as familiar with it as if I had lived there. Important in any monastery is the Chapter House—a sort of house parliament— where all the business of the Abbey is conducted, decisions taken or announced. There are, too, the cloisters—those roofed and arched walks, usually round a square of garden. Why is there always such a feeling of peace in a cloister? Perhaps because so many holy people have paced and prayed there, but the heart of the House is the consecrated church with its long rows of stalls, a great organ loft, an extern chapel—separated by a grille which is always opened for Mass—and a narrow staircase leading to the bell tower from which the bell rings far over the park away to the village and fields. The big park is necessary for health and exercise.

Besides the kitchens, laundries, store rooms and a 'black room' where habits are turned and mended, Stanbrook has three libraries. "You may be enclosed but you needn't have enclosed minds," said the famous Abbess Laurentia. Modern books are there, even novels, and anything of importance in the newspapers is put up on the notice-board or read out in the refectory. There are the printing rooms, a weaving and embroidery room for making the vestments which are sent all over the world; studios, music rooms, offices and studies. This sounds luxurious but every tool and space is needed. The nuns have to earn their living.

Each has her cell, furnished only with a narrow bed, a desk or writing table, a chair and a prie-Dieu which has, below its kneeling ledge a cupboard space for dusters, shoe cleaning brushes, boot polish and furniture polish. Stanbrook is always practical and each nun must look after her cell and herself. Perhaps a painting is allowed, a vase of flowers, the books she needs but they are not 'her' books; from postulancy a nun is trained to say 'ours' not 'mine', but her cell is given her—no-one can come in except the infirmarian and the Abbess—both knock—just as every professed nun has her stall in the church; it is hers for life.

---

*A revolving door with shelves on to which parcels, provisions, books and other necessities from 'inside to outside' 'outside to inside' are put and revolved by, on the enclosure side, unseen hands.

The link with the outside world is through the extern sisters who live in the monastery though do not want to be enclosed; their work it is to drive the cars, shop, answer the endless rings at the doorbell, dispense hot cocoa and bread and cheese to tramps, welcome visitors and show them to the parlours, often receiving someone distraught or sobbing in need of help. They teach catechism to children, serve meals in the guest dining-room, tea in the parlour—every time I see a crocheted teacosy I think of the extern sisters. They man the book and art shop and look after the extern or public side of the church which is thronged on Sundays.

In those five years there were naturally interludes, domestic as well as literary, some successful, some definitely not.

The week before Christmas I always broke off to get ready, usually for the family, planning food and searching around for gifts and remembrances; particularly difficult was trying to think of something that would please the two remaining old Godden aunts, Fa's sisters, Dorothy—Dod—and Mabel who were in a nursing home. I knew that at Christmas the staff were shorthanded and so pressed they could not even take the two sisters to visit one another in their separate rooms, one bed-ridden, the other in a wheelchair. I imagined them at Christmas, immured in these rooms all the long empty day and thought that a parcel, divided into two so that each could have one with many small surprises individually wrapped in pretty paper would amuse and cheer them in their loneliness.

I tried to include all the things I had learned over the years they liked: detective story paperbacks, writing paper, fudge, shortbread and savoury things, a little glass of tongue, paté, chicken paste. I wrapped and tied them all separately. James carried the parcel to the post braving the queues. We had a letter back from Aunt Mabel.

Thank you very much for the good wishes and parcel. I expect you gave the order and someone else packed the things. The parcel was taken in to Dorothy but she felt she could not cope with it in bed and sent it in to me to deal with. It took me nearly three hours opening it and unwrapping the many things. Everything in tissue paper and cotton wool! It was a very tiring job. Coming by post, I see it cost 5/–!

In my diary. 1964

Jon's dilemma, over writing, the critics say, is that she takes too long brooding and thinking before she writes anything—but is it too long? Renoir once told me that when his father, that great painter, was accused of wasting time in different directions instead of settling down to painting, he answered, "Before you can light a roaring fire you have to gather a great deal of wood." I wish I could stand between her and these barbs.

They were uncalled for as Jon was writing her eighth novel, *In the Sun*. Soon we were to work together on an evocation of our childhood, *Two Under the Indian Sun*, the first move towards my books of memories.

How paradoxical it is that, through knowing nuns who are enclosed, I have met a world of people whom otherwise I would not have encountered.

That year I took Ben Huebsch to stay the weekend with the poet, Siegfried Sassoon at Siegfried's great house, Heytesbury.

With Siegfried I had already had a slight contact. On one of my radio readings of poetry for children on the B.B.C. I had read a poem of Siegfried's, 'Cleaning the Candelabrum,'*

> While cleaning my old six-branched candelabrum
> (Which disconnects in four and twenty parts)
> I think how other hands its brass have brightened,
> And wonder what was happening in their hearts:
> I wonder what they mused about—those ghosts—

Soon after I had a letter,

Dear RG   March 11th

Such a delightful surprise at tea-time when the Candelabrum emerged; and as perfectly read.

Yours
SS

I had not, though, visualised meeting him but Siegfried had become Stanbrook's poet.

The literary world still thinks of him as an angry young war

*From *Sequences*.

poet from his short bitingly satirical poems of the First World War. They have become even more well-known since their staging by Peter Barkworth and are in most anthologies, yet slowly, through *Sequences* to *Lenten Illuminations* and *The Path to Peace*, S.S. has become a metaphysical poet, the truest of our century, to be ranked in the clarity of his vision, with Herbert and Vaughan. I still have Dame Felicitas's letter to me about him and Stanbrook.

> He usually appeared on the first evening towards five o'clock, and at least in the first year I'd go to greet him and find him taut, handkerchief in hand, prepared to twist and torture it into endless cat's-cradles. He would look wildly round at the ceiling, the floor, the walls, as if seeking desperately for escape, and finally look at me, say, 'Hello!' in a pleased relieved voice, settle in an armchair, draw out his pipe, fold the handkerchief and put it away, cross his long legs and talk and talk and talk. He was wonderfully handsome and as he talked the years fell away and he looked ridiculously young. He could do anything with that face of his.
>
> There always came a time when he became completely receptive; I used to find him rather frightening then, for he listened to what lay beneath the words, to all that one was determined not to say. The pipe would be removed for an instant, the luminous eyes raised, a quiet question put, an understanding nod, and his sensitive brain registered—and never forgot.

"Go and see him," Dame Felicitas told me.

"Would he want me?"

"He has *asked* for you."

James and I drove seventy-six miles in pouring rain to Heytesbury.

> We found the house, dripping shrubberies, iron gates that would not open, the park with its Constable colours, cricket ground kept like velvet, the horses, two fillies exquisite with their overlong legs, fine necks. We rang and waited perhaps twenty minutes in the rusty porch under Palladian pillars, moss and grass creeping over the terraces. At last he, Siegfried Sassoon, heard and came. An unforgettable two hours followed.

We had tea in the library, he making the tea and talking, talking, talking, with the nervous walking about Dame Felicitas had warned me of, talking, switching the kettle on and off and then, gradually settling down to real talk.

Apparently the room grew colder; neither I nor Siegfried noticed but the unfortunate James, sitting as it were, on the sidelines, eventually asked, in an oddly respectful voice, if he could not make up the fire. "Good God!" S.S. sprang up and with pride dragged up a large model engine, beautifully made that had interior bellows; it blew up the fire in a trice.

At Heytesbury, everywhere you looked was beauty; the high corniced rooms, the wide marble staircase, the sheer size of the house yet there was a strong sense of his not being alone; Heytesbury still held the presence of his mother, his brothers, not the wife who had finally left him or of his son. There was, though, something ineffably lonely about the solitary place laid for dinner at one end of the long mahogany table that could have held thirty, but it was a poet's loneliness; Siegfried had that mark of the true poet, a childlike—not childish which is quite different and to be deplored in an adult—a childlike delight in things, that model engine, his candelabrum which was on his desk—I saw it as soon as we came in—above all in creation.

> That first March blackbird overheard to forward vision flutes and
>   calls . . .
> . . . shadows that bring
> Cloud castled thoughts from downland distances.
> Eyes, ears are old. But not the sense of spring,

something that Ben with all his wisdom, vast knowledge of books and people, his concern with human causes, never knew, could never know, delight and the immanence that is beyond delight.

> This hour, this quiet room, and my small thought
> Holding invisible vastness in its hands.

"My autobiography is my poetry," Siegfried always said.

Until that weekend, he and Ben had not seen one another for forty years. Had Ben, subconsciously, expected still to meet the rebellion and wildness that had so appealed to Ben's wife Alfhilde, equally handsome and unafraid? Ben had found it impossible to accept that Siegfried was now, of his own will, a Catholic. He had been like a fire, all sparks and rockets; now there was a steady shining flame.

You could have said this simple thing, old self, in any previous year.
But not to that one ritual flame—to that all-answering Heart abidant
  here.*

And how did Siegfried find this old man Ben? He still seemed to
think of Ben as the pioneer publisher who had braved American
opinion, upsetting what was thought of, then, as ideals, who now
was its doyen, guide and philosopher, portly, white haired with a
pince-nez.

We had a disastrous dinner at that long dining-table. Siegfried's
housekeeper was no cook; there was underdone fish with bones; a
small bone lodged sharply in S.S.'s false teeth so that he had to leave
us to finish alone. At last we took the wine into the library where,
though it was summer, the model engine came out and we lit the fire
which helped to dispel the chill. Both of them though kept taking me
aside all evening, to lament how old the other had become.

Ben and I left next morning—Siegfried did not come down.
Standing together Ben and I looked over the mossed lawns, to the
cricket pitch so kempt in contrast, as were the thoroughbreds with
their glistening coats. I was sad but Ben seemed oddly serene.

Next day he wrote to me:

I think you know how far I am from the elevated, spiritual life,
especially if it bear only a tiny religious tag, but when I parted with
S. and he held my hand and looked deep into me, I had the firm
feeling that our friendship of forty one years was unimpaired. As
to the most important factor in his life today, he pressed his hand
to his breast and said, with some intensity, "I have peace." It was
as if he wanted to set me at ease and answer the unspoken doubts
of the sceptic that I am. I felt content.

They were both to die in the same year, nineteen sixty-five.

Ben had spent the day before with us in one of the houses we had
been forced to rent after the fire—it took us more than two years
before we could find the house we needed. I was worried about
Ben because he kept falling asleep; when it was time to leave he
held my hand and said, "I don't want to go."

*From *Lenten Illuminations* published by the Stanbrook Press. After S.S. died Dame
Felicitas Corrigan wrote his biography, *Poet's Pilgrimage*.

We begged him to stay but he was catching a plane to Sweden early next morning. We decided James should travel with him to London. "I have a meeting anyway," said James. In the morning, still uneasy, I tried to ring Ben as early as eight o'clock to say goodbye. The Athenaeum Court hall porter answered. "Mr Huebsch please." There was a pause, then, "I am sorry Madam. There has been an accident."

"Put me through to the Manager," I said.

The poor Manager was grateful—fortunately James was in London. Ben had been going to Athenaeum Court all those years but no-one there knew anything about him except that he was a publisher. There was, of course no answer from his New York address—the apartment was closed. Alfhilde was in Sweden; it fell to me to tell her.

The room valet, who had been devoted to Ben, had been told to give him an early call and had found him sitting at his desk writing to his son, Ian. His pen was in one hand, a half-smoked cigar in the other. It must have been instantaneous so that he could not have suffered. I am sure it was as he would have wished.

Ben was cremated with a complete absence of fuss, so complete that it was difficult to take in its austerity. A few words would have dispelled the bleakness, he was a man of words but not one was spoken. Music? He had loved music; we sat in silence. Then I seemed to see him laughing at me gently. "Why cry?" he would have said. "It is time."

He was eighty-nine.

When *In This House of Brede* was in a readable draft, Lady Abbess, as we had agreed at the outset, appointed three of the Dames as 'devil's advocates' whose business it was to fault, challenge or endorse what I had written as need arose. "Three against one," I said. "That's not fair."

It was certainly formidable. This was in the days of the grille; the three sat behind it, upright in their black and white habits,* I, in my working slacks and jersey, was alone on the other side. As

---

*Benedictine nuns have not modified their habits as many Orders have done, making their Sisters look like dowdy Edwardian nurses which is sad as nothing is more becoming to a woman than a wimple and veil and, too, every part of the habit has a meaning, veil, belt, scapular, especially the cowl with those wide sleeves in which Jane had taken refuge.

in Limon the manuscript and notes were passed back and forth in a drawer that opened on both sides.

Once again I should not have been afraid; we thrashed out many good things. One of the nuns, Dame Katharine, ought to have been a detective story writer; I have never met anyone with a stronger sense of plot.

James came to Worcester that weekend and as a refreshment, we drove to Winchester; in any case, in my research I needed to hear the choir, especially the boys' voices. We had forgotten the beauty of the precincts, these twisting ways and lovely houses, the cathedral's long roof of palest stone, the nave fluted with arches.

I went at once to stand by Jane Austen's grave. Set into the stone floor of a side aisle, it looks as small and unpretentious as herself. "So many people ask for her," said the verger. "Was there anything particular about her?"

Simon married Mairie Angela Chisholm at Farm Street's Jesuit Church, the first marriage held there for a hundred and fifty years as it had been a private church.

Simon had gone far beyond me on the way to being a young tycoon, having inherited his father's brilliant flair for business and, since his marriage has been posted to America, Ghana, Malaysia, Vietnam, finally Paris in high positions but, still under the ability and vast preoccupations, the sweetness and wit that, for me, typify Simon are there as they are in his son, my godson, Shaemas, especially the wit. When at ten years old Shaemas saw the Pompidou Museum in Paris with its plethora of outside pipes, he said, "I think Monsieur Pompidou must be the patron saint of plumbers."

People who have read *In This House of Brede* have told me they could not put it down. I could not put it down either, not for those five years. "Promise me" said James, "you will never write another book about nuns. Write one about a brothel."

Ten years later I wrote a book about both.

Shades of Henry James

Rye is officially what is called an 'Ancient Town' attached to the Cinque Ports, those small ports along the coasts of Kent and East Sussex which were fortified against the French; so necessary were they to the Crown that, in twelve hundred and seventy eight, they were given legal privileges: exemption from taxes, the right to rule themselves and appoint their own judges. Rye church, standing high on its hill, makes a landmark across the marshes; the bells from the church were stolen by the French when they sacked the town in thirteen hundred and seventy-seven. Two years later the men of Rye sailed for France and brought the bells back, other 'belles' as well; many a true Rye-er is part French and to this day, instead of celebrating Guy Fawkes on November 5th, Rye has its own 'Rye Fawkes' when an effigy of a French ship is burned on the Salts, the flat ground below the old walls and along the river estuary where the fishing boats come in; after the bonfire there is a triumphant procession of decorated floats and, dangerous in the narrow streets, the letting off of fireworks as it goes through the town.

We were lucky enough to find a house—or houses—in the Citadel as the high ground above the walls is called; if you live outside the walls your address is Rye Foreign. Of the walls, only the Ypres Tower and the Landgate are left but the cobbled streets, the intricate little lanes and twistings, the hidden courts, are still there. Watchbell Street was where the Captains lived; it has its name from the warning bell that hung outside what is now the Hope and Anchor Hotel, then an Inn—the bell was rung if enemy ships were seen. Mermaid Street, now rated as one of the seven most famous streets in the world, was where the ordinary seamen lived—its lower end still holds what we called 'the hovels', cottages so small they might almost be hutches yet they now fetch enormous prices. The Street has, too, the Mermaid Inn, known the world over, and Hartshorn House, once called The Old Hospital because it was where the aristocratic prisoners-of-war from the Armada were kept while awaiting ransom; later, it was a hospital for soldiers wounded in the Napoleonic wars. Hartshorn House was the first house we had in Rye.

I had chosen this Ancient Town because the doctors had told me James would not recover from his breakdown, would not be able to drive a car again, nor dig in the garden, nor cope with any sort of business. In Rye you did not need a car, you could walk across the town in ten minutes; everything was close, almost too close, at hand. Also it had the Dormy Club, well known as a golf club but filled with retired admirals, generals, businessmen, actors, artists with whom James could fraternise. The doctors' gloomy predictions were quite untrue; within a year James drove out, through France and Italy, alone and overnight, to Milan to fetch me when I was taken ill; he became one of the personalities of Rye but never liked the Old Hospital. "It'll fall down," he said. "It must." Its date was fourteen hundred and ninety and he was glad when we were offered Lamb House by the National Trust.

Lamb House is one of the few National Trust houses that are leased privately to a tenant though we had to undertake the opening of the Henry James room and the garden two afternoons a week; also for special groups and occasionally for National Trust entertainments. Henry James lived in Lamb House from eighteen ninety-seven until shortly before his death in nineteen sixteen. It is the 'big' house of Rye, built in seventeen hundred and twenty-two by a local man, James Lamb taking in what used to be three smaller houses on the same site. James Lamb was ambitious and Lamb House is elegant with its brick mellowed to a soft red, its beautifully proportioned Georgian windows and fine canopied front door.

Inside it is a curious house as, though the entrance hall is spacious, none of the rooms is large. The oak parlour, panelled in pale oak, had one of the small fireplaces that were in all the rooms, Dutch tiled with Italian marble surrounds. Above the parlour was the King's Bedroom which sounds grand but was another small panelled room; I slept in it all our time there. It was called the King's Bedroom because George the First, coming back from one of his constant visits to Hanover—he was a Hanoverian and spoke little English—was caught in a storm so violent that his ship was driven ashore on Camber Sands close by Rye. James Lamb as Mayor—he was thirteen times Mayor of Rye—had with his jurors to ride out through the wild windy night to rescue his royal guest for whom he gave up his own bedroom.

It must have been inconvenient for everyone. Poor Martha Lamb was having her fourth baby and was probably hustled up to the attic rooms on the floor above out of earshot; the child, a boy, was born during the night. The King graciously stood godfather, the baby of course was named George and was given a silver bowl inscribed, 'The gift of His Majesty King George to his Godson, George Lamb. Anno Dom. 1725'. A story has grown up from this—for years I thought it was true—that Henry James saw this bowl—it had become by legend, golden—and the sight was the seed that led to his novel, *The Golden Bowl.**

In our first weeks as tenants of Lamb House my familiar poltergeist trouble came back. The old-fashioned kitchen was unbearable—no wonder Henry James's cook, Mrs. Paddington, had been bad-tempered. It was down three steps from the house level so that nothing could be wheeled into the dining room, everything had to be carried; it was dark, airless and dank. We raised the floor, knocked down the back wall making an open scullery which led to a sunny breakfast room once the apple store. The scullery had a glass roof which let in so much light that I was able to grow a plumbago there that climbed to the roof; the trouble was that its pale blue flowers shed their petals into the sink.

Though the renovation had charm, apparently Lamb House or its 'presences' objected to it and we were beset; the new boiler burst—as with Robert Lusty I seemed to cause explosions. New pipes burst, saucepans hurtled off their shelves, electricity fused

*The original bowl was sold by a Lamb descendant; it fetched the, then, enormous price of £1,300 and is now owned by the Marchioness of Cholmondeley.

but I was wiser now. I asked our priest to come and bless us. He did not say, "What? Bless a kitchen?" He even blessed the refrigerator. There was a sudden lull, then peace.

The manifestation was horridly real while it lasted yet in all the years we lived there I never saw the Lamb House ghost.

This was the ghost of James Lamb's brother-in-law, Allen Grebell who, in seventeen hundred and forty-three was murdered in mistake for James Lamb himself who, as Mayor and Chief Magistrate, had fined a butcher, John Breads for giving short weight. That night James Lamb was to have attended a banquet on board a sloop moored by the fishing Salts. Not feeling well, at the last minute Allen Grebell offered to take his place; it was a wet night and, there not being time for Grebell to go back to his house, James Lamb lent him his cloak. Coming back at midnight, Alan Grebell had to cross the churchyard where Breads was waiting with a large butcher's knife; deceived by the red mayoral cloak, he stabbed Alan Grebell twice in the back. Grebell managed to stagger the short distance to his house, opposite Lamb House where his manservant found him next morning in the sitting room by a burnt out fire, still wrapped in the cloak, pools of blood on the floor. He had been dead some hours.

Breads was hanged, his body put on a gibbet for the town people to gape at, while ever since Alan Grebell has haunted Lamb House.

E. F. Benson the novelist saw him:

Sitting in the garden one summer's day with the vicar of Rye I saw the figure of a man walk past. He was dressed in black and he wore a cape the right wing of which he threw across his chest over his shoulder as he passed. The glimpse I got of him was very short, for two steps took him past the open doorway—to Lamb House's secret garden—and the wall hid him again. Simultaneously the vicar jumped out of his chair exclaiming, 'Who on earth was that?' It was only a step to the open door, we hurried but there, beyond it, the secret garden lay basking in the sun and empty of any human presence. There was no way out of the 'secret garden' except the open doorway; it was enclosed by high walls.

The more I discovered about Henry James, the more I admired and lived with the novels, the more I had reservations about him as a man. In all the biographies written about him he seems so kind and gentle, such good company, such a good friend that my feeling seems almost shocking but his valet Burgess Noakes, a tiny rubicund man, still lived in the town. Perhaps because I was a woman and visiting, not interviewing, him, Burgess told me things that showed another side of his master, though not realising I am sure, that they were denigrating; nor did the little man ever swerve in his devotion to 'Mr. James.' Burgess had come to work for him when he, Burgess, was twelve years old and was with him when he died.

Henry James could have for instance prevented the merciless bullying of Burgess by the cook, Mrs. Paddington, whom Henry James called, 'a pearl of great price'. She bullied, as on the day when, at long last, the boy Burgess had saved enough of his modest wages to buy himself a suit, his first. He appeared in it one Sunday. "Think a lot of yourself, don't you?" said Mrs. Paddington and deliberately threw a pan of hot soup over it. Worst of all was an even more horrid story; Henry James had a small dachshund— I am not certain if it was the dachshund, Max, the biographers say he was so fond of, but Burgess was fond of it too, so much so that the little dog would haunt the kitchen. Mrs. Paddington complained, saying it made messes. Finally she told 'Mr. James' she would leave if it did not go. Burgess told me what happened. "Mr. James rang his bell. I answered it. I was told to take Max down to the vet at once and have him put to sleep." Max—if it was Max —was "only young," said Burgess. "He couldn't help hisself but I had to take him down—*and* bring him back in a bag—dead." Burgess winced as he told it.

In the corner of Lamb House garden is a dog cemetery with small plaques on the wall. I wonder Henry James could have borne to look at it.

In the summer he worked in the Garden Room* which had been built apart from the house as a banqueting room. He had begun to dictate his books, having unwillingly accepted a lady secretary of whom Theodora Bosanquet was the last. People passing in the street would hear his voice booming through the big

---

*In the Second World War a bomb fell through the roof of the Garden Room, destroying the whole. It has not been rebuilt except for the wall on the street which bears a plaque with Henry James's name and dates.

wisteria hung window that looked down the hill. It seems sure that it was the dictating that made the books increasingly verbose —those endless sentences with their multiple clauses that made even his usually admiring brother, William James the philosopher, complain.

In the winter the Green Study on the first floor was used; it was awesome for me following the Master there—he was not fond of women novelists with the exception of Edith Wharton who had often come to stay at Lamb House. The Green Study though was 'a perfect place for writing; again panelled, the panelling painted a celadon green, one window looked over the garden and caught all the sun, the other over a side courtyard and away across the huddled roofs of Mermaid Street to Winchelsea, another Ancient Town.

The garden was so large because it had been a 'deese' meaning in Sussex parlance, a drying ground for herring; dried they became the bloaters for which Rye is famed. A deese is common ground but James Lamb poached it, built high walls round it and made a garden, unexpectedly large in that congested town. It used to have a mulberry tree, dating back to when Queen Elizabeth I decreed that the town should grow mulberries, to feed the silk worms she had decided to import from China so that England should have its own silk weaving industry. The mulberry blew down in one of Rye's gales—the town stood so high it caught all the wind—and in our time the mulberry had been replaced by a great white cherry tree which spread above the lawn in snow white glory.

It was at Lamb House that I learned a little about old roses; there was a whole garden of them round a waterlily and goldfish pond where the Garden Room had once stood: the rich crimson Charles de Mills, Tuscany, superb deep crimson fading to purple; Queen of Denmark, glowing pink with green grey leaves, Fantin Latour of the pale pink double blooms, Madame Hardy white with perfectly shaped flowers that has a slightly lemon scent and one, which I came to treasure because of its fragrance, the dark dark red Souvenir du Dr. Jamain. I expect I sound like a garden catalogue; I do not mind if I do.

After Henry James's death no-one thought of keeping his possessions. They were sold at auction, his library dispersed but some of his books came back to Lamb House as gifts to the Henry James Room. Once it had been the telephone room; in his day a telephone was sufficiently rare and important to have a room of its own. It led off the hall; besides manuscripts, photographs, letters, books and a portrait of the Master by Burne Jones, it has James's French writing desk, two Chippendale chairs, a Sheraton-side table and, equally elegant, two of his silver mounted walking sticks, a Georgian wine decanter, a gold cigar cutter and his gold fob watch.

Lamb House could be called a house of authors. Henry James was followed by the Benson brothers, E. F. Benson the novelist and A.C., for years Master of Oxford's Magdalen College—I wonder if anyone has succeeded in editing the twenty-six volumes of autobiography he left. As the brothers disliked one another, E.F. inhabited the house in term time, then went abroad, leaving it to A.C. for the vacations.

E.F. used Lamb House and Rye as the setting of his Mapp and Lucia novels.

> I had seen the ladies of Rye doing their shopping in the High Street every morning, carrying large market baskets, and bumping into each other in narrow doorways, and talking in a very animated manner ... I vaguely began to meditate on some design. I outlined an elderly atrocious spinster and established her in Lamb House. She should be the centre of social life abhorred and dominant, and she should sit like a great spider behind the curtains of the Garden Room, spying on her friends, and I knew that her name must be Elizabeth Mapp. Rye should furnish the topography, so that no-one who knew Rye could possibly be in doubt where the scene was laid, and I would call it Tilling because Rye has its river, the Tillingham.

It would have been an extremely funny book if it had not been so spiteful. I think E. F. Benson must have been a spiteful man which Henry James was not.

In the sixties came Montgomery Hyde, politician, historian and writer of many biographies; he was our immediate predecessor, yielding the Green Study to me. Besides a *Life of Henry James* it was Montgomery Hyde who wrote the excellent small guide, *The Story of Lamb House* which is still sold on open days.

People came in a steady stream; I am told that now they come in two or three thousands but even then, though we employed two guides, I often had to help. It could be amusing. "Is it true Rumer

Godden lives here?" one lady asked me, and when I said "Yes,"
"Do you see much of her?"

"Far too much," I answered truthfully.

"Oh!" she was taken aback. "Is she ... temperamental?" She
was too polite to say, "Horrid."

> 'The pigs must be en pointe'
> 'Bird of paradise plume spines for whiskers'
> 'Five hundred dishes of plaster food for smashing-up'
> 'A tarentella with lettuces'
> 'The rain was *ordered*. Why hasn't it come?'

We had hardly settled into Lamb House when I had a call from
Mr. Stephens of Frederick Warne, publishers of Beatrix Potter. It
was to tell me of the film soon to be made of some five or six of
her books—those books that, she said, "she had made small to fit
children's hands." "Would I," asked Mr. Stephens, "write, for
Warne's, a book, not for the film but about the making of it?" It
was to be produced by Richard Goodwin who went on to make
the enormously successful *Orient Express* and *Murder on the Nile*.
The Beatrix Potter film would be designed by his gifted wife,
Christine Edzard—I think she is a genius—and danced by members of The Royal Ballet, with choreography by Frederick Ashton
who would himself dance Mrs. Tiggywinkle. The combination was
irresistible and made a wonderful change from *In This House of
Brede*.

I suppose I was asked partly because of my long study of Beatrix Potter; I had written an article on her fiftieth anniversary for
The New York Times, given talks on her *Tales* and had a long friendship with Leslie Linder, who had succeeded in deciphering the
secret code in which she wrote her journal as well as having written the best book on her art yet published. Not nearly enough
attention has been paid to Mr. Linder perhaps because he was such
a quiet little man but it should be remembered that, when he died,
he bequeathed his immensely valuable collection of Beatrix Potter's paintings, manuscripts and first editions to the National Trust.
When they were put on exhibition at Petworth House, Sir Frederick was asked to open it. "I can't make speeches," he said in
dismay.

"But you can dance," said Mr. Stephens and, when the moment
for the speech came, to the delight of everyone, Sir Frederick in

his morning coat, striped grey trousers, shoes instead of Mrs Tiggywinkle's black button boots, danced her opening dance.

I had to be at Elstree by at least nine o'clock each morning.

CALL SHEET.   NO: 20

Production TALES OF BEATRIX POTTER   Date Wednesday, Oct. 21, 1970.

Set   Ext. Farmyard and Int. Farmhouse   Stage 4 & 3

Director   Reginald Mills   Unit Call 8.30 am

ARTISTE	CHARACTER	D/R No.	MAKE UP CALL	SET CALL	
Pigling Bland Sequence (Farmyard - to complete)					
Sir Frederick Ashton	Choreographer	370		9.00 Rehearsal	
Alexander Grant	Pigling Bland	380	8.15	8.30 "	
Garry Grant	Alexander	381	8.15	8.30 "	
Sally Ashby	Mrs. Pettitoes	379	8.15	8.30 "	
Suzanne Raymond	Pig	430	8.15	8.30 "	
Anita Young	Pig	431	8.15	8.30 "	
Avril Bergen	Pig	432	8.15	8.30 "	
Graham Fletcher	Pig	433	8.15	8.30 "	
Deputy Dancers:					
Allard Tobin		426		8.30	
Allison Howard		425		8.30	

PROPS: 2 bundles and sticks, peppermints and sweet papers, 2 passports,
        Sandwiches for 2 pigs.

WARDROBE: Handkerchief for Mrs. Pettitoes.

ART: One pig gets it head trapped in gate.

SOUND: Playback required

Int. Farmhouse (to complete)					
Alexander Grant	Pigling Bland	380		From above	
Brenda Last	Black Berkshire	378	1.30	2.00	
Deputy Dancers from above					

PROPS: 2 stools, bundle and stick, peppermint (wrapped), 2 blue striped
        bowls, hot porridge, spoons, various foods including salami and
        sausages.

PLUMBERS: Required on set

ELECTRICAL: Simulated fire

SOUND: Playback required

CATERING: Trolley required for 30 people at 10 and 3.30 please plus
          jug of orange squash on morning trolley.

LUNCH: 1.00 - 2.00 pm

From my notes

On Stage 3. Two trolleys arrive piled with fresh turf. Trees hang
on chains waiting to be swung into position; stone walls in sections
lie about; ferns, outsize foxgloves, lettuces are stacked ready. There
are long trestle tables laid out with dishes of plaster food, highly
coloured glazed lobsters, hams, puddings and cups and saucers
ready for the Two Bad Mice to smash—as well as a plate of fish
that will not smash; it is made of fibre-glass, absolutely indes-
tructible.

All around is the usual paraphernalia of a set; perhaps the huge single camera used for front projection—or a smaller one on tracks, each with its surrounding tables and stands; there is the big play-back for music with its crew of three; tall lights on stands; ladders; giant fans to give life to ferns and flowers and clothes—if you catch the stream of a fan, you shiver while under the lights it is meltingly hot. The continuity girl's desk is moved perhaps two or three times in a day as are the folding canvas chairs, stools, litter bins. Far overhead are the arcs; the light men who tend them walk or sit behind them on narrow gangways; cups of tea and coffee, sandwiches and buns, are hoisted up to them on pulleys. "Save the arcs", the shout comes after every try-out, every shot, as much a part of film sound as the wooden clapper, or cries of, "Quiet please," "Two bells", "Everyone settle down".

Almost always there is a long wooden stand bristling with up-right pegs for the row of animal heads while, in the interminable waits, the wardrobe people play Scrabble and the dancers, in costume, sit on stools or on the grass banks, knitting or sewing, eading newspapers or doing crossword puzzles. Most of the girls bandage their foreheads and necks so that their heads look like graceful little nuns in contrast to the frills and furbelow or fur and feathers of the costumes spread around them; sometimes they keep their mouse or pig heads beside them with an oddly macabre effect.

Beatrix Potter could catch the smallest implications of character; in her *Journal,* she once wrote of the deaths 'by a sad accident' of a family of snails she had kept for a year, all of them distinct and named. 'I am much put out,' she wrote.

They had such surprising differences of character.

Sir Frederick did not despise such minutiae. Each animal, in each *Tale,* is a personality—and as each is well-known in every part of the world, he had to be careful—but his choice of dancers was fitted to the last whisker or frog leap.

The Fox asked for a dancer of panache who could bring smoothness and a grandiose manner to suit the wickedness of that 'sandy-whiskered gentleman'. For Hunca Munca, the bad little she-mouse, Ashton looked for quick neat hands and feet and an endearing quality, and found them in the Royal Ballet's Lesley Collier who, in real life, has the same brilliantly expressive eyes, the pretty movements of head and neck. Jeremy Fisher's prodigious jumps and leaps, each retiré, sauté and temps de poisson, needed a marvellously strong and controlled young dancer—it is not only the height of the jump that matters, it is the control in coming down; the slightest suggestion of a thud and illusion would be shattered. He was found in Michael Cole, a young dancer who had been inhibited by self-consciousness; he danced superbly in a mask.

film, its outdoor scenes shot in the Lake District, begins and ends with Mrs. Tiggywinkle—Frederick Ashton—his feet twinkling in minute black button boots. This delicate, silver-haired man, immaculately dressed—though he hated going to his tailor —could, at sixty-five years old, turn before your eyes into a hedgehog with her busy little hands, wagging petticoats, inquisitive nose and eyes. The mask did not transform him; he transformed the mask.

The masks were made by the Russian master, Rostislav Doboujinsky—whom everyone called Ton Ton—I had a pekingese named after him. No heads could have been more expressive but they were hot to wear, almost impossible to see out of; dancers of the Royal Ballet, though, are disciplined from childhood and the discipline held; there was never a display of temperament on the set. "Different from actors, by gum!" said one of the lights men; the crew had all had plenty of experience with actors!

The discipline was needed. The first sequence to be shot, involving six dancers, was the Mouse Waltz in quick waltz time with an intricate use of tails two-and-a-half yards long. None of the six was used to his, or her, mask and at first, in the waltz, they blundered into one another, tails got looped over heads, masks knocked crooked. "Spacing had to be exact, the use of the tails deft," said Johnny Town-Mouse who, with Mrs. Tittlemouse, was the most prominent. It was very very difficult and finally came down to a matter of using traffic lights with these experienced dancers, and Alexander Grant having to chant through his megaphone, "One two three," till he was hoarse—Alexander, as well as dancing Peter Rabbit and Pigling Bland, was assistant choreographer. They had to try again and again and the schedule was over-run; a day's shooting costs three or four thousand pounds. "One could buy Hill Top Farm for that," one can almost hear Beatrix Potter's shocked voice.

Not all the sequences succeeded but three in particular reached perfection. *The Tale of Jeremy Fisher*, *The Tale of Two Bad Mice*— the dancers were Lesley Collier and Wayne Sleep—and *Pigling Bland*, for which Alexander Grant, quite a heavy man, had to dance en pointe, suffering torture; added to which the male pigs had to wear a crotch in their breeches to keep their legs apart.

All the Ashton light-heartedness is in this *Pigling Bland* ballet, the wit and charm, and something deeper; there are moments, only implicit in the book, that become most moving in the ballet; the parting of Pigling Bland and his brother Alexander from the farmyard and their innocent excitement at being 'sent to market' —their mother, Aunt Pettitoes, knew very well what awaited them there; and the pas-de-deux between Pigling Bland and Pig-wig, the little black Berkshire sow. A classical pas-de-deux is almost always a courtship and this is deliciously tender, though 'tender' is a dangerous word when speaking of a pig—'Dear God, why did You make me so tender?' is Carmen Bernos de Gaztold's *Prayer of the Pig*. The pas-de-deux ends with a lift in which Pig-wig's head touches the rack of sausages and flitches of bacon, the hams and black puddings, hung up in the farmhouse kitchen.

It is always a strange, almost startling sensation for the author of any work to see what was put down on paper take on flesh and blood, but one guesses that when Richard and Christine saw her sketches translated into Ashton choreography, it exceeded even their vision. There is always 'translation'; Christine had not 'copied' Beatrix Potter's dresses and backgrounds, but translated them into costumes and sets; nor did John Lanchbery, Director of Music for the Royal Ballet and, since nineteen fifty-nine collaborator with Sir Frederick, 'copy' Victorian and Edwardian tunes; he translated them into music for *The Tales* exactly as Sir Frederick and his dancers made the characters live. No people could have been further from Beatrix Potter's experience than this quartet, nor she from theirs, yet it is these much travelled sophisticates—if people so unaffected, and simple in their tastes can be called that—who are the only ones who have succeeded in capturing her quality, its unique down-to-earth paradoxical blend of reality with fantasy, into another—and modern—medium.

To watch the film grow and record that growth was, for me, a rich exploration. It was not without problems; well, any dancerwill say you cannot learn without aches and pains and my small experience of film and dance expanded at least three quarters more in those weeks, which was not surprising as I was given help and encouragement without stint by everyone who worked on the picture and with whom I talked or, ideally, let them talk.

When the film was ended, Sir Frederick asked for the curtains of Mrs. Tiggywinkle's kitchen as a memento. I have a letter which is mine:

> Dear Rumer Godden,
>
> The book is beautifully done in every respect with real sensitivity on your part + complete understanding of our medium. You are very kind + flattering about myself
>
> with most grateful thanks.
>
> Fred.

Paula, after the fire, had re-opened her riding school and stables at Udimore near Rye. Though she lived at Lamb House, we seldom saw her as she was so busy and she soon had a full-time head girl, Frances and two younger girls part-time; one of the local dustmen, who had an obsession about horses, acted as night watchman. Besides having horses at livery, Paula provided hunters for the East Sussex hunt, and ponies for children; she taught endless children —"Us wants you to learn us riding," two small boys from the Council Estate told her. For herself she had kept the Arab mare

Titania and bred from her an Arab colt Sweet Sultan, the first foal I had seen newborn, staggering on what seemed legs far too long, with a sweet blunt little face and a pampas flock of a tail. Sultan became a winner.

I think Paula was for the first time truly happy and fulfilled. She had had a thorough, though hard, training first in Devon, then for some time with a well-known show riding family, the Bullens, going on to the Silver Hound. Later she did a course at the elite Crabbet Park which specialised in Arabs. We escorted her and her horsebox there—candidates had to bring their own horse—and were impressed when a voice announced over the intercom, "Miss Foster has arrived with Sultan. Miss Foster has arrived . . ." and a girl groom ran out to take Sultan, this for Paula who had worked so long and hard for other people.

At the end of three months there she—and I with her—went to Leicestershire where she took the British Horse Society Advanced Instructor's examination—she already had her 'Assistant Instructor's Certificate'. The advanced is a qualification held by few men or women in Britain; Paula did not gain the 'Dressage', lacking experience, but passed the exceedingly difficult 'Stable Management', which was slightly awkward as Crabbet Park's own stable manager took the examination at the same time and failed.

Watlands, Paula's stables was, like anything to do with animals, hard work especially on hunting day when each girl, probably with a livery horse each side of her, had to face the long hack home and, when they reached the stables, often wet through, frequently had to walk their charges up and down, up and down, until each had cooled enough to be groomed and fed; too many people returned their mounts in a lather of sweat.

To try and help, I would go up to the caravan which was the Watlands office and restroom, turn on the fire, make tea, hot toast or scones; usually I brought a home-made plum cake. Some of the riders who had ridden their own horses back would come in as well and there was a long horse-gossipy evening.

After one of these, I came back to Lamb House and said to James, "I have seen the man Paula should marry."

"Don't be silly," said James; we all knew what a touch-me-not Paula was, several young men had been given their congé. "He's probably after Frances."

By coincidence, in those years with James I went twice to Israel, once with him, again with Jane, coincidence, because both times the purpose of being abroad had been to go to Cyprus where Anthony was still stationed yet it seemed a pity to be so near the Holy Land and not see it.

Small scenes are still vivid; for one, standing with our guide in a dusty street in Cana when school ended and the children came out. It was an Arab school. A small girl came up to James and stood looking intently at him. Except that she was in school uniform with her dark tangled hair, expressive dark eyes, she might have come straight out of the Bible, especially when she said, "I am Miriam. I live in Cana."

"I am James," said James. "I live in England."

"So-o-!" It was a sigh of wonder, then she was off down the street. . . .

The Hill of Carmel was covered with wild flowers; there were wild hyacinths under the olive trees of the garden of Gethsemane, olive trees so old it seemed they might have been biblical, the leaves still showing silver in the wind. I particularly liked the little church of the hen and chickens as it is called from Christ's cry:

"O Jerusalem, Jerusalem, Thou that killest the prophets, and stonest them which are sent unto thee, how often would I have gathered thy children together, even as a hen gathereth her chickens under her wings, and ye would not!"*

There is another church even smaller, on the shore of Lake Galilee below the Hill of the Beatitudes; it is called the Church of the Primacy because it is the church of St. Peter, suitably built on a rock which is half inside the church, half outside. I stood outside, on the edge of the rock in the very early morning. No-one was about; fishing boats, empty, rode on the small waves that lapped the shore; the boats might have been Peter's, or Andrew's, James's, John's, Zebedee's. In the olive grove beside the church someone had lit a brazier fire; the unmistakable smell of burning olive stones and wood went up. When the fire was red, the same someone laid fish on a grid over it to bake. It might have been two thousand years ago.

*Matthew, Chapter 23, v. 37.

*   *   *

February

Fa died in hospital. He had been so miserable and frustrated that we were all as relieved as we were sad. Mam, we knew, though she did not say it, looked forward to what could have been an Indian summer for her to be happy in, though she too was gravely ill. She could listen to music which had been impossible while Fa was in the room, go to theatres without feeling guilty over leaving him, perhaps travel a little, be free. "I can't help looking forward to it"—in spite of herself it came out—but, though in those last years she could not bear to live with Fa, she could not live without him. She died that August.

My diary—Autumn 1968

> Jon has sold her cottage, a dreadful wrench. Fa and Mam have left Lydd House to Rose, well deserved as she had given up her work in India to look after, first Fa, then Mam. If she and Jon could have lived in the house and cottage side by side it would have been ideal but they could not afford this; Fa's pension died with him.

To begin with it was not easy for either Rose or Jon though Jon was changing into a new gentleness and patience which oddly enough, filled us with dismay as it did not suit her at all—none of us realised how ill she was.

It particularly dismayed me as it invaded her writing; the last two books she was to write, *Ahmed and the Old Lady* and *The Gardener* should have been strong—both had strong plots—but, though beautifully written, especially *Ahmed and the Old Lady* with its Kashmiri scenes, the spark had gone. Yet before these, and exactly in this time of uprooting and adjustment, Jon's old power had flared and she had written *Kitten with Blue Eyes*—called *Mrs. Spark Lives Alone* in America—of which the first chapter is surely one of the most frightening first chapters ever written; the newly widowed Mrs. Starr comes back to her big, supposedly empty, house and realises with a creeping fear that she is not alone in it. I had only to read that opening to recognise, once more, Jon's uncanny power of terrifying.

I had known all along that, when *In This House of Brede* was published I would have to face scepticism, scorn, sometimes real hostility—Christians have faced that since there were Christians but, as with them, it cost me dear. For one thing it lost me the interest and approval of many people I valued, for instance Noel Coward. As long ago as nineteen forty-six he had liked and applauded *A Fugue in Time*, even wanting to make a play of it—I wish he had but when he heard I was writing one myself he told me to persevere. "Never, never mind what the critics say," was one thing he taught me. "They don't—and can't—know." "Never have an efficient secretary," was another. "You'll come to rely on her so much that she'll get so close she could write your books for you—almost."

After one meeting with him—it was at a party—we went outside and talked—I wrote:

> It is difficult to describe what good the talk with Noel Coward did me; long and technical and full of wisdom. All the sillinesses fell to the ground. (I was stupidly overdressed for instance.) "Don't *you* go into the fashionable stream," he said. "Hold fast and use your head."

But now, "If she's going to write about nuns"—he had a phobia about nuns—"I've finished with her."

Nearer home in dismay because she was intrinsically part of me was Jon. "If you must write this you must," she had said, "but I would rather not read it."

"Why do you want to write this book?" Ben had asked at its outset. "Don't tell me *you're* religious." I, added to Siegfried, was nearly too much for Ben. "Why?" he had demanded, and my writing self, which is the more truthful, had answered, "Because nuns are dramatic. Theirs is the greatest love story in the world."

I still think it is.

Anthony's term in Cyprus had come to an end.

My diary.

> Jane, Anthony and the four children weary, dirty and crumpled arrived from Cyprus. Emma was on the verge of hysterics. She had cried all the way in the aeroplane, sticking her toes in at the airfield. "I want to go home." They got in after midnight and to bed at 3 A.M. Air travel is cruel on small children.

Anthony had left the army and was opening a branch of his brother-in-law's firm in Scotland; while he and Jane looked for a house we had the children in Rye. With flaxen polled Mark I have always had an affinity; Elizabeth who came next was one of those naturally—or unnaturally—good children. The first time I took her shopping she came back and told Jane, "I don't want to tell you but I think you ought to know; Grandmother goes into shops and buys things and doesn't pay for them." When Jane told her of accounts she was enchanted by them. "Could I have one?" Like Jane, Elizabeth had endearing freckles which to her, as to Jane, were a grief; both she and Emma had inherited the Hingley blue eyes.

The youngest was Charlotte, a witch of a child.

Rye. June 19th

I realise that for more than a hundred years there has not been a child at Lamb House.

James and Martha Lamb had had nine, including the small George of the King's silver bowl; their descendants must have had more but the last Lamb, Augustus Lamb was a celibate clergyman. After his death, in eighteen sixty-four the house was sold to a Mr. Bellingham; there is no record of his having any children. In eighteen ninety-seven, his heirs leased the house to Henry James who was succeeded by the Bensons, all bachelors. During World War II the house was empty until taken by an elderly lady, Mrs. Fullerton whose son was grown up. Montgomery Hyde, the next tenant, was also elderly as were James and I.

Now suddenly Lamb House was alive with those shrill, sometimes piercing child voices, scampering of feet—thumping of feet. There was sliding down the banisters, toys left on the stairs, a new untidiness, a quickening of life and, sometimes, in the hurdy-gurdy I had a strange sense of 'presences', two other children, silent, well-behaved. It was as if they were watching. Soon I knew who they were, Miles and Flora.* Our own children had brought them out of the Green Study where Henry James had conceived them. After our four had gone I had the feeling Miles and Flora were still there.

*Miles and Flora are the two children in Henry James's immortal story, *The Turn of the Screw*.

*　　*　　*

It was strange that Emma who, of the grandchildren had been the silent timorous one, should at five years old become the most original, outspoken of them all with a powerful turn of phrase. In their new home in Scotland, after years in Cyprus where there was then little television, they encountered it and became such little addicts, so disobedient over watching it that Jane, in a flash of temper cut the television cord which, I must say, shocked the village as much as it shocked the children, but Emma rounded on Jane; "You are the horriblest mummy in the world. I wish a tractor would run over you and grind you into dust." It could though be endearing; listening to Anthony's lame old father describing how he limped out to feel the sun and waves on a visit to beaches in Spain, Emma said, "I wish I were a walking stick and could have been with you."

She was unusually interested when in nineteen seventy-two I won the Whitbread Prize for Children's Literature—the first time it had been awarded.

I had written a book for children about a gypsy child in an English village and had not thought much of it, though James said it was special. Shortly after it was published, Peggy came and told me that I was wanted on the telephone by Whitbread's who had 'good news' for me. I could not think why a brewery should want to speak to me but imagined I had won a cask of beer in one of Rye's innumerable raffles. Instead, the voice told me *The Diddakoi* had won the Whitbread Literary Award for the best children's book of the year.

When Emma heard she exclaimed, "Has Grandmother won a horse? Oh I hope she has!" She had seen the Whitbread drays with their teams of shire horses. James told Major Whitbread this who immediately said, "Of course Emma shall have a horse. We'd be only too glad." Apparently, after years in the streets of London, the horses are retired and, if possible, good homes are found for them. Sadly, not even Paula could accommodate one of these mighty horses.

There was a splendiferous luncheon and a thousand pound cheque in a silver cigarette box. Kingsley Amis said of the book, "I only wish adult fiction was written half as well," which was warming. That luncheon was the last time I saw Harold Macmillan; frail as he was he came, and wrote to me afterwards.

From the Rt. Hon. Harold Macmillan

Telephone: 01 836-6633

4 Little Essex Street,
London, W.C.2.

26th October 1972.

It gave me great pleasure
to be present on Tuesday when you
received the Whitbread Literary
Award for your children's book
'The Diddakoi'.

This is indeed a great honour
for you, and for us as your
publishers

The Diddakoi won Holland's Silver Pen for the Children's Book of
the Year and was made into a beautiful, and truthful children's
television series directed by Dorothea Brooking who had made her
mark with her film of *The Secret Garden*. The series had to be called
Kizzy because it seemed that only in Sussex dialect is a diddakoi
someone only half gypsy. Everywhere else it means a 'tinker' or
'traveller' whom true gypsies despise.

October was a fortunate month for me. An advance copy of
another book for children arrived, this time a picture book for
smaller children, *The Old Woman Who Lived in a Vinegar Bottle*. An
old folk tale, this version used to be told to Mam by her nurse on
hair-washing nights. Mam told it to the four of us; I told it to Jane
and Paula; Jane told it to her children—on hair-washing nights—
so that in our family alone it is four generations old.

Why it was, and is, told on hair-washing occasions I do not
know either but the two went so well together that the story is
always connected in my mind with the warmth of the sun or of a
fire seen through tangles of wet hair, the smell of damp towels
and the fresh scent of shampoo.

As far as I know this was the first time this version had been written down; I added the cat, Malt.

It was illustrated by Mairi Hedderwick who, like the Old Woman, used to live in the Hebrides. She made the book perfection. How lucky I am that Marni could find illustrators like these.

In those years of living in Rye we had some, in Rye eyes, startling visitors; though plenty of overseas tourists visited the old town they did not usually stay in people's homes. We had, of course, many Indian guests and I had kept my link with Japan; *The Old Woman who Lived in a Vinegar Bottle* was printed in Tokyo which led to an embarrassing situation; sheets were sent over which Marni pronounced perfect. Then there was a long silence, so long with letters unanswered that she finally telephoned Japan to ask what had happened. An unwilling—and embarrassed—voice at last answered her; the book though in English, had been printed in Japanese fashion, back to front. It was such a loss of face that the whole print was burnt though I begged to have a copy as a souvenir.

Then there were the two Japanese Professors who came down from London for lunch and to interview me. One of them was, of all unlikely things for a Japanese to be, an expert translator of the Scots poet, Robert Burns, and regularly went to Dumfries for Burns's night when the haggis comes in accompanied by bagpipes, the Burns sonnet in honour of the haggis is recited and much whisky is drunk. At a different end of the literary scale, the other Professor had translated one of my books for children for a Japanese publication and wanted to record an interview to take back to his students.

It was a long and painful luncheon. James could not be there, added to which one of the pekingese was desperately ill, I thought dying, upstairs. Peggy and I took it in turns to escape up to him.

Knowing Japanese like fish for an opening course I had chosen smoked trout, as a Scots delicacy in honour of Burns; the trout were whole, on the bone; both Japanese ate the bones, spine and all. (Was it Japanese custom or did they think they had to, I wondered?) They had already had a difficult time when our dear but choleric neighbour had knocked the cameras out of their hands when they tried to photograph him on his doorstep. "I *will not* be photographed on my *own* doorstep as I am coming out of my *own* front door."

Three times Joan, Mrs. Manders' successor, approached with the main course, and had to retreat. At last the last bone was gone. We began to clear the plates when Professor Number Two announced that he had written a poem in honour of the occasion and would like to read it. "Afterwards?" I ventured—the lamb was spoiling.

"Now," said the Burns Professor.

It was a long poem. I heard the vet arrive. Peggy slid out but, in honour bound, I had to hear the poem through.

It seemed aeons before we were back in the drawing room for coffee. "What did the vet say?" I whispered to Peggy. "He'll be back in the evening," which was ominous but I could not go upstairs; it was time for the recording. Fortunately the Professors had been charmed and were happy; questions burbled out; I did my best to answer them, trying to think of those unknown students in that strange faraway classroom. It seemed to go well, the little Professor was all smiles when the bell rang. It was the taxi come to fetch them for their train.

They had begun to bow when Peggy, who was always practical, said, "Wouldn't it be wise to test the tape?"

We rewound it, set it going. There was not a sound, absolute silence. The little Professor had forgotten to press the button for sound.

There was no time to make another, their train had to connect with the flight back to Japan. "We'll record and send the tape to you," I promised. "But it will not be *my* voice with yours," he said in misery. Worse than that; again face had been lost. They literally crept out of the house.

Doctor Leon Edel, who had written the classic biographies of Henry James—there are several books—was one of the people connected with Lamb House I had most wanted to see; he had driven over from Lewes where he was staying.

Unfortunately, from my point of view, he had largely lost interest in Henry James and was avid for anything to do with the Bloomsbury Circle of which we had little, except that Virginia Woolf had come to Lamb House in Henry James's time, while later, Clive and Vanessa Bell had wanted to rent it, "Turned down because they hadn't a title," we were told which, of course, was not true; none of us tenants had had a title* but to Dr. Edel's

*Until Sir Brian Batsford who took it in nineteen eighty became the first.

as from The Athenaeum
Pall Mall SW1

11 August 73

THE SHELLEYS HOTEL
LEWES
SUSSEX
TELEPHONE: LEWES 2361-2

Dear Rumer Godden

What an enchanting visit we had yesterday! Lambs House was never more beautiful and the garden (in the bright sunlight) was exquisite. I felt profoundly — perhaps more than I showed — your dedication to the memory of the master.

Leon Edel

delight we were able to conjure up Barbara Bagnall, probably the last of the Circle; she had worked with Leonard and Virginia Woolf at the Hogarth Press so that he talked to her not to us. However he sent a handsome letter which added,

> I quite grudged the minutes you so generously made available to me for Bloomsbury. But, I shan't forget the vividness of your little ghostly tale of the missing pages.

The ghostly tale was another something that has never been explained, unless it was that my poltergeist had been at work again. On a day when I and James were quite alone in the house, though Peggy Bell was to come at two o'clock, at the end of the morning's work I left the book on which I was working, as yet only a few pages of manuscript, on my table in the Green Study and took, as is my custom, the pekingese out for a noontime walk. After it we had lunch and I went upstairs; the pages were gone. "James, did you take them?" he had not been into the room. Peggy Bell had arrived. "Peggy, have you seen . . . ?" She had not even been upstairs. Knowing what a careless person I am and forgetful, all three of us searched, even outside the study, turning out cupboards, looking on shelves, from the attic top bedrooms to the kitchen. No pages were found.

Two days later when I came into the Green Study in the morning they were back on my desk.

When I told that to Dr. Edel, "Ah!" he said, "Things like that do happen in Lamb House."

"Only to some people," I protested.

"Only to some," he agreed and added, "Perhaps you have to be a writer."

I was silent, thinking of my pen. It was at that same time and in the Green Study that I had come to the last word of the long stint that had been *In This House of Brede*. With the pen that had served me all the way through it I wrote, The End, the date and laid down my pen. It split from top to bottom.

It was good too, at Lamb House to be able to entertain, in such surroundings, some of the many Americans who had entertained us in the States, in particular Marilyn Marlow of Curtis Brown, New York, and the Orville Prescotts.

Was there a time when I did not know Orville and Lilias? There must have been because Lilias has shown me a stiff little letter beginning 'Dear Mrs. Prescott . . .' but it is hard to visualise it.

The only time, since I grew up that I have felt jealous was when Orville—Bill as he likes to be called by those near to him—in his bi-weekly/weekly literary column in *The New York Times* wrote, as a review of her new book of poems, *A Love Letter to Phyllis McGinley*. "You never wrote me a love letter," I complained.

"Didn't I?" asked Bill.

His book, *In My Opinion, An Inquiry into the Contemporary Novel* was the result of getting on for three decades of reading and reviewing: some cult idols came in for rough handling—Bill cannot bear any kind of pretence and several myths were exploded but to me he was gentle, including me in a chapter called, 'The Essence of Experience'.

He wrote:

Contemporary novelists are all citizens of the same unhappy world. When the winds of wrath blow up a tempest in Korea, Cambodia, Iran or the Potsdamer Platz they all shiver with equal apprehension. Whatever their nationality, their philosophy or their metabolism, they walk in the dark beside the same haunted graveyard. Some try to exorcise their fears with shouts of fierce defiance. Some, and they are a select and superior company, choose to speak in a quiet voice about less horrendous matters, the timeless truths of character and experience which are always the same, yesterday, today and to-morrow.

This is not a literary 'escape' (oh much abused word!), but a fitting and proper example of the shoemaker sticking to his last . . .

A few writers can persuade their readers that they have cast a ray of light into the secret places of the heart, that they have increased by a mite the sum of human understanding about life and love and death, grief and loneliness and the misery of growing up. Theirs is no mean feat. It is a high art to distil the essence of experience into fiction. And to do so without adding to the general din, in a quiet voice, with taste, simplicity and sure technical craftsmanship, is to contribute something rare and fine to a world sadly in need of it.

I did not need a love letter after that.

My Jane and the Prescotts' daughter, Jennifer, made firm friends; Jennifer's children have become my American grandchildren. Jane's youngest, Charlotte, when she was ten years old flew out by herself to stay with them in New England; the two small Prescott granddaughters came to stay with us in Scotland and in Rye, and so it goes on. Now, every time I cross the Atlantic, my first port is the haven of Bill and Lilias's small stone built house in New Canaan, Connecticut. I know it by heart; the white carpeted sitting room where the paintings Bill, with so much discernment has collected from all over the world; Lilias's flowering terrace garden under its pergola of clematis in lavender, purple, pink and red; my bedroom looking down on the dogwood trees. I always beg them, "Don't change anything—ever."

They came, of course, to Lamb House and, "What are you working on now?" was always Bill's first question.

Norah Smallwood of Chatto and Windus rang up. "We have here some albums of the most remarkable photographs of India I have ever seen. Can you and Jon come?"

Norah was the first woman publisher of eminence in London—in her own firm she was queen. She was Jon's publisher not mine but since *Two Under the Indian Sun* she had tried again and again to get us to do another book together. "A Life of Indira Gandhi," she had suggested.

"Norah dear, we know nothing about politics," and now, "You know about this," she said as she opened the albums.

There were three; one of them was entirely of patterns, patterns that escape most people's eyes, sand ripples, shadows of leaves, reflections from rods in a river, the mottling of the inside of an elephant's ear. Another was of people, chiefly portraits—I remember a ragged child looking on while other people ate; the third was of scenes, street scenes, country scenes, mountains, rivers, trees. Stella Snead, a tall sun-bronzed blonde, utterly unconventional, said she photographed by instinct—inspiration was nearer. Jon and I were captivated; Jon really stirred to new life.

A book of photographs usually has a short accompanying text, sometimes only captions; it remains a book of photographs. Books written about places and their people often have photographs as illustrations; they are illustrated books. *Shiva's Pigeons** does not come into either category—perhaps it does not come into a category at all—because it is an attempt to do something more, an attempt at what we, Jon and I, have always thought a book about India should be, a concept of a whole; this does not mean comprehensive—no-one could write or photograph a comprehensive book about India, not in twenty lifetimes—but whole in the way the rishis† saw all life as a whole, a concept in which photographs and writing should balance, neither being dominant but both blending and woven so closely together that to take away one photograph or to let a sentence run over its allotted page would disturb that balanced whole.

It was a formidable task. The chief difficulty was that Stella worked only in Bombay or New York which meant continual letter writing or telephoning. Jon and I, dyed-in-the-wool novelists, had not imagined what discipline it would be to follow the dictation of the photographer nor where she would take us. Above all we had to re-encounter India, she, whom up till then, we thought we knew so well.

*Shiva, third god of the Hindu Trinity.
†India's ancient sages.

India is always spoken and written of as 'she'; other countries are too, but the Indian 'she' has something of the quality of her own great universal Goddess, Durga or Kali; she has many different aspects and many other names because; she is manifold and has the feminine attribute of 'shakti' or energy. She is the wife or female aspect of Shiva; he is her Lord, which is why we reverently, we hope, took his name in the title.

At Lamb House in the breakfast room we had made from the old apple store there were two long trestle-like tables; on these we spread the photographs trying to arrange them so that a thread could be found to run through them to make a whole. They were on those tables for months as we eliminated, changed them round, put in extras, often cabling or telephoning Stella for an essential link which she hated to photograph saying it would be posed. It is remarkable that we have stayed friends.

Shiva's Pigeons makes no claim to be more than a conglomeration of glimpses, like one of Udaipur's embroidered patchworks that have little diamonds and rounds of mica mirror stitched into them so that the colours reflect and inter-reflect; move, and the colour reflections change; another person looks from another angle and sees a different pattern. It does not matter; little human points of view wax or dwindle as the cycles turn. Stella's camera could only tell what it had seen, and we could only try to interpret our pooled experience, what we had seen, heard, touched, smelled, and tasted since our babyhood days, learned since—there is always so much to learn—and always remembered because, like the pigeons, our spirits haunt the places we loved.

For us, with India it will always be the same. I had been back several times, once going out to stay with Dick and Nancy in their beautiful Company's house in Aurangzeb Road, New Delhi. Dick was its chairman now with an equivalent house in Calcutta. "You had better come soon," Nancy had written. "Dick retires next year."

If I were rich I should spend every winter in New Delhi, waiting until the flowering trees, jacaranda, acacia, golmohurs came into bloom before I left to escape the coming heat.

Perhaps I managed to convey a little of Delhi in the last novel I wrote of India, *The Peacock Spring*—seen through the eyes of Una, a fifteen year old girl; Una, with her governess the half-caste Alix:

The early morning was chill enough to be exhilarating; sunlight, though pale, seemed to spin round the car as they drove; every garden gave glimpses of lawns and roses. "Delhi is called the city of fountains and flowers," said Alix.

"Parts of Delhi," Una might have said. The roads were as busy and crowded as ant passages, with workers on their way to offices, shops, hotels, hundreds of brown legs, thin for the most part, walking or pedalling bicycles or rickshaws, or driving phut-phut taxis. The street cleaners sent dust up with their twig brooms, and little piles of leaves smoked on the sidewalks, giving off a clean acrid smell.

Dick took us where I had never been, to Rajasthan, in particular to Jaiselmur The Golden City which had few tourists then; we were the only Westerners walking in the fabulous Street of Carvings where every house, balcony and eave was carved, fretted in golden coloured sandstone, a miracle so far out in the desert.

Our visit there was under the auspices of our friend, Muchu Chaudhuri, who was then Commander-in-Chief of the Indian Army, travelling in a military and escorted plane, met by the Rajah of Jaiselmur and a parade of troops. Muchu and Dick were entertained with a banquet and dancing girls while Nancy and I had luncheon in the harem. When it was time to leave, again in Muchu's plane, with another in escort, as soon as we were airborne, out of the lavatory, veiled and salaaming, came a dancing girl, dressed in turquoise satin tunic and trousers, small scarlet slippers and tinkling with jewellery. It seemed Muchu had, from politeness, admired her and she was a present from the Rajah. Poor little creature! The plane turned round, went back, and she was ejected under escort.

I went to South India where I had not been since I was a child, but this time to Periyah one of India's finest game reserves where we stayed, not in its hotel but in the official's bungalow rest house on an island apart. The charm of Periyah is that you do not go to see the animals by car or caravan as in most reserves but by water, so quietly that you can come silently close. We had a light native boat, small enough to be paddled by our guide—I was with Eric da Costa, perhaps India's most esteemed journalist. We started before dawn and on the second morning, "Hush," whispered the guide. "See that." On a spur of land hemmed by water, elephants were walking in a circle, round and round, bull elephants, one behind the other, so close that trunks and tusks touched tails. Inside the ring were the cows with their young calves, all facing inwards and in the centre—we could not see clearly because of the huge legs and waving trunks—but, "An elephant is being born," whispered the guide.

What I remember about Periyah even more vividly than that rare sight is something that still gives me nightmares. My room was, as usual, stonefloored, level with the verandah which was some four feet above the garden; there were no doors, only palm leaf shutters half-way up. The room held a bed, mosquito netted, a wardrobe, chair, bedside table, and had an old-fashioned Indian bathroom.

I said goodnight to Eric who had work to do, heard him go away, it was to seem far away, down the long verandah.

I went into my room and stopped. In the middle of the floor was an enormous tarantula, quite eight inches across, pale grey, black and orange with thick black legs, its huge malevolent eyes looking at me. I knew how poisonous were tarantulas but not if they attacked on sight.

Backing out, I called till I was hoarse. A gnome of a watchman with a lantern and a stick was supposed to be on guard; there was no sign of him. I did not even know where Eric's room was. He was probably typing and could not hear. At last, step by step, watching the monster, I went towards the bathroom which, being primitive would have, I knew, a stool where if you took a bath you sat to pour water over you with an outsize mug made of metal. It was the mug I wanted. Thank God it was heavy.

Slowly, cautiously I came up behind the tarantula, clamped the mug down over it on the smooth stone floor, holding the mug down with both hands—the spider was amazingly strong; it pushed and leaped almost jerking my hands away but I managed to push it, inch by inch, to the edge of the verandah. There, in one movement, I took off my hands and with a kick sent mug and beast flying into the darkness, rushed into the room, opened the net and leaped on the bed not waiting to undress. I did not dare to get out all night.

Next time I went to Delhi was to check my Indian novel, *The Peacock Spring*. Nancy and Dick were gone.

They had bought a beautiful old house—Erasmus had once lived there and it still has part of a Roman Wall—in the same village, Aldington in Kent as Jon and Rose. Delhi seemed strange without Nancy and Dick—Nancy had lived in India longer than any of us—and it dawned on me that now I did not know a single Western person in the whole city, except that I had an introduction to the American Ambassador. All my friends there were Indian. I liked that.

> Two young women, overheard talking in a train about Rumer Godden, agreed that she seemed to know as much about the running of a large household as if she were accustomed to doing it herself. "But of course she couldn't possibly," one of them concluded. "She probably has to have everything done for her because she needs all her time for writing."

This was in an article sent to me by an American magazine. I remembered the interview and the interviewer and how, with mutual sympathy, we had talked once again of the difficulties of a professional woman's life, the everlasting conflict between the domestic 'angel in the house' and the 'creative angel'—though 'demon' might be a better word. The kind lady had written that she thought,

> Rumer Godden simply accepts them as 'angels,' and follows the guidance of whichever needs to take precedence at that moment,

which I suppose in a way I do—in any case there is, after all, no option—but by providence, for a great deal of my life I have had things done for me and have had at least some staff. 'A staff of hope to lean upon.'

Our first real gardener was at Little Doucegrove; we could not do otherwise but employ him as he went with the house. Percy Piper and his sister Dolly had been born in the middle cottage of our three; "Fifty-seven years I've lived here," said Dolly. Though they had no water, not even a sink, they were content. I hope that white squirrel, Sheila Kaye Smith, looked in at their window to see the new pipes, sink and loo we were able to give them. "We have found a father and mother," Dolly said which was disconcerting as she and I were the same age.

Percy was more than content when he realised what James was doing in the garden. Percy worked slowly, methodically, we never knew him hurry; if you asked him the time he would slowly straighten up, take from his waistcoat pocket a small Colman's

mustard tin; inside the tin was a handkerchief which he un-
wrapped; in the handkerchief was a large silver watch—I think it
is called a 'turnip watch'; he would open its case, look and tell you.
Then it had all to be put carefully back again.

When it was time to stop work at four, he would break off
five minutes early, put on his coat—he was wise enough to know
you must not stand about in the least wind if you have been
sweating—then meticulously clean his tools and put them back in
the shed. One of the workmen borrowed his spade and broke the
handle. "It was old," was said in defence. "Aye," said Percy. "It
lasted me fifty years and would have lasted another fifty—proper
handled."

He had no need of weather forecasts as he could tell the weather
in advance and in his own language. "T'will be a butterfly day,"
he would say of a day of sun and cloud. "There'll be a tempest,"
he would predict.

After Little Doucegrove was burned down and the new owners
had rebuilt it, every Christmas Percy and Dolly would come and
see us in Rye, he bearing a sack of perfect sized logs for a town
house, Dolly with a bunch of the prize chrysanthemums she grew
in her minuscule greenhouse. There were never a brother and sister we honoured more.

Living in so many different houses in so many different places
we had, willy nilly, many changes of staff so that many faces,
many voices say, "Remember me. Remember me." I can only pick
out one or two who made the deepest mark.

I have hardly ever had to send anyone away; the partings came
about through circumstances but I had to dismiss Arlette and will
not forget it.

A fiery little Belgian, and pretty, with truly violet eyes, she came
to us at Lamb House when our prop and support Mrs. Manders
was ill and it seemed likely she would have to retire. Arlette had
a pathetic story; in her first post she had got into trouble and had
an illegitimate child—all her employers had been, it seemed, vil-
lains of unspeakable cruelty. She had never stayed anywhere for
long, which ought to have warned me but I knew François, the
little boy, was the pivot of Arlette's life and, "She has never had a
chance," I told James. "You try living in someone else's house
with a child on sufferance. Let's give them a home"—we found
them a small flat and helped to furnish it. "She'll last a week,"
friends told me. "She's been with us three months already," I was

able to retort but Arlette, it seemed, had to destroy; there began to be a falling out, with Peggy Bell, with our cleaner, Mrs. Simms, tradespeople, even visitors.

It culminated on a day when I was being interviewed for radio —the interviewer was to stay for lunch. Shut away in the Green Study we had not known what was happening in the rest of the house but, as we came out at half past twelve, we heard a fracas from the kitchen. I hastily took my interviewer to the oak parlour, introduced him to James, went to the kitchen, opened the door and narrowly escaped being hit by a frying pan thrown, not at me, but at Mrs. Simms, who retaliated with the mop she was holding— Mrs. Simms had a temper too. Arlette had picked up a heavy kettle when, "Stop this. Stop it at once," I thundered.

Both were scarlet in the face; Mrs. Simms I could see was close to tears. Both gave me notice at the top of their voices.

"Nonsense," I said to Mrs. Simms who was shaking. "We're not going to part from you. Come upstairs." I put my arm round her and took her away leaving Arlette standing by the cooker panting with hate, her eyes venomous. "Put on your coat and go home," I told her over my shoulder. "I'll talk to you this afternoon."

"I go. I go now, and not come back."

I paused. "Arlette," I said, "think of François."

"François is my business. Mine." I thought she would spit.

She did more than spit. We were having a lunch party next day, too large for me to cope with; mercifully, Mrs Manders, who always rescued us, came back. It was in honour of Ben Travers the playwright's birthday, the same Ben, urbane, simple, delightful who wrote *Cuckoo in the Nest, Rookery Nook* and, when he was ninety, *The Bed Before Yesterday*. I had planned what he especially loved, a summer pudding made with all the fruits of early summer. Mrs. Manders brought it in personally, oozing juice and goodness but as one guest after another tasted it they put down their spoons. It appeared Arlette had made a secret visit to the kitchen and changed things round, putting salt where the castor sugar was kept and other such things.

She had gone round the town as well. Our fishmonger rang up. "Your thirty-nine pounds of salmon have arrived. Would you like them sent up?"

"Why thirty-nine, not forty," James groaned.

"Arlette is an artist," I said.

The butcher was more sensible. "*Five* saddles of lamb is an awful lot of meat. Are you sure, Madam?"

I had to admire the ingenuity of the revenge but James and I were both sorry about François, jerked so suddenly out of a place he had learned to love and trust.

Chief of all staff, for us, was Mrs. Manders.

She walked into our lives at Little Doucegrove on a cold dark February evening, walked in through the back entrance—she knew the way—and unannounced, knocked at my study door. If it had been the Archangel Gabriel, it could not have been more blessed.

All winter the tug-of-war between writing and domesticity had gone on, tearing my work and time—and me—into rags. The too big house, the demands of the church, James at home all day. Why, oh why had we left London where cooks were not difficult to find, and come to live in an isolated house in the country where it seemed no-one except Fay who cleaned and did the church flowers would consent to work?

That evening, putting the finishing touches to a chapter between dashes to the kitchen, I was near despair. Then came that knock. "Who is it?" I called impatiently.

In came a short, plump person, wearing boots, mitts and such a large anorak with a fur-trimmed hood that she looked like an Eskimo—but an Eskimo with fair hair and blue eyes who beamed confidence and, better still, capability. She had heard, she said, we were needing. . . . Heaven obviously had sent her but I was still doubtful.

"But can you come in the evening?" I asked.

"Why not? I always did."

She had, it appeared, been cook for a while to Sheila Kaye Smith and Penrose, but I still thought of our two miles' distance from the village—"There's a bus," said Mrs. Manders—the quarter-mile of dark and lonely drive. "I know this place like the back of my hand," said Mrs. Manders. "But waiting in the lane, in the dark and cold, for the bus to take you home?" I said doubtfully.

"I have my torch," and, "I'll be in tomorrow," said Mrs. Manders. There were to be tomorrows and tomorrows.

Mrs. Manders was not simply a cook, she was a chef with long years of training under master chefs in big houses, on the Train

Bleu and finally at the Dorchester Hotel. She had been cook to the Countess of Warwick which had been the highlight of her career after whom, "Respectfully," she said, she had named her son, Warwick. She had a tremendous veneration for birth and breeding—and could tell you as much about the Royal family as anyone in England but, then, choosing beer for herself rather than sherry, she would say, "Proper common I am." Yet she loved, and could look after, linen and embroidery, upholstery, clothes, silver, polished furniture. Sir Osbert Sitwell's cook used to advise him on modern paintings. Why not? A true artist has an instinctive understanding of all arts.

"*Look* at this beautiful cabbage!" Mrs. Manders would say. "Look at the firmness and the colour! It still has the dew on it, it's so fresh."

One evening I was, again, in my study writing when Mrs. Manders burst in, her face flushed, eyes blazing with excitement. "Look!" she cried. "Look!" What a beauty," and down on my table, on and among my pages and notes and books she plopped an open cardboard box, from which waved two enormous pinkish apricot things like claws or pincers. "Isn't it a beauty—straight off the boat!"

"But what is it?"

"He, not it." Mrs. Manders was put out. Then, "He's a crab. The biggest, finest crab I've ever seen and so fresh! Mr. Manders has just been down to the boats. We'll have it tonight! It would be a sin not to."

Mr. Manders was often pressed into service. He brought home-grown tomatoes and vegetables; in sweet-pea time there were bunches of sweet-peas, and in spring, lilies of the valley.

It was not only in favourable times. As Mrs. Manders tells in the book we eventually wrote together:*

There was that early morning, in the soaking rain, when our doorbell rang and there was Miss Godden with her daughter, both ashen white under smoke and grime. The old house had been burned down in the night and they had brought the pekingese to me to ask if I would take them in. Those two scamps of pekes have spent much of their time with me ever since.

*Mrs. Manders' Cook Book. I still use her recipes.

We were left homeless, possessionless and for more than two years we had to camp in furnished houses, Mrs. Manders still came though the kitchens were awkward, the cookers sometimes dirty, the china poor with queer oddments of plate.

In her cook book I wanted her to put as much as possible in her own words. There is a chapter called 'Parties':

> I love the feeling of a house when there is going to be a party; the bustle and expectation, the planning of the menu, the table and flowers, the getting out of china and glass. It gives a new thrill to the usual domestic round and conjures up the resources of the house. I love the cooking, though it is hard work, as I like to do it all myself—with someone to act as kitchen maid if possible—'Me', R.G.
>
> I remember a June party, a buffet for twenty-four when the cloth was white, embroidered with white roses, and we had real white roses to match. The cut glass glittered, and the silver shone in the way I like to see.
>
> Miss Godden says I make it all sound too splendid. Well, it was splendid but not at all splendiferous; everything was home-made and we did it all ourselves, she, her husband and me.

Before the Reformation there was a belief that, even if the food was simple, the home poor, every time the table was laid for a meal it was a humble reflection of the Last Supper; food was holy, not in a ritualistic sense, but as a blessing from God. That reverence seems lost in our lives today yet still a belief persists—and I have heard doctors endorse it—that if food is cooked with care and love, and, however plain it is, served without haste and invitingly, there will be no indigestion or bad tempers in the family. That was true of Mrs. Manders' cooking; there was always a feeling of well-being and ease after her food.

Shining Popacatapetl

There are two things in my long working life that have perhaps been of use and have also given me pure pleasure, pure because they were without alloy in that nothing happened to spoil them. They hold no tinge of regret; one is my work for children's literature—in Winona, Wisconsin, a children's library has been called after me—I went to Winona to open it, how I wish May Massee could have been there; the other is that in England for some ten years, among schools, state schools, especially primary schools and especially in Kent, my family county, I became known to children as 'the poetry lady'.

My diary. November 1973.

On a dingy afternoon in one of the dingiest streets in London, suddenly, in the dirt and slush, above the grind and din of the traffic, lorries, vans, cars and buses—their scarlet the only bright colour in the November afternoon—I hear children's voices. There is nothing unusual in that; it is half-past three, the time children come out of school, but these are not children's voices in their usual chattering noise; they are chanting two words, 'Shining Popacatapetl',* and I

*From W. J. Turner's "Romance":

When I was but thirteen or so
I went into a golden land,
Chimborazo, Cotopaxi
Took me by the hand.
I stood where Popacatapetl
In the sunlight gleams.

I walked in a great golden dream
To and from my school—
Shining Popacatapetl
The dusty streets did rule. . . .

298

feel an unforgettable surge of pleasure, gratification and reward because these children, an hour earlier, have been at one of my poetry
readings.

In the tour of that autumn I had read poetry to more than eight
thousand children of all ages and backgrounds, some of them even
tougher children than those grubby little London sparrows—and,
as had happened time and time again, some, at any rate, of the
poetry had stayed.

It had begun quite fortuitously. As a writer for children I needed
to be in touch with them and after the poetry readings at the
B.B.C. I told David Davies of the then *Children's Hour* that I was
going to try and do some readings 'live'. He said "Where?" Without thinking I answered, "The London Libraries." He said, "They
will never let you, and, certainly, never pay you." They did and
they have.

My idea was to show children that poetry is meant for pleasure,
exploration, entertainment as well as learning which did not mean
we read only light verse. Of course we read some—but, even for
children as young as seven years old, we gave them Shakespeare,
Milton, Chaucer, Wordsworth, Manley Hopkins, Dylan Thomas. I
say we because for each season I engaged two young actors, pref-
erably straight out of drama school—L.A.M.B.D.A. was the best
—a boy and a girl amenable to training—we had to rehearse and
rehearse. They became extraordinarily versatile, necessary because,
though we had programmes on different themes, *Round the Day*
and *Round the Year* were two of the popular ones, we never gave
exactly the same programme twice; I had to gauge our audience
as we went along and would say, in an aside, "Leave out the
Thomas. Read *Celandines* instead." "Cut . . . such and such." "Read
such and such again."

Both boy and girl wore casual clothes; we had no props except
three large hollow wooden cubes painted pale grey and large
enough to sit on; they could be built up like a child's bricks to
make a tower, a post box, a milestone, put together for a couch;
we also had a red spotted handkerchief and a stick. During those
years, though often in London, we travelled around the country
from Kent to Yorkshire. James drove us; we and the actors stayed
in the same hotel but they were free to do as they pleased when
not working. We paid them two pounds a reading, worth perhaps
twenty pounds today. It was hard work, often we gave four read-

ings a day so that, with expenses, they earned a good total each week and gained a great deal of experience.

I tried not to have the children sitting in rows but in a circle round us; if teachers were there we asked them to sit among the children or at the back and I always asked the headmaster or mistress if they would mind if we made a noise as, for instance, when the children joined in for the refrain of a ballad. William Morris's *Two Red Roses Across the Moon* was a favourite.

> There was a Lady lived in a tower
> Two red roses across the moon . . .

Then

> There was a Knight came riding by
> Two red roses across the moon.

The refrain sank to a whisper when the Knight passed by the Lady—he had to as the battle was set—rose to a shout as,

> You scarce could see for the scarlet and blue
> A golden helm and a golden shoe.

—William Morris always had wonderful colours—

> So he cried, as the fight grew thick at the noon
> Two red roses across the moon.

It almost raised the school roof. It was like conducting an orchestra.

It was not always easy; as with speaking you had to win your audience; even the time of day made a difference. What could be more unpropitious than giving a poetry-reading at nine o'clock in the morning to sixth form boys as happened to us at Dover College but I tried not to refuse a challenge; also it was good for our young actors to stand up to adversity—they would have plenty later on. Inevitably we had our failures, but they were ten wonderful years. I especially remember Smeeth Primary School in Kent.

When we went into the country where schools were smaller, one school would act as host to perhaps three others to get enough children of the right age to make an audience. This happened at Smeeth. Smeeth School was host but so many children applied that we had to do two readings with a coffee break between. For the

Shining Popacatapetl | 301

second reading the Smeeth children who had been at the first were told they could choose either to go out to the playground and play or come to the second reading. We did not know this, only that our audience seemed unusually large; they had all chosen to hear us again.

Added to this, while we were having coffee, the 'infants', five and six year olds, who had been banished to another room were allowed to come in and look at the place where we had been, our blocks, stick, spotted handerkerchief and books. I thought this a little pathetic and after the second session asked the headmistress if she would let us repeat the last two poems, a pantomime and a carol* and allow the infants in, which she did.

Afterwards we realised that the Smeeth children had sat through two forty-five minute recitals plus ten minutes for the repeat—a hundred minutes of poetry. How many adults would do that?

I was not surprised. Children are naturals for poetry because they and poets are akin; perhaps an unusual view of children yet it is true.

Upon this planet there dwell two strange races of people. The first is a tribe small of stature and delicate of limb, the members of which make their way into civilised society one by one, arriving among us entirely unable to look after themselves and quite ignorant of our language. After a little while, they learn our speech and something of our habits ... but they take little interest in the things we prize most; their ideals are not our ideals ... they see a universe quite different from that which is familiar to us. Our eyes are lamps in which the oil of reason burns, their eyes are charmed casements through which the moon of imagination pours—until we teach them to forget. We have to teach them or the work of the world would never get done. Yet there are a few, a very few, who do not forget ... and these form the second race of strange beings; they are the super-children, the Johnnies-head-in-air, at whose stumbles the world laughs because it cannot see the stars on which their gaze is fixed ... they take no part in that all absorbing task of our civilisation: the acquisition, transformation and distribution of matter ... but they are the true creators ... they bring cosmos or beauty into a world which is without form and void. And so they have the name 'Makers or Poets.'†

*The programme was *Round the Year* which ended with Christmas.
†*The Shakespearean Scholar*. Professor Dover Wilson.

Until I read that I did not know that the word 'poet' came from the Greek word for 'maker'.

We kept to our ideal of poetry for pleasure, making it not only alive but part of every day, giving perhaps a richness, a new light to the world around us—and we were rewarded as, for instance, when we gave a late afternoon reading for seven to ten year olds in the library of one of the poorest of the poor parts of London; the librarian told me that in the holidays and on Saturdays, the children lived in the library and how she hated having to turn them out into the streets, especially in winter, when the library had to be locked while the staff went to lunch.

We always liked coming to St. Luke's but that afternoon, Anne and David, the two young actors who came with me, had asked if they could get away promptly as they had a date that evening. We read *Round the Day* which ended with poems about stars.

First we read part of Gerard Manley Hopkins's

> Look at the stars! look look up at the skies!
> O look at all the fire folk sitting in the air . . .

as read by David it was wonderfully evocative—everyone looked skyward. Then Anne came softly in with a concluding jingle which, jingle or not, is poetry.

> Star light. Star bright.
> Last star I see tonight.
> I wish I could, I wish I might
> Have the wish I wish tonight.

The reading was over but we were surrounded.

"Miss. Miss. Can we write that last poem down?" Mysteriously, bits of paper and pencils had appeared. "Miss. Can we?"

"I'm sorry. There isn't time. David and Anne have an appointment."

"Oh, *no!*" Devastation. "No! Please, Miss. *Please.*"

Both David and Anne elected to stay, going among the children to help them. I can still see the small heads, bent over the tables, the little vulnerable white necks, as the magic words were softly caught on paper.

Star bright. Shining Popacatapetl.

In those last years at Lamb House a quietness fell on our lives. Mrs. Manders had died but, in any case, though she had excellent successors, we had to do less and less because James had developed diabetes, the 'maturity onset'.

It is impossible for anyone to know the distresses of diabetes unless they have lived with it; the 'sugar turns' as they are called, are often mistaken for drunkenness which is cruel. Not allowed any sugar, when these turns come, the victim has to take sugar and quickly; I learned to carry it and a bottle of Coke everywhere we went; Coke is a marvellous help as it is full of sugar and it is easier to get a large frenzied man to drink it than to eat some dozen sugar lumps. James tried valiantly to be normal but on our usual visits to London, eating out, as he loved to do, became more difficult; the restaurant had to be airy, tables not close together. More and more we relied on the Hyde Park Hotel's spacious dining-room where the waiters knew us and were wonderfully helpful. At the first sign of trouble, I would signal to the head waiter or his second; in minutes a glass of Coke would appear, reinforced with sugar.

Graham wrote to me after he and Dorothy had dined with us one evening at the Hyde Park; in the evenings the restaurant was magical, its long windows looking into the Park and its lights.

> What a nice civilised hotel is the Hyde Park.
> Poor James, I hope we didn't overtire him. He is marvellously brave in coping with such a tiresome complaint and marvellously resilient in refusing to allow it to hamper him.

But we soon had to give up London. I had to sell the cars; it was too dangerous for James to drive and he would not let me. Slowly, everything he most prized began to be taken away from him.

Parties, of course, were over except that we gave a dance for Paula, she who had always had a horror of parties and dances. "You're not going to make me have a *dance*," she had said on her twenty-first birthday. Instead we sent her on a trip to India and Kashmir where she went to Dove House. Now suddenly she wanted a dance.

Banquets had been given at Lamb House in James Lamb's

day but I do not think there had been a dance. It was difficult to organise in that congested town. I was worried about the band keeping our neighbours awake and asked that, after midnight, it would try and play quietly. As it was, many neighbours watched from their upstairs windows. I had gone round to see them all to warn them and found as I might have known, they knew all about it already.

It was a harvest festival dance with the terrace transformed into a pergola of vines and grapes, old farm implements we had found, sheaves of wheat, cornucopias of apples and, a Sussex speciality, corn dollies hung on yellow ribbons.

The man who came to help us position the wooden ploughs and haycocks, hang up the yokes, sickles and sheaves, set up the supper tables, was he whom I had seen in the caravan at Watlands.

A year later he and Paula were married in our little church around the corner.

To me, perhaps the best bonus of Rye was that little Catholic church of Saint Anthony. A terrace church, it was almost joined to the houses each side of it because it dated from when Roman Catholic churches were not allowed to be built in Britain. The story is that the priest used to stand in its small forecourt on the street and beg for bricks, even one brick, to finish it.

It was a graceful little church, with a marble altar and a small cloister on one side leading to the Lady altar.

I took to going there every lunch time when it was empty; there, I found I could 'recollect'—that good old Catholic word—collect myself together in quiet. Tuck, now my senior pekingese, came with me, sitting solemn and still as a Buddhist should in the pew beside me. Often we were joined by Father Wilfred's cat.

The best years were when Father Wilfred, a Franciscan, was our priest. Father Wilfred was the nearest any human can get to sanctity but he was convinced he was a failure; frail and an artist, he was certainly no use at bazaars, boys' clubs and the like. His sermons were poor. "I can't go telling people what to do," he used to say and, to his congregation, "It would be better if I read you the gospel again," but when he left—Franciscans often change places—and there was as usual a collection for a farewell gift, where those for other priests had amounted to perhaps a hundred pounds, for Father Wilfred more than eight hundred poured in and from all over the town.

*   *   *

It was Father Wilfred that people of any creed or no creed asked for when they were dying but when it came to James, Father Wilfred had been moved to Liverpool.

My diary. October 10 1973.

James died in Hastings Hospital. I do not want to be consoled—ever.

By chance, Father Wilfred had come down on holiday—he had an aunt in Winchelsea. As soon as he heard that James was in intensive care in Hastings Hospital—it had become impossible to keep him at home—Father Wilfred went straight to him.

For days James had been in violent delirium recognising no-one. No-one could reach him in those agonising spasms—it took three nurses to control him. "It's no use," they told Father Wilfred who took no notice but went and stood by the iron railings that had had to be put round the bed.

"James."

James opened his eyes.

"James, do you know me?"

"Father Wilfred . . ." It was a hoarse whisper, the words could hardly come out.

"James, you are dying," said Father Wilfred. "Would you like me to bless you?"

Another struggle to speak. At last, "Please."

Father Wilfred blessed him. Before he left, James had gone into a peaceful coma. He died next day.

It would have been completely suitable if I too had died, though four years later, on my seventieth birthday, such a marvellous day that it would have made a good exit—but life does not arrange itself into a tidy pattern like that.

The years nineteen seventy-three to nineteen seventy-seven were difficult, to put it mildly. James had so protected me that I had come to take it for granted that all was well and had no idea that, perhaps for two years, he had been unable to cope with our affairs. They were in a hideous tangle.

To add to the problems I had now three houses.

It had become clear that I had to get James out of Lamb House, though our lease had still six years to run. It was too public. As well as diabetes, he had been attacked by arterial sclerosis which at times made him violent. At all costs, I thought, I must keep him at home but where in Rye could I find another house big enough?

In a panic I bought Chapel House, a villa I did not like, bought it simply because it was large enough to give James a bedroom and a private sitting room, with a room for a nurse next door, while there was a small study for me. No sooner had I bought it than the house I had always wanted in Rye came on the market, a Queen Anne house with a wisteria. Large houses in Mermaid Street were rare and much sought after but I was offered it privately. I took a deep breath and bought it as well.

Providence, as always came to my rescue—when will we learn to trust? Graham and Dorothy Watson took over Lamb House, Graham was now semi-retired. Our doctor, who had long wanted a house that could give him a surgery and waiting room as well as living quarters, pounced on Chapel House and I was able to juggle finance for Number Four Mermaid Street.

It was, like the Old Hospital, in need of repair. Once you touch an old house in an ancient town like Rye you are in trouble; Rye's plumbing alone is a mystery. I shall not forget the winter I had to spend alone in Lamb House while the work was being done— fortunately Graham and Dorothy were not in a hurry, but there were not even the guides for company as Lamb House was closed from October to April.

All my helps, including Peggy, went home at two o'clock so that the house seemed suddenly huge. "It is the silence," I told Jon. Going up to bed past James's shut door was an ordeal. I do not think I could have stood it without the pekingese who brought some life and warmth.

My diary. January 1974.

A gale, force ten, the garden blown to shreds; the big apple tree came down. All day rain drove across the town but in the afternoon three pairs of eyes looked at me imploringly, every other second opening and shutting in hope, and then gave up in mute sorrow. "Very well then, we'll go out." Harnesses, leads. It had to be a walk in the town, the rain was so fierce I could not see to drive the car. I put on my oldest woollen clothes—I detest raincoats they are so stiff.

We go. In two minutes we are soaked to our spines; feathers are clogged, ears streaming water. The Salts are deserted. We walk by moored fishing boats and over squelching grass. The rain not only deluges, it is bitingly cold. Tails sink. Am I cruel to take them out in such rain? We trail home; I wring the three of them out in the kitchen like washed dusters, wrap them in towels, then change and dry myself.

Hey presto! There is a carnival of spirits, chasing from room to room, round and round, in and over. The house resounds with scampering and joy. Cruel!

When another crisis, more than thirty years ago, had taken me to Jinglam, a tea garden near Darjeeling and into isolation I had written a note in my diary:

How to be happy when you are miserable.

Plant Japanese poppies with cornflowers and mignonette, and bed out the petunias among the sweet-peas so that they shall scent each other. See the sweet-peas coming up.

Drink very good tea out of a thin Worcester cup of a colour between apricot and pink shell. Have Rafael (Jane) paint a truly good picture. Have letters from America ...

It was the small things that helped, taken one by one and savoured. 'Make yourself savour them,' I told myself. 'Misery can become a habit,' and presently, I could say with the psalmist 'I have been through the bitter valley and found springs.'

Life came back to normal, especially when I moved almost next door and Graham and Dorothy came to live at Lamb House though, 'Always remember,' I schooled myself, 'your friends are almost certainly more important to you, than you are to them. Do not encroach.'

Again it was the pekingese that helped me back to writing. I had had to shelve a novel, it was too introspective but thought I could do something purely objective and that would be fun to write. The result was *The Butterfly Lions, a History of the Pekingese in Legend, History and Art*—*not* a dog book.

The seed of the idea had been sown sometime before when Bernard Levin, my favourite journalist, especially when he wanted to provoke, had written, as his customary fourth leader in the *Times*, a *Malediction Against Dogs*, enough to stir outrage throughout dog minded Britain. He had excluded pekingese from his vilifications, saying that they were not dogs but cats. That had been more than I could bear and my pekingese wrote to Bernard Levin that, while they agreed with most of what he said, they had to point out that they were not cats but 'spirit' dogs. There is a legend:

> Once upon a time a lioness grew tired of the brute attentions of her mate and yielded to the delicate caresses of a butterfly; (if you have ever been given a butterfly kiss, someone else's eye-lashes fluttering against your cheek, you will know how delicately teasing that is). The result of this mating was a pekingese and ever afterwards these little dogs have to be as brave as lions and dainty as butterflies.

I have not enjoyed writing any book more; it lifted me out of myself and so helped assuage the grief. The research was fascinating, going back to the Chou dynasty in China about 1000 B.C.

One of the first pekingese to come to England from China was brought by a young Lieutenant Dunne who found her after the sacking of the Summer Palace in the Opium Wars of the eighteen thirties. He gave her to Queen Victoria who unashamedly called her Looty; her portrait hangs in the Lord Chamberlain's Office. I discovered all the correspondence about Looty when I was allowed to research into the archives at Windsor Castle, no-one had found them until then. The Queen also gave me permission to see the Royal Kennels and the dog graves in the private part of Windsor Castle grounds.

Many of the originals of paintings I needed to use were in Peking; Alan Maclean of Macmillan wrote to the Cultural Attaché of the Chinese Republic in London, asking if he could help in tracing paintings or any remnants of pekingese history. The Attaché wrote back: 'We have no knowledge of these luxurious parasites.' My pekingese have been called luxurious parasites ever since.

On the other hand, Taiwan was most helpful. We cast our net wide and had surprises: an exquisite embroidery picture of a 'flowered' or parti-coloured pekingese lying on a cushion came from Kalamazoo Public Museum, Michigan. We found an Imperial Dog Cage in cloisonné and white jade in Philadelphia. The Field Museum of Natural History in Chicago came up with an album leaf of two court ladies watching pekingese dogs coupling but added to my researcher, "We feel sure your employer will not want to include *this*!" I discovered grave dog pekingese in the Oriental Department of the Royal Ontario Museum in Toronto.

A day or two after the book was published, Dorothy Watson telephoned. "Have you seen the *Times?*"

I had been tempted to send Bernard Levin a copy—he had written a typical Levin letter back to my pekingese—but it had seemed too much like angling for notice. There, in the paper where the fourth leader was customarily positioned, was part of the scroll of *A Thousand Pekingese*, the Manchu Empress's stud book I had used as an illustration for *The Butterfly Lions* and far more than a mention of the book in the accompanying article. "No-one," said Dorothy, "could have bought that for you."

As a break from writing *The Butterfly Lions*, Peggy and I drove round to deliver the customary parcels to my private sort of pensioners. After Mrs. Manders died we had tried to look after Mr. Manders; for Christmas he always had a jar of the Stilton cheese he loved. On top of the parcel for Percy Piper I always put a box of chocolates for Dolly, the prettiest box I could find, because I had discovered that in all her long life Dolly had never had a box of chocolates.

I suppose Peggy and I felt a little like lady bountifuls—she did much the same in her husband's parish—or those, too good to be true, ministering children of Victorian times and what happened? Mr. Manders had a bottle of whisky for me, dry sherry for Peggy. "You said you liked it dry." The Pipers produced more logs, a fresh chicken, and bunches of chrysanthemums.

Our last call was to Burgess Noakes, now living in a terrace cottage surrounded by neighbours. We found him in a white apron making Christmas puddings, helped by five or six children who were eating most of the raisins. "I always made the Christmas puddings for Mr. James," said Burgess. His face was red and cheerful, the kitchen spotless, the fragrance of the puddings wonderful. "One is for you," he told me. "And you, Miss." He could never accept that Peggy, in a working position, was Mrs. but was sure that, like Mrs. Paddington's, it was a courtesy title; most cooks then, married or not, were Mrs. to give them authority. He had made mince pies for us too. We came back more laden than when we went out.

From my diary. December 1977.

I heard the church clock strike nine as I went down into the garden—it was warm enough to walk. There were a few last roses glimmering in the lights from the French windows. This is the last night I shall be sixty-nine. How sad there is no-one to tell, or is there? No other flowers were out in the garden, yet I seemed to smell the strong scent of nicotiana, and with that another smell, a cigar. I had put on a record of James's beloved Mozart but James had not smoked cigars nor was there anyone near who did. The scent came with me as I walked, and I felt a companionship.

Rye had a new bookshop called The Martello run by a young couple devoted to books and so touching in their eagerness to succeed that I had agreed to do what I normally avoid doing, signing books in a shop. The book in question happened to be the one about a brothel and nuns, *Five for Sorrow, Ten for Joy*.

After *In This House of Brede*, publishers as well as readers had been insistent that I should write a successor. "How can I?" had been my answer. "I haven't a story." Then I was told about an unusual Order of nuns, so unusual that many people still do not believe they exist, Les Soeurs de Béthanie in France.* At least half their communities or maybe more than half are ex-criminals— some may even have committed murder—ex-prostitutes, alcoholics, drug addicts and the like while the other Sisters have been 'called' in the accepted way. As all are anonymous, having names like Sister Marie de la Croix, nobody knows which are which, except the Prieure Générale and her Council. In all the time I spent with them I never knew or even guessed who had been in the first category.

The book had brought many visits to France and Paris where I spent long hours at the Cour d'Assize listening to trials. One whole night was spent in the streets; from midnight until three o'clock my French agent, Georges Hoffman, drove us—Dorothy Watson was with me—taking us to such notorious places as the Place Cliché and the Latin Quarter, chiefly Arab where, though Georges had two large dogs in the back, he locked the car doors and said, "Don't ask me to stop because I won't." After three in the morning, Georges and Dorothy had had enough but I knew I

*They now have many houses in Germany, Austria, Italy, America and one in Britain.

had to finish and went on foot, with a little housekeeper from the hotel, Adèle whom I bribed to come with me. She only agreed if her boyfriend, who drove a taxi, drove close behind us—the boyfriend was a strapping young black man which was reassuring. It was quite frightening but worth it as I saw what Georges had told me no longer existed, drunks being picked up from the gutter by the police and being thrown into the 'panier des salades' as they called their vans; we saw the prostitutes waiting at their doors in the Rue Saint-Denis and there was even the little café where Lise, my heroine, found the fourteen year old Vivi drunk and asleep with her head on one of the zinc-topped tables.

The date The Martello chose happened to be my seventieth birthday.

I had thought no-one knew except Graham and Dorothy who had asked me to, I thought, a quiet lunch; in the evening I was to go over to Jon, Nancy and Rose at Aldington for a family dinner, no more.

I was in the kitchen feeding the pekingese when the first van arrived, a van loaded with flowers; flowers from Jane, Paula and the children. Well, I had expected that, but there were flowers from the Simons, Macmillan, Curtis Brown London, Curtis Brown New York, The Viking Press. Peggy who loved flowers and loved doing them was hardly able to cope. Then came the post, cables and telegrams. When it was time to go down to the bookshop—I had that always terrible thought, 'Suppose nobody comes'—people were standing in their doorways smiling and waving; in the High Street even my bank manager came out with good wishes in spite of my overdraft. There was a queue at the bookshop. I signed and signed, thankful that The Martello had sold some books; but there is an even more wonderful feeling of reward though, when people bring you a book bought so long ago that it is tattered and worn by being treasured, passed on to sons and daughters, perhaps grandchildren. I am old enough to have experienced that; recently I signed three copies of the same book for Carol I, Carol II, Carol III.

At one o'clock Graham came and rescued me. The lunch was at Lamb House where I found, to my amazement, he and Dorothy had invited all the people most dear to me in the literary world; they had come not only from round about but from London including Alan and Robin Maclean and Marni. In the evening I drove across the marshes by twilight with the pekingese—they had been invited; we had a family dinner, with all my favourite things.

My cup was full.

Next day I had to tell, first of all Peggy who really knew, then the staff, Mrs. Simms, Mr. Almond, the part-time gardener, the dear cook Joan, who had succeeded Mrs. Manders, that I was going to leave Rye. As soon as a little new home was ready I would live in Scotland. "Scotland!" they cried as if I had said the North Pole. Joan burst into tears, while, "You're making a mistake," said Peggy.

Everyone said that but, "I must do this while I am still not too old to adjust," I said. "I have seen too many people clinging on to a house they can no longer manage," and, "I need to be near Jane and Paula." The newly-weds had bought a farm near Anthony and Jane. "You can be a nuisance to your family," I said. "You mustn't be a nuisance to your friends."

Epilogue

I am a story-teller. Well, if I were asked which of two great writers I would choose to be, Proust or Robert Louis Stevenson, much as I honour and enjoy Proust, I would unhesitatingly choose Stevenson but, of course, there is no choice; story-tellers are born not made.

A short while ago I was sent one of those publisher's publicity questionnaires. It ran to several pages, wanting to know every fact about me from the day I was born—everything that has little or nothing to do with writing. I am afraid my answers were mostly negative. Education?—in my case almost nil. Qualifications?—none except for dancing. Politics?—none. Hobbies?—none—but the last question temporarily floored me, 'What makes you think your books are different from anyone else's?'

At first I decided not to answer it; it seemed impertinent, besides I had never thought that. Then, slowly, I began to see it is a vital question—and absolutely relevant; in fact there is only one answer. 'What makes you think your books are different from anyone else's?' The only answer is, 'Because they were written by me.'

That sounds conceited but it is not; all authors should be able to say it, whether they are a lion or just one of many sparrows. Fulfilment can be all sizes.

Like everyone else I am a house with four rooms. As a child the physical room was barred to me, I had to fight my way to get into it. The room of the mind has always been mine. In the emotional,

I have been marvellously lucky; with the spiritual, it was a long time before I would do more than peer in; now it is where I like best to be alone.

All of us tend to inhabit one room more than another but I have tried to go most days into them all—each has its riches.

My house is, of course, slightly worn now but I still hope to go on living quietly in all of it, finding treasures, old and new until the time comes when I shall have, finally, to shut its door.

Rumer Godden
Ardnacloich

Appendix

Four Poems for Emily Dickinson

These beautiful poems were sent to me by James Kirkup after he knew I was writing this book.

In the House of Emily Dickinson

At this small table, hardly
Bigger than a checkerboard,
She told with birdlike hand
The coming of the word.

Over the square-paned casement
A muslin curtain, bright and still.
A hedge away, the country lane,
The fields, the railroad of the will.

She could see out, but they
Could not see in. The heart's long mile
Was all she trod, her world a room.
It did not cramp her style.

A spirit here was not confined,
But wandered high and far,
From yards of death to leagues of life,
From slowest candle to the quickest star.

Elegy for Emily

Robed in her usual white, withdrawn
In her white casket she was borne
Out of the sunny back door, over the lawn,
Along the ferny bridlepaths of May
To the burial ground on Pleasant Street.

The Irish workmen, her friends and servants,
Conducted her in a funeral like a game,
Some grave children's celebration,
The toecaps of their black boots
Burnished with buttercups.

O she was strange and rare
As a Red Indian brave—dark hair,
Pale face, great eyes, rich mouth.
At her throat, she wore in death
A posy of violets, and one pink cypripedium.

With two heliotropes by her hand
She floated over the pansied grass;
Through the hedge of flowering may
Fled like a flock of linnets,
Leaving behind her a buzz of bees.

The sun shone in her grave sprigged with yew,
Scented with earth and flowering trees.
Dark hair, pale face, great eyes, rich mouth.
—Her burial was an ascension, for

It is she who remains, and we,
Alone, are the departed.

At the Grave of Emily Dickinson

Leaving the florist's on the other side of Pleasant Street
With a posy of corn, thistles, rushes, pink immortelles,
I cross the vulgar road you would not recognize, and turn

Into the burial ground. Behind its black iron railings
Your father's tall stone still casts his shadow over you.
But on your other side, Lavinia—the one you loved.

Being apart, in this hilly Amherst graveyard haunted
By weathered flags on worn tombs of forgotten warriors
And later ones—flags whose faded stripes, extinguished stars

The sunset glows through as if they were of glass—
Surrounded by obelisks, yews, maples aflame with fall,
Congregationalist, you lie with them, and lie apart.

Below the yew, your father's stone, bolt upright. But yours
And Lavinia's lean back a little, half-fastidiously.
"Called back," says the inscription. (Whither?) "May 15, 1886."

Upon your tomb I pressed two autumn leaves, gathered from my
    garden,
But the wind flung them away. Behind your tilted stone
I planted the posy of corn, thistles, rushes, pink immortelles.

I have come all this way across the world to speak to you,
As you so often came to speak to me, but found you
Not quite there: myself, remote and blind, not there at all.

Why am I telling you this? As the tears finally flow for you,
I know you are with me, as always, watching these words I
    write
To one who was also not altogether of this world.

Emily in Winter

Born in December, from the start
You knew a sunstruck winter of the heart.

Gales now blow clouds of snowdust ghosts, that bloom
With rainbows round your black-railed room.

I come once more with flowers and alone
To speak with you behind your stone.

You who can move upon the crusted whiteness
And leave no track; I press

My handprint on the snow, and feel the heat
Above the buried breastbone where your heart once beat.

James Kirkup

Amherst
(from *White Shadows, Black Shadows: Poems of Peace and War*, and from *The Body Servant: Poems of Exile*, Dent.)